W9-AKW-142

GARY P. LATHAM
University of Washington

KENNETH N. WEXLEY
Michigan State University

Increasing Productivity Through Performance Appraisal

ADDISON-WESLEY PUBLISHING COMPANY

Reading, Massachusetts • Menlo Park, California
London • Amsterdam • Don Mills, Ontario • Sydney

THE ADDISON-WESLEY SERIES ON MANAGING HUMAN RESOURCES

Series Editor: John P. Wanous, Michigan State University

Fairness in Selecting Employees
Richard D. Arvey, University of Houston

Organizational Entry: Recruitment, Selection, and Socialization of Newcomers
John P. Wanous, Michigan State University

Increasing Productivity through Performance Appraisal
Gary P. Latham, University of Washington, and Kenneth N. Wexley, Michigan State University

Managing Conflict at Organizational Interfaces
David Brown, Case-Western Reserve University

Employee Turnover: Causes, Consequences and Control
William H. Mobley, Texas A & M University

Library of Congress Cataloging in Publication Data

Latham, Gary P
   Increasing productivity through performance appraisal.

   (Addison-Wesley series on managing human resources)
   Bibliography: p.
   Includes index.
   1. Employees, Rating of. I. Wexley, Kenneth N., 1943– joint author. II. Title. III. Series.
HF5549.5.R3L367   658.3'125   80-14894
ISBN 0-201-04217-7

Reprinted with corrections, February 1982

0-201-04217-7
JKLMNOP-AL-8987

Series Foreword

Widespread attention given to the effective management of human resources came of age in the 1970s. As we enter the 1980s, the importance placed on it continues to grow. Personnel departments, which used to be little more than the keepers of employee files, are now moving to the forefront in corporate visibility.

The difficulties encountered in effective human resource management are without parallel. Surveys of managers and top level executives consistently show "human problems" at the top of most lists. The influx of the behavioral sciences into business school programs is further testimony to the active concern now placed on human resources as a crucial element in organizational effectiveness.

The primary objective of this Addison-Wesley series is to articulate new solutions to chronic human resource problems; for example, the selection and entry of newcomers, performance appraisal, leadership, and conflict management. The aim is to communicate with a variety of audiences, including present managers, students as future managers, and fellow professionals in business, government, and academia.

John P. Wanous
Series Editor

To William P. Latham and Helen Wexley

for being models of exemplary performance

Foreword

Most people agree that employee appraisal is important. But until now, no one approach has proven completely satisfactory, particularly, for large categories of professional employees. This book describes an effective approach to measuring an individual's performance that not only provides a solid basis for promotion and compensation decisions, but stimulates employee productivity as well. Most important, it eliminates the pro-forma "happiness file" appraisals that clog most personnel records and replaces them with a decision making approach that satisfies legal requirements regarding the treatment of an organization's human resources.

This book provides a behind-the-scenes look at ten years of scholarly work by the authors that has been published in leading scientific journals in the United States and Canada. The authors have integrated their research findings into this easy-to-understand book that should prove invaluable to managers and students alike.

Peter Belluschi, Vice President
Weyerhaeuser Company

Acknowledgments

The authors wish to thank the following people for their comments on one or more preliminary chapters in this book: Abraham A. Arditi, Attorney, Northwest Labor and Employment Law Office; Walter C. Borman, Vice President, Personnel Decision Research, Inc.; Herbert Heneman III, Professor, University of Wisconsin; Loretta Schmitz, Graduate Student, University of Wisconsin; John R. Hinrichs, President, Management Decisions Systems, Inc.; Dean A. Messmer, Attorney, Bogle & Gates; Terence R. Mitchell, Professor, University of Washington; Melvin Sorcher, Director of Management Development, Richardson-Merrell, Inc.; Patricia Cain Smith, Professor, Bowling Green State University; and James Taylor, Personnel Manager, Weyerhaeuser Company.

We are particularly indebted to Lise M. Saari, Graduate Student, University of Washington, for her editorial assistance in writing this book; and to Stephen Conway, Vice President, Weyerhaeuser Company, Edwin A. Locke, Professor, University of Maryland, and John Wanous, our editor, for reviewing this book in its entirety.

Seattle, Washington   G. P. L.
August 1980   K. N. W.

Contents

Overview

1

INTRODUCTION

What are the chances that an employee will get a raise? Land a job in the Chicago office? Be promoted to top management?

If a person works for a small company, the answers may depend on a series of informal judgments made by managers who know the employee well. But in a large organization, the employee's chances may hinge on something much less personal: an evaluation form completed by a supervisor and then reviewed by another executive who makes the final decision.

Most organizations are growing more and more dependent upon formal performance reviews before making personnel decisions. These companies do not want to rely on informal evaluation systems because they know that they are in a better position to avoid conflict with equal employment opportunity laws if they can justify their decisions with valid appraisal standards. More importantly, they know that well-developed appraisal systems increase the probability that they will retain, motivate, and promote productive people.

Yet many appraisal systems are being severely criticized from all sides. Managers find them troublesome, particularly when they have to criticize an employee personally and put the criticism in writing. Employees charge that the appraisals are often too subjective, and the federal courts frequently agree with them. Most disappointing of all, many executives themselves realize that existing performance appraisal systems do not bring about a positive change in their employees' behavior. A 1977 report by the Conference Board (Lazer & Wikstrom, 1977) notes that over half of the 293 organizations it surveyed had developed new appraisal systems within the last three years, but despite these efforts, the report concludes that current systems are still widely regarded as a nuisance at best and as a necessary evil at worst.

In short, performance appraisal systems are a lot like seat belts. Most people believe they are necessary, but they don't like to use them. As a result, appraisal systems are often used reluctantly to satisfy some formal organizational or legal requirement. In many cases managers are ingenious at finding ways to bypass them. This is unfortunate because performance appraisals are crucial to the effective management of an organization's human resources, and the proper management of human resources is a critical variable affecting an organization's productivity.

PRODUCTIVITY AND HUMAN RESOURCES

The productivity of most organizations is a function of the way at least three variables are managed, namely: technological, capital, and human resources. Many organizations have been leaders in realizing dollar opportunities from technological development and capital investment. Many of these same companies, however, have failed to maximize productivity by failing to take full advantage of the abilities of their people.

Increases in performance due to investment from capital or technology can be measured in traditional accounting terms (e.g., profits and costs, as measured by output/input). The influence of an individual employee on productivity in most jobs is difficult to measure in traditional accounting terms. The influence of an organization's human resources on productivity, however, can be measured in terms of *what people do* on the job. What people do can be appraised in terms of such traditional measures as attendance, accidents, turnover, and grievances. Also, what people do can be measured directly in terms of observations by managers, peers, and subordinates as to the frequency with which employees do those things that are critical to job success. What people do or do *not* do should be a source of concern to all organizations. Current employee practices such as coming to work late, stopping work early, and filling work orders incorrectly are costing one of our client companies $80,000,000 compounding at 7 percent annually. Such ineffective employee behavior can and should be changed. Cost increases for such items as equipment and energy are areas over which most organizations have little control. What people do *is* an area that managers can influence to their benefit and to the benefit of their subordinates. However, most organizations have not yet totally explored the development of effective human resource systems in a systematic manner.

HUMAN RESOURCE SYSTEMS: THE KEY ROLE OF PERFORMANCE APPRAISAL

Selection, performance appraisal, training, and motivation principles are four key systems necessary for insuring the proper management of an organization's human resources. Of these four systems, an argument can be made that performance appraisal is the most important because it is a prerequisite for establishing the other three.

The efficient use of an organization's human resources begins with *selection,* namely, choosing the right person for the job. However, before a selection test can be developed for predicting who will be the right person for the job, the word *right* must be defined. That is, correct on-the-job behavior must be defined. The core of the performance appraisal process is the definition of effective employee behavior. A valid selection test cannot be developed until the organization agrees upon an acceptable definition (i.e., measure) of employee behavior. This is because the validity of a test is determined by measuring the performance of people on the test and measuring the performance of the same people on important aspects of the job. If there is a significant correlation between these two measures the selection procedure is valid.

Selection is important for two reasons. A proper selection procedure can minimize difficulties with government agencies such as the Equal Employment Opportunity Commission (EEOC) and the Office of Federal Contract Compliance Programs (OFCCP). More important, properly developed selection techniques increase productivity because they assist organizations in screening out applicants who work at less than acceptable standards. The amount of money saved by effective screening can be enormous. For example, one company in 1979 estimated that it costs over

$16,000 over a six month period before a machine operator is performing at the same level as a skilled predecessor. This figure is based on the assumption that the right person is selected as the replacement. If the wrong person is chosen, this cost figure increases dramatically. Thus a selection system can literally make or break an organization.

Validated selection procedures can predict who is likely to be absent, who is likely to quit, who is likely to be dissatisfied with the job, and who is likely to perform the job well. However, if performance appraisals are based on biased or inaccurate observations, no degree of care in the development of selection instruments will improve selection/staffing decisions. This is because the validity of a test is determined by correlating the test scores of individuals with their performance on the job. Therefore, to the extent that the performance appraisals are biased, the effectiveness of the selection instruments is reduced.

No approach to selection is foolproof. Therefore, once a person has been selected for a job, the problem becomes one of monitoring and maintaining a high level of performance. Again, this is where performance appraisals play a critical role.

The definition of performance appraisal is not limited to one-on-one situations where a supervisor discusses with an employee areas deserving recognition and areas where improvement is needed. A *performance appraisal* is any personnel decision that affects the status of employees regarding their retention, termination, promotion, demotion, transfer, salary increase or decrease, or admission into a training program.

A properly developed appraisal instrument serves as a *contract* between the organization and an employee in that it makes explicit what is required of that individual. Appraising performance is necessary because it serves as an audit for the organization about the effectiveness of each employee. Such a control system, based on key job behaviors that serve as standards, enables a manager to specify what the employee must start doing, continue doing, or stop doing. *It is the combination of performance feedback and the setting of specific goals based on this feedback that enables the performance appraisal to fulfill its two most important functions, namely the counseling (motivation) and development (training) of employees.* These are the primary purposes of performance appraisal because it is on the basis of an employee's motivation and training that decisions are made regarding that employee's retention, promotion, demotion, transfer, salary increase, and termination.

During the performance appraisal interview the supervisor may determine that the person is not fulfilling job responsibilities or behaving in a satisfactory manner due to a lack of knowledge or skill. Where this is the case, *training* that actually brings about a relatively permanent improvement in an employee's behavior is critical for effective human resource development (Wexley & Latham, in press). The job analysis on which the performance appraisal instrument should be based in order to satisfy legal challenges (see Chapters 2 and 3) plays a key role in identifying training content. That is, the job analysis reveals the knowledge and skills in which employees as a group are deficient. In this way, the job analysis specifies *what* must be taught in a training program. The performance appraisal identifies *who* should receive the training.

To the extent that a person has both the knowlege and skill to do the job, but is doing it in an unsatisfactory manner, the problem may be one of *motivation.* The key components of effective motivation strategies include *feedback* that allows an employee to learn how well he or she is doing, *goal setting* that specifies what the person should be doing, *team building* that allows the employee to participate with peers and the supervisor in solving problems that impede their productivity, and monetary *incentives* that reward good performance.

Performance appraisal lies at the heart of motivation because it is through the appraisal interview that the employee receives feedback from a manager and/or others (e.g., peers) regarding job performance. In addition, goals are set in relation to this feedback, problems that surface are resolved through manager-employee discussions, and monetary rewards can be given contingent upon satisfactory performance.

In summary, performance appraisal is a fundamental requirement for improving the productivity of an organization's human resources, because it is through an appraisal that each individual's productivity is evaluated. It serves as the basis for counseling and developing an individual to maintain or increase productivity. Performance appraisal is critical to selection systems because the job analysis on which the appraisal instrument is based enables the manager/researcher to hypothesize the selection instruments that are likely to identify effective employees. Once an individual has been hired, it is necessary to determine whether the selection procedure worked. It is the correlation of employee evaluations on a selection instrument with the evaluations on the appraisal instrument that determines whether the selection instrument is *valid*. After the individual has been on the job, the performance appraisal identifies who is in need of training and/or motivation.

Viewed in this way, the primary purpose of a performance appraisal system is to provide a measure of job performance that will facilitate counseling and development of an employee. In addition, at a time when managerial freedom to make personnel decisions is increasingly circumscribed by law, performance appraisal records should provide the documentation a manager needs if and when these decisions are challenged in court. All too often personnel files yield no more than a succession of "Satisfactory," "Good," or "Outstanding" ratings, which are *not* defined. As documentation against possible legal challenges, or as an aid to improving employee effectiveness, most appraisal systems fall far short.

ORGANIZATION OF THE BOOK

Most organizations do not realize that a performance appraisal is considered a test in the eyes of the law and thus is scrutinized by the courts as closely as selection procedures for adverse impact on members of a protected class. Therefore, before an organization develops an appraisal system, or modifies an existing one, it must take into account current laws. Chapter 2 focuses on laws prohibiting employment discrimination, the roles of the OFCCP and the EEOC in enforcing these laws, and court decisions regarding performance appraisals.* In addition, the 1978 Civil Service Reform Act is discussed because it specifies procedures to be followed in conducting performance appraisals with federal employees.

At a minimum, organizations need to check their appraisal systems and the uses of such appraisal systems, to determine whether decisions regarding retention, promotion, demotion, pay, or admission to a training program are affected by the race, sex, religion, color, national origin, or age of employees. If adverse impact is evident, that is, if performance appraisal decisions are different for one group (e.g., women), the organization must either abandon the appraisal system or justify its continued use.

Justifying an appraisal system is not easy. Chapter 3 examines different ways of defining and developing measures of an individual's productivity.

---

*For an extensive treatment of legal issues on recruiting and hiring applicants, the reader should consult Arvey (1979).

Special attention is given to job analysis, that is, identifying the critical requirements of a person's job, and with this information developing the performance appraisal instrument. The second focus of Chapter 3 is on the meaning of the word *valid* in both the legal and psychometric sense of the word. In order to continue using an appraisal system that has been shown to affect one or more groups (e.g., blacks, women) adversely, an organization must demonstrate that the system is valid. That is, the organization must show that the appraisal decisions are job related and that the appraisal instrument taps a representative sample of critical job duties.

The appraisal instrument is only as good as the people who use it; an appraiser must accurately observe significant aspects of the employee's job performance. Careful observation is a necessity not only for making valid recordings of behavioral measures, but also for evaluating the meaning of so-called objective criteria such as tardiness, absences, and accidents (Smith, 1976). In fact, "human judgment enters into every criterion from productivity to salary increases" (Smith, 1976, p. 757). Thus, once a valid appraisal instrument has been developed, managers must decide *who* will use the instrument.

There are at least six possible sources of an appraisal. Observations can be made by managers, peers, subordinates, employees themselves, outsiders or some combination of the above. Chapter 4 discusses the advantages of each of these sources for using the appraisal instrument.

Regardless of who uses the appraisal instrument, human beings are notoriously poor in recording accurately what they observe. For example, a professor who is outstanding on one aspect of the job (e.g., research) may be evaluated erroneously by the university as being outstanding on all aspects of the job (e.g., teaching, advising students). Chapter 5 describes a training program that increases observer accuracy and objectivity in making performance appraisals. This program is essential to minimizing bias and thus feelings of inequity among employees due to managers' using different frames of reference for evaluating people. It is not uncommon for two employees who do the same quantity and quality of work to be rated differently by two different managers or even by the same manager. Uniformity and objectivity are mandatory for maintaining feelings of equity among employees, particularly when the function of the appraisal is to motivate them through recognition, promotion, etc. Uniformity and objectivity are also a "must" when monetary rewards are tied to performance. A minimum requirement for money to serve as a motivator is for employees to believe that their performance is being recorded objectively by management.

Chapters 6, 7, and 8 are concerned directly with increasing employee productivity. If productivity does not increase or remain at a high level, there is little reason from a motivational standpoint to provide the results of a performance appraisal to the employee. In Chapter 6 detailed descriptions are given of motivational procedures such as goal setting, reinforcement, team building, and monetary incentives that have been shown to increase an individual's productivity after the appraisal instrument has been validated and the observers have been trained to record objectively what they have seen an employee do on the job.

Chapter 7 describes ways of conducting a formal appraisal interview. In addition, suggestions are given for ways to appraise and motivate employees on a daily basis using the principles discussed in Chapter 6. Fig. 1.1 provides a diagram of the activities involved in an appraisal and serves as an outline for this book.

Chapter 8 contains a case description of an organization that incorporated the ideas described in Chapters 2 through 7 and the results that were obtained. Having described a performance appraisal system which we believe is applicable to most, if not all, organizations, we conclude this book with suggestions in Chapter 9 on how to implement this approach to performance appraisal. These suggestions are based on our successes and frustrations in this area during the past ten years.

CLOSING REMARKS

In closing this first chapter, it is important for the reader to be aware that this book does not provide a comprehensive review of the literature on different performance appraisal systems. For example, little or no mention is made of the merits and criticisms of graphic scales, forced choice techniques, written essays, and the like. This is because for 50 years industrial psychologists have examined the measurement properties of various appraisal scales without bringing about substantial changes in an employee's behavior. For example, ranking systems do not provide concrete information for improving performance; they tell only how well one person did versus another. Further, it is difficult to combine rankings

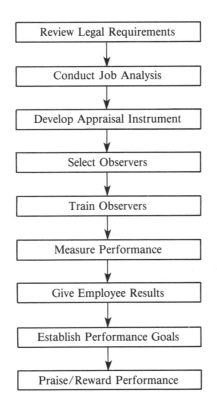

Figure 1.1 *The Performance Appraisal Process*

of employees in different departments because the highest ranking individual in one department may be only average in other departments. Finally, as will be discussed in Chapter 2, rankings have been prohibited by the 1978 Civil Service Reform Act.

The same criticisms can be made about forced choice procedures where the appraiser is asked to choose one item out of three or four that best describes the employee. In constructing clusters of items, an effort is made to equate items on desirability so that the rater is not tempted to bias the ratings for or against an appraisee. As an additional safeguard to prevent the appraiser from biasing the ratings, the one item within each cluster that has been found to differentiate the effective from the ineffective employee is kept secret by the Personnel Department. Because the appraiser does not know the importance given to the different items by the Personnel Department which affect the employee's score, feedback, counseling, and development with this method are difficult, if not impossible, to accomplish with the employee.

Nor do we discuss various philosophies of performance appraisal or different approaches to job analysis. Of the various approaches that can be taken in conducting a job analysis (see McCormick, 1976) only one—the critical incident technique—in our opinion is tailor-made for maximizing feedback and the use of motivational principles, identifying training needs, and conforming with legal requirements for performance appraisals.

Nor do we present extensive discussions on the merits of having one appraisal system for meeting developmental needs of employees and another for making organizational decisions for administrative purposes regarding salary increases, terminations, and the like. It is a naive employee who believes that failure to use feedback and grow with the job will not affect promotions, demotions, or salary increases. To pretend that two different systems should be used is to insult the intelligence of most employees. They know what will happen if they do not satisfy job requirements. The purpose of this book is to describe a system that will increase the probability that managers can help employees know and accept what is required of them.

In summary, this book describes an appraisal system that is valid, that satisfies legal requirements and, most important, defines and stimulates employee productivity. The system is based in part on three milestones in organizational psychology—the critical incident technique, goal setting, and principles of reinforcement (Dunnette, 1976). The latter term refers to making positive consequences the result of engaging in desirable behavior. For a historical look at performance appraisal we recommend reading *Performance Appraisal* by Whisler and Harper (1962) and literature reviews by Smith (1976) and Wexley (1979).

SUMMARY

Performance appraisal can play a key role in bringing about and maintaining satisfactory performance on the part of an individual employee in the following ways. First, it provides a means of measuring the employee's effectiveness on the job. Second, it identifies areas where the employee is in need of training. Third, it maintains a high level of motivation through feedback and the setting of specific goals on the basis of this feedback. However, the definition of performance appraisal is not limited to the actual presentation of information by a supervisor to an employee regarding the extent to which job requirements/responsibilities are being fulfilled. Performance appraisal is any judgment or decision that affects an employee's status in an organization regarding retention, termination, promotion, demotion, transfer, salary increase, or admission into a training program that affects any of the preceding factors, regardless of whether the rationale behind these decisions is made known to the employee.

Selection, performance appraisal, training, and motivation principles form the core of effective human resource systems that affect the productivity of an organization at the level of the individual employee. Of these four systems, an argument can be made that performance appraisal is the most important because it is a prerequisite for establishing the other three. For example, the effectiveness of selection systems is determined by comparing the performance of people on the selection procedures with appraisals of their performance on the job. The job analysis on which the appraisal instrument should be based can reveal important areas where training is needed in the organization. The performance appraisal identifies who in the organization should receive the training. Moreover, it is the combination of performance feedback and the setting of specific goals in relation to this feedback that enables the performance appraisal to fulfill its two most important functions, namely, the training and motivation of employees. Goal setting and feedback are primary components of most, if not all, motivation theories (Locke, 1978).

Performance Appraisal and the Law

2

INTRODUCTION

Although the purposes of performance appraisals are laudable, there is increasing concern on the part of the federal government as well as organizations themselves that most performance appraisal systems are not satisfying the objectives for which they were designed. However, before existing systems are modified or new systems are developed, current laws must be taken into account. Violation of federal laws regarding performance appraisal can easily cost an organization several million dollars for legal fees, court costs, damages, and back pay, not to mention the drain on an organization's time and personnel in preparing for a case.

The government is concerned primarily with the impact of an appraisal system on an employee's status within the organization. Title VII of the 1964 Civil Rights Act states that it is against the law to affect an individual's status as an employee because of race, color, religion, sex, or national origin. The Age Discrimination in Employment Act provides similar protection for people between the ages of 40 and 70.

A negative performance appraisal can directly affect an individual's employment status. More often than many of us care to admit, factors such as an employee's race, sex, or age may lie behind negative comments couched in objective terms. In recognition of this fact, legislative acts and court decisions have subjected performance appraisals to close scrutiny and rigid requirements to eliminate discrimination. Such requirements affect all aspects of personnel systems, including recruiting, hiring, training, upgrading, compensation, demotions, layoffs, and so on. What most managers fail to realize is that the legal requirements for performance appraisal systems are essentially no different from those for any selection test, namely, reliability and validity. Reliability refers to consistency in measurement. Validity refers to the extent to which a test truly measures what it purports to measure. These two key concepts are discussed in detail in Chapter 3.

The purpose of this chapter is to introduce important equal employment opportunity laws. After all, before one can discuss the proper construction of performance appraisal instruments, it is mandatory to know the legal requirements affecting appraisal systems and the steps that must be taken to comply with them. In this chapter we also explain how some of the main enforcement agencies operate, since the intensity of enforcement efforts by these agencies is expected to increase in the years to come.

HISTORICAL BACKGROUND

On July 2, 1964 Congress passed the Civil Rights Act of 1964, which became effective July 2, 1965. Title VII of that act is concerned with discrimination in all conditions of employment by four major groups—employers, public and private employment agencies, labor organizations, and joint labor-management apprenticeship programs.* Any of these four groups found to be discriminating on the basis of race, color, religion, sex, or national origin is in violation of the law. The Equal Employment Opportunity Commission (EEOC) was created as the governmental agency to administer Title VII.

In 1965 the Office of Federal Contract Compliance (OFCC) was established as the administrative body responsible for insuring that federal contractors and subcontractors conform to Executive Order 11246, which also prohibits employment discrimination on the basis of race, color, religion, and national origin. It was later amended to include prohibition against sex discrimination. In 1975 the OFCC merged with the Department of Labor and became the OFCCP—Office of Federal Contract Compliance Programs.

---

*It does not apply to such organizations as Indian Tribes, religious groups, or private clubs.

On March 24, 1972 Congress passed the Equal Employment Opportunity Act. It extended the powers of the EEOC to include federal, state, and municipal employees as well as employees of educational institutions. It also required any organization with 15 or more employees who work for 20 or more weeks to comply with Title VII. The EEOC was authorized to bring suit in its own name against nongovernmental agencies.

In the past the Department of Labor (DOL) was responsible for enforcing the Equal Pay Act of 1964 and the Age Discrimination in Employment Act of 1967. Effective July 1, 1979 the EEOC assumed the responsibilities of DOL in this area. The Department of Justice has primary responsibility for initiating court action and for prosecution against the government, a government agency, or a political subdivision. Enforcement by private plaintiffs is also permitted in all of these areas regardless of whether the defendant is a government body or a private company.

For most organizations the OFCCP and the EEOC are the most visible agencies in monitoring alleged discrimination in employment. For this reason, this chapter will concentrate on these two federal agencies. In addition, the Civil Service Reform Act of 1978 is discussed because it deals specifically with the performance appraisal of federal employees.

THE OFFICE OF FEDERAL CONTRACT COMPLIANCE PROGRAMS (OFCCP)

The OFCCP is concerned with discrimination in such areas as hiring, upgrading, demotion, transfer, recruitment and recruitment advertising, layoff or termination, rates of pay or other forms of compensation, and selection for training, including apprenticeship, by any employer who holds a federal contract of $10,000 or more.

The OFCCP requires that all federal contracts of $10,000 or more include special clauses by which a contractor agrees to refrain from engaging in discriminatory practices and to require that all subcontractors refrain from engaging in discriminatory practices. If the OFCCP finds that a contractor or a subcontractor has failed to meet the nondiscriminatory requirements of the contract, it can: (1) publish the names of the contractor and/or the union, (2) cancel the contract, (3) bar noncomplying employers from bidding on future federal contracts until they are in compliance with the law, (4) recommend to the Department of Justice that appropriate action be taken against the contractor or subcontractor when there is an alleged violation of Title VII, and (5) recommend that the Department of Justice bring criminal action against anyone supplying false information to any federal agency or to the Secretary of Labor.

The OFCCP's contract compliance coverage is broad in the sense that nearly all manufacturing operations in the country do at least some work as federal contractors or subcontractors, and thus are subject to the jurisdiction of the OFCCP. In addition, it is important to note that, although only one facility of a company may hold a nonexempt federal contract (that is, an aggregate of $10,000 or more in any 12 month period), *all* facilities of the company are subject to the requirements of the OFCCP. This policy may cause unexpected legal difficulties for some organizations. People at an organization's headquarters are frequently unaware of specific practices at outlying facilities. For example, one multidivisional company had discriminatory practices within only one of its divisions. That division had no federal contracts. Nevertheless, the discriminatory practices led the OFCCP to take action against the entire company.

When a large chemical plant had received a complaint from several Mexican-Americans regarding alleged discrimination against them in promotions to supervisory jobs, the OFCCP reviewed all aspects of the plant's employment practices (e.g., promotions, layoffs, hiring procedures, recruiting, training). Their recommendations were not restricted solely to the promotional practices of one plant, but rather were broad and applied to the entire company.*

Complaint Investigations

Any individual may file a complaint alleging discrimination with both the OFCCP and the EEOC. The two agencies, however, try to avoid duplication of effort and have agreed that only one of them will usually assume jurisdiction over an individual complaint.

Unlike the EEOC, which will be discussed shortly, the OFCCP does *not* have to defer to a state agency before proceeding with its investigation.

---

*The EEOC, too, can bring nationwide charges against a firm that engages in discriminatory practices. However, in 1977 the Commission decided to no longer do this because of the difficulty of putting a case together. A major problem with such cases is that the employment practices of a large company, such as Sears, vary across the country. Thus, current EEOC policy is to limit job bias charges against a large employer to a specific community.

The OFCCP is *not* concerned with a contractor's violation of a local or state law, but rather with violations of federal contract compliance requirements described previously. A sample OFCCP case might proceed as follows: A maintenance foreman has been asked to work weekends. The foreman, however, states that his religion prohibits him from working on Saturdays. As a result, the foreman receives a poor performance appraisal, is demoted to a lesser job, and is denied an opportunity to attend further training programs. This foreman may file a complaint with the OFCCP area office within 180 days, alleging employment discrimination on the basis of religion. That area office would then commence an investigation of the employer's practices. In doing so, the OFCCP can investigate *all* aspects of employment practices having possible discriminatory consequences. In other words, the agency does not have to confine itself to the specific complaint. If a violation is found, the OFCCP may take any of the actions enumerated in the previous section.

Compliance Reviews

An employee complaint is not necessary in order to trigger an OFCCP compliance review. OFCCP compliance officers on their own initiative can conduct on-site reviews. Two to three weeks advance notice is normally given to a facility to allow for the assembly of its employment records.

A local compliance officer has the right to request employment data broken down by race, sex, and national origin of an employer's departments and promotional lines. The officer is likely to inquire about the possible existence of segregated departments and/or jobs. Another question may involve the promotional history of minorities and women employed by the organization. A compliance officer has the authority to inspect employment records and to inquire into general personnel and employment practices to answer any of these problems.

The OFCCP is concerned particularly with the employment status of minorities and females in six job categories: (1) officials and managers, (2) professionals, (3) technicians, (4) sales workers, (5) office and clerical workers, and (6) skilled craftsmen. Organizations should take special care to maintain promotional records, seniority rosters, applicant flow data, and applicant rejection ratios to provide data on minorities in these categories. Note, however, that information disclosing the race, sex, national origin, and the religion of applicants as well as current employees *must* be kept separate from the forms used in selection and performance appraisal systems. The information should *not* be recorded (even in code) on the application blank, interviewer report, paper-and-pencil tests, or any other selection-appraisal document. One suggestion is to record this information on either index cards or a tear-off sheet, which will not be available to anyone in the organization directly involved in making selection or performance appraisal decisions.*

The possibility of contract cancellation is considered so serious by most organizations that OFCCP field officers frequently are able to exert more influence upon the personnel practices of the organizations they review than is justified by their legal authority. This situation is particularly true regarding the soundness or validity of performance appraisal systems. The official position of the OFCCP is that their field officers are to gather evidence regarding the validity of an organization's appraisal decisions. This evidence, if it exists, is to be reviewed by the OFCCP in Washington, and the final decision is to be made by that office rather than by local compliance officers. The OFCCP has an advisory committee, which includes industrial-organizational psychologists experienced in business, industry, and government to assist it in examining the soundness or validity of appraisal procedures. An organization confronted with a negative review from a local agency that it believes is erroneous should request a review of the evidence by the OFCCP in Washington.

In general, the adoption of quota systems (a fixed percentage) for the transfer, promotion, or admission of employees into training programs that is race or sex conscious is to be avoided unless the organization has been found guilty by the courts of employment discrimination, or it has job categories where the employees are predominantly of the same race and/or sex. To do otherwise is to invite a reverse discrimination suit (alleged discrimination against a nonminority group member which is also prohibited by Title VII of the Civil Rights Act). Nor do written affirmative action policies guarantee that an organization will be free from OFCCP scrutiny. The real measure of an employer's good intentions regarding

---

*The EEOC's (1979) advice is as follows: "Wherever a self-identification form is used, the employer should advise the applicant that identification by race, sex, and national origin is sought, not for employment decisions, but for record keeping in compliance with federal law" (p. 23277).

affirmative action (affording employment and training opportunities to women and minorities) is not a written policy but, rather, *evidence* that over a period of time minority representation has increased at all levels and in all portions of the work force where deficiencies had existed. Thus, an organization should not adhere to a specific number of females or minorities who will annually be promoted or admitted to a special training program; rather it must show that it is increasingly allowing these people access to these employment opportunities. This issue will be discussed further in the section regarding major court cases.

THE EQUAL EMPLOYMENT OPPORTUNITY COMMISSION

The EEOC is an independent federal agency that was created by Section 705 of Title VII of the Civil Rights Act. When it receives a charge that an alleged violation has occurred, it has the legal power to: (1) subpoena and question witnesses under oath, (2) recommend a conciliation between the complainant and the company, and (3) contact the OFCCP if a federal contractor or subcontractor is involved.

In contrast to the OFCCP, the EEOC does not have the power to order an organization to discontinue a practice that it believes is discriminatory. However, in March 1972 Congress passed legislation giving the EEOC direct access to the courts to present evidence of alleged discrimination. Most court cases involving alleged discrimination stem from charges filed with the EEOC, rather than the OFCCP. OFCCP cases are more likely to be settled out of court because a company does not want its contract suspended while waiting for the litigation to end.

The EEOC has the authority to investigate the practices and records of organizations that employ 15 or more people who work for 20 or more weeks for an organization. It can require organizations to maintain records regarding the race (particularly of blacks, American Indians, Hispanics, Asians, and whites), sex, religion, and national origin of all applicants/employees.

Deference to Other Agencies

The EEOC is required to defer to state fair employment practice commissions (e.g., Washington State Human Rights Commission) before initiating its own investigation. Persons who believe that they have been subjected to discrimination must file a complaint within 90 days with a local agency. Sixty days after the charge has been filed with the local agency for review, the EEOC may begin its own investigation. In conducting its investigation, the EEOC is not bound by the findings of a city or state agency. If the EEOC finds the charge to be substantiated, it provides the complainant with a notice of right to sue. Within 90 days following such notice, the individual must file suit with the court to preserve the claim.*

Investigation of Charges

The EEOC investigates a complaint by first interviewing the complainant. Next, it reviews the employment practices of the company. This may include investigation of hiring, promotion, seniority lists, test files, performance ratings, race identity files, and files on all job openings. It may include information on departments and jobs in addition to those covered by the specific charge. If a finding of probable cause is reached, the role of the EEOC is to attempt to bring about conciliation. The objective of conciliation is for the EEOC to get the organization to correct the original situation and any other employment practices determined to be in violation of Title VII. Conciliation remedies can include relief for the complainant (e.g., reinstatement, back pay, promotion), relief for other similarly affected individuals, changes in the organization's discriminatory practices, and affirmative action steps involving recruitment of minorities. If a conciliation cannot be reached, the EEOC can refer the case to the OFCCP if the organization is a federal contractor or subcontractor, and it can file a suit against the organization.

An employee can file discrimination charges with two or more agencies (e.g., the EEOC and the OFCCP). Consequently, an employer can be required to conduct a defense with more than one agency at the same time. The employee, however, must ultimately choose the remedy designated by only one agency. In this way employers are not asked to pay twice for one discriminatory action.

---

*The EEOC does not have to accept the person's request to withdraw the complaint. It can go ahead on its own and file suit with the court. It is likely to do this if it believes the individual was threatened or bribed into withdrawing the complaint, or if it believes that the likelihood of a similar complaint being filed against the company is high.

Employees who were not involved in the original complaint, but who claim similar discrimination as being members of the affected class, may also join in a suit seeking relief. Employers found guilty in such cases may be required by the court to publish a notice inviting members of the class to apply for jobs and back pay.

Class action suits can result in a finding of discrimination on the part of an organization even if the court finds that the original complainant's claim is without merit. The claim of each class member is considered on its own merits, and discriminatory practices may have affected other class members even though the original complainant is found, for example, to have been treated properly.

EEOC Guideline Changes

The EEOC made several significant changes in its guidelines in 1978. These changes include the definition of tests, the 80 percent rule, and the bottom-line alternative strategy.

The 1970 guidelines defined *tests* to include any paper-and-pencil test or *performance measure* used as a basis for any employment decision. This definition included any and all formally scored, quantified, or standardized techniques used for selection and performance appraisal purposes. The adoption of the guidelines resulted in many organizations abandoning *formal* selection and performance appraisal systems in favor of informal, intuitive procedures. Consequently, the 1978 Uniform Guidelines redefined test to also include unstandardized, informal, and unscored appraisal procedures. In short, *any* and *all* personnel decisions affecting an employee's status in an organization are defined as tests, and tests that adversely affect people in a protected class must be valid. That is, where adverse impact exists, an organization must be able to present evidence showing a relationship between decisions based on assessments made by a given procedure, and subsequent criteria such as job performance, performance in a training program, permanence, advancement, or other critical job behavior.

As of August 1978, the EEOC and other federal agencies adopted a rule of thumb for determining whether they would take an organization to court. This rule of thumb concerns the definition of adverse impact. *Adverse impact* is defined as a substantially different rate of selection in hiring, promotion, or other employment decisions that works to the disadvantage of members of a race, sex, age, or ethnic group. If a selection rate for any race, sex, or ethnic group is less than four-fifths or 80 percent of the selection rate for the group with the highest rate of selection, a test is considered to have an adverse impact on the former group. This four-fifths rule is simply a rule of thumb followed by the EEOC. It is not intended as a legal definition of discrimination. It is simply a practical way for the EEOC to focus its attention on serious discrepancies in rates of hiring and promotion that may result from discrimination (EEOC, 1978).

For example, if the promotion rate for whites is 60 percent and for nonwhites it is 40 percent, then the nonwhite rate is only four-sixths or 67 percent of that for whites. Thus, adverse impact may exist for nonwhites.

The courts, however, have ruled that if an employment practice is shown to be valid, it is not considered discriminatory even though it may have adverse impact. However, the thrust of the new Uniform Guidelines does not require an employer to validate an employment practice; but, rather it encourages an *alternative strategy,* namely, to engage in voluntary action programs that are conscious of race, color, sex, or ethnic origin.

The new guidelines imply that a voluntary action program is an appropriate defense for an organization against charges resulting from the use of employment practices that have had an adverse effect on a group (e.g., blacks, males). Thus, it would appear that the new guidelines have in many ways abandoned the concept of equal opportunity for all employees for the concept of equal results (e.g., an equal proportion of whites and nonwhites). This apparent abandonment of individualism for collectivism violates three axioms of psychology: (1) Individuals differ in many ways. (2) Individual differences in personal characteristics and backgrounds are often related to individual differences in behavior on the job. (3) It is in the best interest of organizations and employees that information about relevant differences between individuals be developed and used in making personnel decisions.

In 1979 Division 14 (Industrial-Organizational Psychology) of the American Psychological Association withdrew its support of the Uniform Guidelines.* The role of well-developed and uniform professional opinion

---

*As of this date, the APA Committee on Psychological Tests and Assessment has also refused to endorse the Uniform Guidelines. A series of five letters to the APA, Division 14 of the APA, and the EEOC concerning this issue has been printed in its entirety in the February, 1980 issue of *The Industrial Organizational Psychologist.*

in influencing the courts is of importance for organizations to take note of because in 1977, the Supreme Court supported a lower court opinion in *United States* v. *South Carolina* that: "To the extent that EEOC Guidelines conflict with well-grounded expert opinion and accepted professional standards, they need not be controlling."

An organization must carefully consider this *alternative strategy* in comparison to a validation strategy. Title VII does not command that the less qualified employee be preferred over the better qualified employee simply because of minority origin. The employer who chooses this alternative strategy runs the risk of violating both the Civil Rights Act and the Constitution. Taking simply a numbers approach (quotas) referred to by the Uniform Guidelines as the *bottom line,* instead of validating employment practices, may well lead to legal challenges, not to mention a decrease in productivity.

For an indication of how challenges to appraisal practices will be resolved in the future, let us examine major court decisions concerning performance appraisals. Because employers have been winning only five percent of the race, sex, and age discrimination cases that end up in court, present and potential managers are well advised to examine these decisions closely (Mitnick, 1977).

MAJOR COURT DECISIONS

Griggs v. *Duke Power* (1971)

This was the first Supreme Court decision involving Title VII. Duke Power had employed only blacks in one department and only whites in other departments. A high school diploma or a satisfactory score on two standardized pencil-and-paper aptitude tests was required for employment in the four departments where the whites worked.

The effect of the Court's decision is as follows. First, it made the EEOC Guidelines the law of the land by explicitly endorsing the guidelines as "expressing the will of Congress." Second, it ruled that any and all employment criteria (e.g., educational requirements) that adversely affect a class member (e.g., women and nonwhites) must be shown to be job related. While the specific term *validation* was not used, the Court did endorse the procedures called for by the 1970 guidelines that do require validation. Third, the Court ruled that employment procedures, "neutral in intent," are not justifiable if they result in discriminatory practices. Finally, the Court's opinion states by inference that quota systems are contrary to the Civil Rights Act and, further, that it is equally illegal to discriminate against members of nonminority groups. In this regard, the decision reads:

> Congress did not intend by Title VII, to guarantee a job to every person regardless of their qualifications. In short, the Act does not command that a person be hired simply because he was formerly the subject of discrimination or because he is a member of a minority group. Discriminatory preferences for any group, minority or majority, are precisely and only what the Congress has proscribed.

As a final note, it is appropriate to quote from the closing statement of the Supreme Court's opinion:

> Nothing in the Act precludes the use of testing or measuring procedures; obviously they are useful. What Congress has forbidden is giving these devices and mechanisms controlling force unless they are demonstrably a reasonable measure of performance. Congress has not demanded that the less qualified be preferred over the more qualified simply because of minority origins. Far from disparaging job qualifications as such, Congress has made such qualifications a controlling factor, so that race, religion, nationality, and sex become irrelevant. What Congress has commanded is that any test used must measure the person for the job, not the person in the abstract.

Brito v. Zia Company (1973)

The Zia company was found to be in violation of Title VII when a disproportionate number of protected group members were laid off on the basis of low performance appraisal scores. In its findings, the Court commented that the performance appraisal system used by Zia in determining layoffs was, in fact, an employment test. Moreover, it stated that the company had not shown that its performance appraisal instrument was valid in the sense that it was related to *important* elements of work behavior in the jobs where the employees were being evaluated. In short, the court found that the evaluations were based on the best judgments and opinions of supervisors ". . . but not on any identifiable criteria based on quality or quantity of work on specific performance that were supported by some kind of record."

In reviewing this case keep in mind that discharges prompt the majority of discrimination cases (Mitnick, 1977). Discipline and discharge procedures must be applied in a uniform manner. Documentation of the steps taken is essential. The following incident (Stanton, 1976) demonstrates the necessity for documentation.

The case involved a 56-year-old laboratory technician in a midwest manufacturing company. He claimed that he was discharged because of his age. His employer stated that even though the man had been employed for a long time, the quality of his work was consistently poor and his attitude and attendance had been unsatisfactory. The company further claimed that the employee had been advised repeatedly of the company's dissatisfaction with his work before he was finally terminated.

The employee responded by stating that his work was, in fact, acceptable, that his attitude was good, and that he had never been advised that the company was not pleased with his work. He further stated that he had received regular pay increases.

The court ruled in favor of the employee. It ordered the company to give him back his job and to pay back wages and legal costs, *because* the company could not offer sufficient written documentation that the employee's work performance had been bad enough to warrant discharge. The attendance records could not prove that his attendance was poor. The employee's personnel file contained no evidence that he had ever been considered a poor worker, or that he had been spoken to by his supervisor about unacceptable work. The only thing the file indicated was that the employee had received regular pay increases.

Wade v. Mississippi Cooperative Extension Service (1974)

In this case, black employees alleged that the evaluation instrument used to appraise their performance discriminated against them as a class. The Court held that the Extension Service had the burden of demonstrating that the appraisal instrument was job related (i.e., valid) and served a legitimate employment need.

In finding the Extension Service guilty, the Court noted that what the company called an "objective appraisal of job performance" was in fact based on supervisory ratings of such general characteristics as leadership, public acceptance, attitude toward people, appearance, grooming, personal conduct, outlook on life, ethical habits, resourcefulness, capacity for growth, mental alertness, and loyalty to the organization:

> As may be readily observed, these are traits which are susceptible to partiality and to the personal taste, whim, or fancy of the evaluator. We must then view these factors as presently utilized to be patently subjective in form and obviously susceptible to completely subjective treatment.

Albermarle Paper Company v. Moody (1975)

In this case, the performance appraisals were not criticized as a test, per se, but rather as the criteria (or performance measures) against which the selection tests for hiring purposes had been validated.* The Court ruled that in the process of validating their tests, the company had not conducted a job analysis to identify the critical requirements of jobs. Instead, the selection tests had been validated against supervisory rankings where the basis of the ranking of employee performance was undefined. To make matters worse for the company, employees were ranked against one another without regard for the fact that the employees were doing different jobs. The court concluded that:

> . . . there is no way of knowing precisely what criteria of job performance that supervisors were considering, whether each supervisor was considering the same criteria—or whether, indeed, any of the supervisors actually applied a focused and stable body of criteria of any kind.

---

*As noted in Chapter 1, the first step in validating a selection instrument is to define how performance will be measured, which should be done through a systematic job analysis. A job analysis identifies the important tasks, duties, and responsibilities associated with a job. Second, on the basis of the knowledge gained from the job analysis, psychologists develop tests that should predict who will do well on the performance measures. Third, people are measured on how well they do on the test and they are measured on how well they do on the job performance measures. If the correlation between the two sets of measures is significant, the test is considered valid (see Arvey, 1979). In Albermarle v. Moody the correlation was significant, but the court did not like the performance measures against which the test was validated.

United Steelworkers of America v. *Weber* (1979)

In a case involving admission into a university (*Bakke* v. *Regents of the University of California,* 1978), the Supreme Court decided that explicit quotas for minorities were wrong. Sixteen seats in the medical school had been reserved for nonwhites. Justice Powell wrote: "The guarantee of equal protection cannot mean one thing when applied to one individual and something else when applied to a person of another color." However, the Court did make it clear that preferential-treatment programs are appropriate when they remedy past instances of discrimination against minorities. There was no history of past discrimination at the university where Bakke had applied for admission. Thus, the Court decided in Bakke's favor. The decision set the stage for a suit filed by Brian Weber against Kaiser Aluminum and Chemical Corporation and the Steelworkers Union.

Kaiser and the Steelworkers Union agreed to set up affirmative action training programs. Blacks accounted for less than 2 percent of the 273 craftsmen at the plant. Blacks constituted 39 percent of the local work force. To close the gap, the company and the union decided to accept whites and blacks into the program on a one-to-one basis. When Brian Weber was rejected from the program he sued both his employer and the union charging that he had been illegally excluded from a skilled-craft training program that would have made him eligible for higher paying jobs, such as electrician and repairman. Weber had more seniority than two blacks who had been admitted into the program.

By a 5-to-2 vote, the Supreme Court ruled that employers can indeed give blacks special preference for jobs that were traditionally held by whites. Moreover, the court stated that whether or not it had discriminatory job practices in the past, a company can use affirmative action programs to remedy "manifest racial unbalance" in employment without fear of being challenged for its efforts in the courts. This latter statement is important for employers. It means that companies and unions can establish affirmative action plans under similar conditions without fear of losing court suits on the basis of reverse discrimination. Equally crucial for organizations is the provision that organizations that set up affirmative action programs are not required to admit to discrimination in the past. Admission of past discrimination could create costly lawsuits.

Thus, quotas are acceptable if: (1) they deal with job categories that have traditionally been segregated, and (2) they are *temporary* in nature.

Justice Brennan noted that when the percentage of black skilled workers at the Kaiser plant approximates the percentage of skilled blacks in the local labor force, the program will end.

In conclusion, it is likely that the EEOC will use this ruling to push companies to accept outright quota systems for minorities. However, keep in mind the following issues. First, the Court was sharply divided on the decision. Burger and Rehnquist dissented forcefully, pointing out that the two lower courts that had decided in favor of Weber had followed the letter of the 1964 law by banning discrimination in employment, no matter whether the bias is against blacks or whites. Brennan, who wrote the majority opinion, conceded this point. Further, Burger and Rehnquist pointed out that Congressional proponents of Title VII had argued "tirelessly" for 83 days of debate that the Act would be used neither to require nor permit quotas. Burger concluded: "Congress expressly prohibited the discrimination against Brian Weber the Court approves now."

Second, to be safe from Weber-type challenges, personnel decisions must not exclude whites altogether; whites must not be fired to make room for nonwhites; goals/quotas must deal only with jobs that have traditionally been held by employees who were predominantly of the same race or sex, and the goals/quotas must be temporary. Quotas must end as soon as there is no evidence of adverse impact. Our recommendation is to (1) actively recruit females and minorities in addition to whites and males, (2) validate personnel decisions in accordance with the procedures discussed in Chapter 3, and (3) select, promote, reward, transfer, demote, and terminate the most appropriate people.

In the Weber case, there was no indication that he was superior in performance skills to the blacks who were admitted into the training program. There was evidence that Bakke's skills were superior to those minority individuals who were admitted to the medical school. In *Reeves* v. *Eaves* (1977) the court ordered a police department to stop hiring less-qualified individuals on the basis of race. The court required the development of validated procedures for making personnel decisions. Quotas or a bottom-line strategy were not recommended.

THE 1978 CIVIL SERVICE REFORM ACT

Section 430 of the 1978 Civil Service Reform Act deals specifically with the establishment of performance appraisal systems for all federal employees except those in the Central Intelligence Agency, the Foreign Service, the General Accounting Office, as well as judges, physicians, dentists, nurses, and individuals appointed by the President. The act is noteworthy because it specifies a sound straightforward approach to performance appraisal. Moreover, it is likely that these requirements will be applied to the private sector within the next decade. It is only a matter of time before a federal judge decides that an organization's appraisal practices that adversely affect minorities must be completely revised. In searching for guidelines for the organization to follow, it is likely that a judge will recommend part, if not all, of this Act.

In brief, the Act states that each agency shall develop one or more appraisal systems that encourage *employee participation* in establishing performance standards. The standards are to be based on *critical* elements of the job. The method or procedure (e.g., job analysis) by which such critical elements are established must be clearly recorded in writing. The employee must be advised of these critical requirements before rather than after the appraisal. Finally, and most important, an employee's appraisal must be based on an evaluation of his or her performance of the critical requirements of the job. "An appraisal system must not include any controls, such as a requirement to rate on a bell curve, that prevent fair appraisal of performance in relation to the performance standards" (Federal Register, 1979, p. 3448). In short, an employee must be appraised solely on how well the job is being performed, rather than on a comparison (ranking) with other individuals.

The appraisals are to be conducted and recorded in writing *at least* once a year. The results of the appraisal must yield information that can be used for making decisions regarding the "training, rewarding, reassigning, promoting, reducing in grade, retaining, and removing employees" (Public Law 95-454, 1978, 92STAT., p. 1132). An employee whose reduction in grade or termination is proposed must receive 30 days advance written notice of the proposed action that identifies the critical elements of the employee's job involved in each instance of unacceptable performance. The employee must be allowed to respond to the charge orally and in writing.

Because of the importance of performance appraisals in rewarding and/or punishing (e.g., terminating) an employee, each agency is required to provide training to those individuals who conduct appraisals (see Chapter 7 for one approach to training). In addition, each agency must establish procedures for conducting periodic evaluations of the effectiveness of its appraisal system *and* use the evaluation data to refine, alter, or improve the system. The Office of Personnel Management is responsible for determining whether an agency is fulfilling the requirements of the Act, and it has the authority to direct an agency to implement an appropriate system or revise an existing system to meet the requirements of this Act.

CLOSING REMARKS

We will conclude this chapter with a list of key legal considerations affecting performance appraisals:

1. Any person who employs 15 or more people for at least 20 weeks is responsible for keeping accurate records on the results of employment decisions for groups constituting 2 percent or more of the total labor force in the relevant labor area. These records must be kept separate from both selection and performance appraisal programs.

2. The courts have ruled that any and all decision-making processes, from background checks to supervisory performance ratings, that affect an employee's status in an organization are tests and thus are subject to scrutiny for adverse impact.

3. Employers sometimes attempt to distinguish among a hiring, a promotion, or a performance appraisal decision. They sometimes assert that there are no lines of progression within the organization, and that a transfer should not be regarded as a promotion. However, the courts generally find such distinctions irrelevant. It is the employment practices that are subject to challenge, and the question is whether the organization's practices are discriminatory (*Domingo* v. *New England Fish Co.,* 1977).

4. An employee who files an action under Title VII has the burden of establishing a prima-facie case (i.e., on the surface it would appear that discrimination exists) of employment discrimination. This burden may be met by the employee with statistical proof, although proof of specific instances of actual discrimination are sometimes required. Once the employee has presented a prima-facie case, the organization has the burden of proving that its appraisal decisions were made on a nondiscriminatory basis (*Albermarle* v. *Moody,* 1975).

5. In establishing a violation of Title VII, it is not necessary to prove that the defendant *intentionally* discriminated against one or more people. "Congress directed the thrust of the Act to the consequences of employment practices, not simply the motivation" (*Griggs* v. *Duke Power,* 1971). The inquiry must therefore be directed to the impact, rather than the intent of an allegedly discriminatory personnel practice or performance criterion (*Domingo* v. *New England Fish Co.,* 1977). However, the courts do make a distinction between adverse impact and disparate treatment. A plaintiff can claim that a superficially neutral practice has an adverse impact on nonwhites. The issue is then characterized as an adverse-impact case and intent becomes irrelevant. Alternately, the plaintiff can claim that there is disparate treatment—such as where a nonwhite is reprimanded/ dismissed for something whites can allegedly do with impunity. Here, intent is an issue.

6. The crux of statistical proof in discrimination cases is the presentation of percentage differences between majority and minority groups sufficiently substantial to support an inference that such differences would not exist in the absence of discrimination. The burden then shifts to the company to dispel the inference. If it is unsuccessful, the court may proceed as if discrimination explains the observed differences, even in the absence of *direct* evidence of discrimination (*Domingo* v. *New England Fish Co.,* 1977).

7. The numerical methods used to assess the adverse impact of performance appraisals depends, according to Edwards (1976), on the nature of the personnel decision it supports. If the decision is a dichotomous one, such as to retain or to layoff, then direct comparison of proportions of minority and majority persons assigned the same status should be made. If the performance appraisal results in assigning employees to rating categories such as excellent, above average, average, and below average, then statistical comparisons of the frequencies of minorities and non-minorities in each category should be made.

If a numerical score is assigned to individuals, such as is the case for behaviorally anchored rating scales (see Chapter 3), then the averages for minority and nonminority groups should be statistically compared. In each of these comparisons, if the sample is large enough to be statistically significant, and if the odds of observed differences occurring by chance alone are less than one in 20, the courts are likely to determine that the statistics suggest an inference of discrimination (Edwards, 1976).

8. Employers often argue that comparative employment statistics (e.g., number of female engineers versus number of male engineers in the organization) are insufficient to establish a prima-facie case of discrimination. They state that discrimination can only be shown by demographic statistics where the employer's work force is compared with the work force available in the appropriate geographic area where the employer is located. The 1978 EEOC Guidelines appear to disagree with this argument. The courts, in fact, do disagree with it. Comparative statistics from an employer's work force are often used as evidence of discrimination (*James* v. *Stockham Valves and Fittings Co.*, 1977; *Wetzel* v. *Liberty Mutual Insurance Co.*; *Pettway* v. *American Cast Iron Pipe Co.*, 1974). Comparative statistics are especially applicable in cases involving performance appraisal decisions.

9. Where demographic statistics *are* ruled admissible, employers often contend that the labor market can only be defined in terms of the geographic area where the employer hires its employees. But the courts (e.g., *Domingo* v. *New England Fish Co.*, 1977) have ruled that this limitation is improper, especially where the employer seeks to use the area it chooses to find employees instead of the area surrounding the place of business. The area where an organization chooses not to hire its employees is considered as relevant to the courts as the areas where it does hire. The courts have not adhered to one formula in defining the relevant labor market, but rather have treated the issue as a question of fact to be legally determined.

10. The courts have developed a deep skepticism of appraisal techniques involving supervisory judgments that depend almost entirely on subjective evaluation (*Rowe* v. *General Motors,* 1972). The courts have specifically condemned procedures based on trait scales that are discussed in Chapter 3 (*James* v. *Stockham Valves and Fittings Co.,* 1977). In brief, trait scales consist of vague terms such as commitment, initiative, and aggressiveness, that are not defined in terms of overt observable behavior.

11. The best defense against a charge of adverse impact in performance appraisal is a properly validated appraisal system. In order to show that a measure is valid "there must be a proper job analysis to determine appropriate measures of job performance. These job analyses are required so that the study's author may select the most important behaviors or measures

of job performance for correlation to the test results" (*Dickerson* v. *U.S. Steel*, 1978). "Without a job analysis to define the knowledge, skills, or behavior required on the job, and a description of how the appraisal instrument samples critical and/or frequent components of a job, a claim of validity cannot be substantiated" (*Albermarle* v. *Moody*, 1976). In *United States* v. *City of Chicago,* the appellate court rejected a study that had no job analysis in it. In short, the performance appraisal system must be shown to be job related if adverse effect is shown (*Griggs* v. *Duke Power*, 1971). Job analysis, as previously noted, identifies the important tasks, duties, and responsibilities of a job.

12. Employers often state that employment decisions do not have to be validated unless adverse effect has been shown, which is true. But, it is somewhat imprudent to wait until a charge has been filed to validate a performance appraisal system. If comparative statistics are ruled admissible by the court, there are few employers who could win their case, because few employers currently have approximately the same percentage of females and nonwhites in jobs other than entry level as they do males and whites. And, many companies do not even have a substantial number of nonwhites and females in entry-level jobs.

13. The adoption of the bottom-line strategy (i.e., quotas) in place of validated personnel systems is inadvisable unless the organization is under a court order to do so or has job departments where the employees are predominantly of the same race, sex, or national origin. Regardless of what the EEOC implies, discriminatory preference for any group, minority or majority, is prohibited by law.*

14. An organization would be well advised to study the 1978 Civil Service Reform Act as a model for developing an appraisal system. In brief, the Act requires that employees participate in identifying the critical elements of their job, that employees be evaluated solely on the extent to which they fulfill the critical requirements of the job, that rewards should be tied directly to performance, that the appraisal should take place one or more times a year, that the individual should receive 30 days notice of a

---

*Note that this is not a criticism of equal employment opportunity laws, but rather a direct criticism of the EEOC as an agency whose responsibility it is to enforce equal employment opportunity laws. For a discussion of the agency's strengths and weaknesses, the reader is directed to Pati and Reilly (1977).

decision regarding demotion or termination, and that the individual should have an opportunity to respond to the decision orally and in writing.
15. The Uniform Guidelines, the 1978 Civil Service Reform Act and the courts state that performance measures must be based on critical or important requirements of the job. We were recently amused by a client who wanted to validate a selection test against performance measures that would not be used for performance appraisal or any other business purpose. If the performance measures are not useful to the company, other than being handy for correlating them with test scores, they cannot be critical and they should not be used.

SUMMARY

Title VII of the 1964 Civil Rights Act states that it is unlawful to make employment decisions on the basis of an individual's race, color, sex, or national origin. Employment decisions include those regarding the training, rewarding, reassigning, promoting, demoting, retaining, and removing of employees. The Act applies to any organization that employs 15 or more people for 20 or more weeks.

The two primary government agencies concerned with employment discrimination are the OFCCP and the EEOC. These agencies are particularly interested in the sex (female) and race (blacks, American Indians, Hispanics, and Asians) of employees in six job categories: (1) officials and managers, (2) professionals, (3) technicians, (4) salesworkers, (5) office and clerical workers, and (6) skilled craftsmen.

The OFCCP investigates manufacturing operations who have federal contracts of $10,000 or more. If the OFCCP believes that an organization is engaging in discriminatory practices it can suspend/cancel the organization's contract, which can be very costly to an organization.

Unlike the OFCCP, the EEOC does not have the power to directly order an organization to discontinue a practice it believes is discriminatory. It can, however, take a company to court. Approximately 5 percent of the court cases involving employment discrimination are won by defending organizations.

In accepting a prima-facie charge of discrimination (on face there appears to be discrimination), the courts have generally relied on demographic or comparative statistics. A prima-facie case of discrimination may be shown by demographic statistics when the employer's work force is compared with the work force available in the surrounding community, and the percentage of eligible minorities/females in the community is significantly greater than that which is employed by the organization. Where comparative statistics are used, the court simply examines the percentage of female/minority with the percentage of male/majority within one or more job classifications within that one organization. If the statistics indicate that adverse impact exists, the burden of proof is then on the defendant to explain why the statistics are not the result of discriminatory personnel practices.

The government recommends two methods of defense against a discrimination charge. The first involves a validation strategy. That is, the defendant must be able to present evidence showing the job relatedness of appraisal decisions. This procedure is in accordance with the science of psychology. The alternative strategy urges the adoption of a bottom line. That is, organizations are encouraged to engage in voluntary affirmative action programs that are conscious of the race, color, sex, or ethnic origin of employees.

In finding organizations guilty of discrimination, the courts have pointed to the use of racial quotas where there was no history of past discrimination, the use of tests or experience requirements that cannot be shown to be related to satisfactory performance on the job, the use of appraisal instruments that are not based on a systematic job analysis, the use of poorly defined traits on the appraisal instrument, and the ranking of employees who were doing different jobs against one another.

The 1978 Civil Service Reform Act serves as a model for organizations to follow in developing performance appraisal systems. In brief, the Act states that performance standards must be based on critical elements of the job, the employee must be advised of these critical requirements before rather than after the appraisal, and the employee must be evaluated solely on how well the job is being performed rather than on a comparison with other individuals.

The Development and Validation of Appraisal Systems

3

INTRODUCTION

The appraisal of employee performance is a key process for an organization trying to increase or maintain its effectiveness because the actions of employees affect the optimal use of the organization's capital, technological, and marketing resources. Despite the obvious importance of making accurate appraisals of an employee's performance, most appraisal instruments, if they exist at all, consist of a list of key traits (is a team player, is conscientious, shows initiative) or cost-related variables (sold 15 trucks). Both appraisal instruments are limited from the standpoint of counseling and developing an employee. In this chapter we discuss these limitations, the importance of a job analysis to identify critical job behaviors, the construction of the appraisal instrument, and the different ways of assessing reliability and validity of the appraisal system.

APPRAISALS BASED ON TRAITS

Traits such as commitment, creativity, loyalty, initiative, and the like are words surrounded with ambiguity. Telling a person to be a better listener or to show more initiative may be good advice, but it doesn't tell the individual *what to do* to accept this advice. These words must be defined explicitly for the employee.

For example, a director of research and development was told by the vice president to work on her communication skills. Because she was from a foreign country and felt ill at ease speaking before a large group, she enrolled in a three-day course to improve her oral skills at a cost to the organization of $3,000. At her next performance appraisal interview six months later, the vice president repeated the same criticism to the employee. She became highly irritated and explained to the vice president the value of the course she had taken to improve her skills. Astonished, the vice president replied that all he wanted was for her to send him carbon copies of memos she sent to a rival vice president!

As another illustration of problems with trait-oriented appraisal instruments, ask ten people to write a description of an aggressive employee. Many people will write a positive description. However, several people will almost always describe the person using such words as obnoxious, pushy, or inconsiderate.*

Finally, as pointed out in Chapter 2, a trait-oriented appraisal instrument is likely to be rejected by the courts. And yet, most firms continue to use forms containing such words as "decisiveness, stability, and integrity" (Lazer & Wikstrom, 1977). Examples of appraisal instruments emphasizing traits or personality characteristics are shown in Tables 3.1 and 3.2. These two instruments are currently being used by two organizations to appraise people.

One advantage of trait scales is that they can be developed quickly. It does not take considerable time or imagination to brainstorm a set of words that are considered positive, complimentary, and necessary for all employees (e.g., dependable, unselfish, tactful). A second advantage of trait scales is that they can be used across jobs. Thus the organization can often get by with only one appraisal form. But, these two advantages are illusory. Feedback and training must be specific if they are to bring

---

*In a review of the literature, Kavanagh (1971) concluded that trait-related scales are almost as good as performance-based scales. We argue in Chapter 5 that prior to training supervisors in the skills necessary for observing and recording employee job behavior, it doesn't matter what type of appraisal instrument is used. None is very good from the standpoint of reliability or validity. *After* supervisors are trained to improve their objectivity in observing and recording employee behavior, trait scales are clearly inferior to other scales. The major point of the present discussion is that traits are generally undefined in terms of observable employee job behaviors. Moreover, as Borman (1979) has pointed out, they refer at best to potential predictors of performance rather than to performance itself. Thus they are poor from the standpoint of feedback and goal setting with the employee on ways to maintain or improve performance.

TABLE 3.1

A Trait-Oriented Performance Appraisal Rating

Name

Department | Section | Position

Reporting Period:

a = superior | d = below average
b = above average | e = unsatisfactory
c = average

1. Ability to Adapt	9. Practical Talent
a d	a d
b e	b e
c	c
2. Diligence and Application	10. Potential
a d	a d
b e	b e
c	c
3. Cooperation with Others	11. Communication Skills
a d	a d
b e	b e
c	c
4. Quality of Work	12. Planning
a d	a d
b e	b e
c	c
5. Making Decisions	13. Capacity
a d	a d
b e	b e
c	c
6. Manner and Appearance	14. Leadership
a d	a d
b e	b e
c	c
7. Job Contribution	15. Calmness
a d	a d
b e	b e
c	c
8. Initiative	16. Personal Conduct
a d	a d
b e	b e
c	c

TABLE 3.2

A Trait-Oriented Performance Appraisal Rating

Name			PLC/CO	Class	Date	Situation		
S = Sufficient D = Deficient								
	S	D		S	D		S	D
Bearing			Integrity			Initiative		
Enthusiasm			Decisiveness			Judgment		
Justice			Endurance			Dependability		
Physical Courage			Knowledge			Unselfishness		
Tact			Loyalty			Moral Courage		

Remarks: Comment on all weaknesses. Unobserved traits will not be
        marked.

	Overall Evaluation (Circle One)		
(Use reverse, if necessary)	Satisfactory	Unsatisfactory	Marginal
Plt. Ldr	Rank	Card Initials	

about a relatively permanent change in an employee's behavior. Further, the feedback and training must be related to critical or important aspects of the job if they are going to meaningfully affect an employee's performance. What is critical or important in one job is not necessarily critical or important in other jobs. Appraisal instruments must be designed for the job or job family in question if the appraisal process is to be effective.

We will close this discussion of traits with the following statement:

An employer has no business with a man's personality. Employment is a specific contract calling for specific performance, and for nothing else. Any attempt of an employer to go beyond this is usurpation. It is immoral as well as illegal intrusion of privacy. It is abuse of power. An employee owes no "loyalty," he owes no "love," and no "attitudes"—he owes performance and nothing else. . . Management and manager development should concern themselves with changes in behavior (emphasis added) likely to make a man more effective. (Drucker, 1973, pp. 424–425)

APPRAISALS BASED ON COST-RELATED OUTCOMES

Senior level management, stockholders, and consumers are generally concerned with economic or cost-related outcomes of an organization. That is, they are concerned with quantitative measures or performance outcomes such as profits, costs, and returns on investment. Thus, it would appear logical that profits, costs, and returns on investment should be a major responsibility of a manager. Therefore, it could be argued that an appraisal document should measure the manager, if not individual subordinates, on the extent to which these measures are satisfactory. Such measures usually serve as excellent indicators of an organization's effectiveness. Nevertheless, they are generally inadequate indicators by themselves of a single person's job effectiveness for several reasons.

First, cost-related measures are almost always deficient in that they often omit important factors for which a person should be held accountable (e.g., teamplaying as defined by a superintendent in one district loaning equipment to a superintendent in another district). This deficiency is a major criticism of management by objectives (MBO) where the performance goals or standards are usually set in terms of cost-related targets.

Emphasis is placed primarily on tangible results that are perceived to be easily measurable. Consequently, many employees feel that there is an overemphasis on quantitative goals because they are not measured on nor do they receive credit for important aspects of their jobs which cannot be spelled out in quantitative terms (Ivancevich, Donnelly, & Lyon, 1970). For example, a marketing manager might specify that a major objective of the forthcoming year is to increase the number of accounts by 10 percent in the Vancouver area. A personnel manager, however, would have difficulty expressing the desired end results of a new career development program in percentage figures. The latter problem has caused much frustration and anxiety among MBO participants (Ivancevich et al., 1970).

Industrial psychologists have historically preferred these concrete, tangible measures because they believed that these "objective" measures eliminate errors in observation (see Chapter 5) and judgment that often occur when ratings are used. However, Smith (1976) has cogently argued that careful observation is a necessity for evaluating the meaning of hard criteria such as tardiness, absences, and accidents, as well as for making valid ratings on so-called soft measures. "Human judgment enters into every criterion. . ." (Smith, 1976, p. 757).

Second, as alluded to in the first point, cost-related measures are difficult to obtain on employees in many jobs. For example, a cost-related measure of a logging cutter's effectiveness might be the number of trees cut divided by the number of hours worked. But what cost-related measures exist for a personnel manager, engineer, or newspaper reporter? Economic measures are obtainable only when the employee produces a distinguishable output. But such output is generally more typical of blue-collar than white-collar or managerial employees; and most blue-collar union contracts contain clauses that prohibit the collection of these data for individual performance appraisal.

Even when such measures can be obtained, they are usually applicable only for the work group as a whole, because no one worker has substantial control over the output measured. Employee performance is often affected by the performance of others. If they do poorly, the employee does poorly. Work groups should be evaluated, but performance appraisal is concerned with the individual employee. Employees should not be evaluated on factors that are beyond their control. Thus, a third problem with the exclusive use of cost-related measures is that they often take into account factors for which the individual is not responsible.

Situational factors over which an individual may have little or no control, but which can affect a person's performance negatively, include tools and equipment, materials and supplies, budgetary support, time availability, and the work environment that includes noise, heat, and light levels (Peters, O'Conner, & Rudolf, 1980). To the extent that these situational factors constrain performance, the motivation level of employees is reduced because their belief that effort leads to performance is decreased (Peters & O'Conner, 1980). Thus, to the extent that only performance outcomes are measured and situational constraints affect them adversely, employee feelings may become so strong that the employee chooses to either quit the job or lower commitment to those goals for which situational variables inhibit goal accomplishment (Peters et al., 1980). This is particularly true for employees with high levels of ability and motivation. Situational inhibitors obviously have a minimum effect on the potential performance of persons with little ability or motivation. The consequence can be an organization populated by the latter group of people.

Cummings and Schwab (1973) argue that it is particularly unfair to distribute organizational rewards on the basis of these cost-related measures unless the employee has substantial control over the output measured. However, they do point out that group productivity data may be useful for evaluating the supervisor of the work group. We would argue that even here the evidence (e.g., Likert, 1967; Curtis, Smith, & Smoll, 1979) suggests that this is not always appropriate, because the performance of work groups is usually affected by other work groups with whom they are linked. Moreover, the leader's performance is often directly affected by the performance of subordinates whom he or she may lack the authority to reprimand or replace. Further, the performance of groups can be affected by the situational constraints that affect the individual employee.

Fourth, the sole use of these measures can encourage a results-at-all-costs mentality that can run counter to both corporate ethics policies and legal requirements. Moreover, a results-at-all-costs mentality can run counter to the overall productivity of the organization. For example, loaning a truck to a fellow superintendent may hurt the monthly cost sheet of the loaner, but it may significantly increase the profits of the organization as a whole. Nevertheless, the person whose appraisal is based primarily on minimizing costs is unlikely to loan the truck unless coerced to do so.

Finally, and most important, economic measures or performance outcomes by themselves do not inform employees what they need to do to maintain or increase productivity. This is not to imply that cost-related measures should be ignored. They should be down played for counseling and development purposes only, unless the critical behaviors that an employee can engage in to influence them are defined explicitly. This is because cost-related measures alone may indicate whether an employee is or is not meeting a set of objectives, but the answers to the questions of how or why can remain elusive.

For example, telling a baseball player that he just struck out will not come as a surprise to him. He will already have that information. What the player needs to know, and what a good appraiser-counselor should be able to tell him, is exactly what he must do (strategies, tactics) to at least get on first base, and possibly hit a home run. It is for these reasons that many industrial psychologists (Campbell, Dunnette, Lawler, & Weick, 1970) have become increasingly vocal about the need to measure and evaluate an employee in terms of *observable job behaviors* that are critical to job success or failure.

We will close this discussion of performance outcomes with the following statement:

> . . . the perception of causes of poor performance may lead to inaccurate appraisals and points of conflict . . . . the data suggest that supervisors make attributions and responses partly as a function of the seriousness of the outcome. In work settings these outcomes may be completely out of the subordinate's control (e.g., whether a patient falls out of bed when the railing is down) . . . . supervisors would be more efficient if they concentrated on trying to change the behavior that caused the incident rather than focusing on the outcome. What our analysis suggests is that when poor performance occurs but the outcome is not serious, the supervisor is more likely to overlook the problem. This strategy can lead to serious negative consequences at some later time and is clearly not an effective means of feedback. To change behavior we must focus on the behavior, not the outcome. (Mitchell & Wood, 1980, p. 138)

BEHAVIORAL CRITERIA

Behaviorally based appraisal measures can account for far more job complexity, they can be related more directly to what the employee actually

TABLE 3.3
Examples of Behavioral Measures for Evaluating Foremen

---

1. Explains job requirements to new employees in a clear manner (e.g.,
   talks slowly; shows them how to do it).
   Almost Never   0   1   2   3   4   Almost Always
2. Tells workers that if they have questions or problems to feel free
   to come and talk to him or her.
   Almost Never   0   1   2   3   4   Almost Always
3. Distributes overtime equally taking into account seniority.
   Almost Never   0   1   2   3   4   Almost Always

---

does, and they are more likely to minimize irrelevant factors not under
the control of the employee than can cost-related indexes. Behavioral
criteria developed from a systematic job analysis serve as indicators of
productivity, attendance, and accidents. Examples of behavioral measures
for foremen are shown in Table 3.3. If an individual foreman is suddenly
doing poorly on the job, the manager can use the appraisal instrument to
diagnose what the foreman must do to improve performance. Good cost-
related outcomes (e.g., profits) do not come about through osmosis.
Someone must do something to make them good or bad. Behavioral
measures based on a job analysis indicate precisely what is being done
by an employee to warrant recognition, discipline, transfer, promotion,
demotion, or termination. Examples of behavioral measures of logging
supervisors are shown in Table 3.4 (Latham, Pursell, & Wexley, 1974).
The relationship between the behavior of loggers and both cords per man
hour and attendance are shown in Tables 3.5 and 3.6, respectively.

Although not shown in Tables 3.5 and 3.6, behavioral measures can
encompass cost-related measures. For example, in the baseball example,
coming to work, striking out, and hitting a home run are all performance
outcomes. Similarly, reducing costs by 10 percent, selling 52 cars in a
month, and turning a report in on time are performance outcomes. What
makes behavioral criteria more comprehensive than cost-related or economic measures by themselves is that they not only measure the individuals
on factors over which they have control, but they also specify what the
person must do or not do to attain these outcomes (swinging level of
bat, stepping into the ball).

TABLE 3.4
Examples of Behavioral Measures for Evaluating Logging Supervisors

1. Evaluates a tract of timber in terms of production cost and profit before agreeing to harvest it.

   Almost Never   0   1   2   3   4   Almost Always

2. Sets a goal of how much wood he will harvest on a daily or weekly basis.

   Almost Never   0   1   2   3   4   Almost Always

3. Keeps spare tools, parts, and/or supplies in his truck (e.g., chainsaw, gas).

   Almost Never   0   1   2   3   4   Almost Always

TABLE 3.5
Expectancy Table for Predicting Cords per Man Hour

PERFORMANCE APPRAISAL SCORE	CHANCES IN 100 OF BEING PRODUCTIVE
69 and above	84%
56–68	65%
37–55	50%
30–36	35%
0–29	16%

Note: A person who receives a score of 69 or higher on the appraisal instrument has an 84 percent chance of being highly productive. This was determined by correlating appraisal scores with the productivity measures of the same employees.

TABLE 3.6
Expectancy Table for Predicting Attendance

PERFORMANCE APPRAISAL SCORE	CHANCES IN 100 OF HAVING GOOD ATTENDANCE

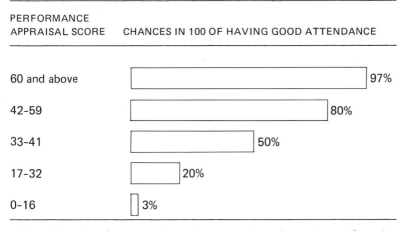

60 and above	97%
42-59	80%
33-41	50%
17-32	20%
0-16	3%

Note: There is a 3 percent chance that a supervisor who receives a 16 on the appraisal instrument will have a crew with a good attendance record. This was determined by correlating scores on the appraisal instrument with the attendance records of employees. This information enables supervisors to know exactly what they are doing that affects the attendance of their subordinates.

In summary, a well-constructed appraisal instrument includes the behavioral strategies necessary for employees to affect the bottom line. The bottom line defined in cost-related terms is a primary measure of an organization's effectiveness. The purpose of the appraisal instrument is to specify what each employee needs to do to influence that bottom line. The instrument will do this to the extent that the behavioral criteria are based on a systematic job analysis, and the instrument is reliable and valid.

MINIMUM STANDARDS FOR APPRAISAL INSTRUMENTS

There is general agreement in the psychological literature as to the characteristics that define a good appraisal instrument. This agreement is compatible with court cases (see Chapter 2) that cite the presence or absence of three characteristics as essential issues to be examined when appraisal systems are challenged on the basis of race, sex, or age discrimination. Moreover, this agreement coincides with the fact that these are the same three characteristics that are necessary if behavioral criteria are to serve as indicators of cost related outcomes. These three characteristics are a *job analysis* that yields a *reliable* and *valid* instrument.

JOB ANALYSIS

The Critical Incident Technique

The cornerstone in the construction of the appraisal instrument is the job analysis. The federal government's Uniform Guidelines (1978) make this explicit by stating that:

> *There shall be a job analysis which includes an analysis of the important work behaviors required for successful performance. . . Any job analysis should focus on work behavior(s) [emphasis added] and the tasks associated with them. (Sec. 14.C.2)*

Where a job analysis has not been performed, the courts have struck down claims of validity for an instrument—even when the instrument was evaluated by six subject matter experts. Specifically, the court rejected the notion that the experts "had in their heads a job analysis sufficient to satisfy legal and professional requirements" (*Kirkland* v. *New York Department of Correctional Services,* 1974).*

A number of acceptable procedures exist for conducting a job analysis, each differing in terms of its possible contribution to the objectives of management. One way of classifying job analysis techniques is through the use of: (1) task or activity statements that culminate in a definition of the job-oriented content of the job(s), or (2) behavior statements that culminate in a definition of the worker-oriented content of the job(s).† For developing an appraisal instrument we prefer to focus on behavioral statements because they make explicit what is required of an employee.

---

*Measures of the results or outcomes of work behaviors such as production rate or error rate may be used without a full job analysis where a review of information about the job shows that these criteria are important to the employment situation of the user. Similarly, measures such as absenteeism and tardiness, or turnover, may be used without a full job analysis if these behaviors are shown by a review of information about the job to be important in the specific situation." (EEOC, 1979, p. 2319)

†A summary of job analysis research has been published by McCormick (1979) and Prien and Ronan (1971).

One of the most frequently used job analysis procedures for developing behavioral criteria is the critical incident technique (CIT) (Fivars, 1975; Flanagan, 1954). The CIT requires observers who are aware of the aims and objectives of a given job and who *see* people perform the job on a frequent basis (e.g., daily) to describe to a job analyst incidents of effective and ineffective job behavior that they have observed over the past 6 to 12 months. Thus supervisors, peers, subordinates, and clients may be interviewed about their observations of the *critical requirements* of the job. The specific steps in conducting a job analysis based on the critical incident technique follows:

1. (Introduction): I am conducting a job analysis to determine what makes the difference between an effective and an ineffective _____ (e.g., supervisor, dentist, secretary). By effective performance I mean the type of behavior that, when you saw it occur, you wished all employees would do the same thing under similar circumstances. By ineffective performance I mean behavior that, if it occurred repeatedly or even once under certain circumstances, would make you doubt the competency of the individual.

I am talking with you because you are aware of the aims and objectives of the job, you frequently observe people in this job, and you are able to discern competent from incompetent performance. Please do not tell me the names of any individual to whom you are referring. (Note: Job incumbents are not interviewed concerning their *own* behavior. This is because incumbents are usually objective in describing their *effective* but not their *ineffective* behavior (Vroom & Maier, 1961).

2. (Interview): I would like for you to think back over the past 6 to 12 months of specific incidents that you yourself have seen occur. (Note: The emphasis on the past 12 months is to insure that the information is currently applicable. For example, behaviors that were critical for a salesperson in the 1950s may no longer be critical in the 1980s. Moreover, memory loss may distort the facts if the analysis is not restricted to recent incidents. The requirement that the interviewer report only first-hand information maximizes the objectivity or factual nature of the information to be reported.)

Can you think of an incident? (Note: If the answer is no, the following comments may stimulate recall.)

● Write down the five key things that an employee *must* be good at in this job. What is the first thing you wrote? Can you think of an employee who within the past year demonstrated that point? What was the second thing you wrote? The third, etc.?

● Tell me the first initial (in order to maintain anonymity) of the most effective person you know in this job. Suppose I could argue that this person is ineffective. What incidents can you cite to change my opinion?

You have thought of an incident. Good. For each incident you recall, I am going to ask you the same three questions, namely:

● What were the circumstances surrounding this incident? In other words, what was the background? What was the situation?

(Note: This question is important because it establishes *when* a given behavior is appropriate.)

● What exactly did the individual *do* that was either effective or ineffective?

(Note: Generally effective incidents are requested before ineffective incidents. There is no empirical evidence to support this decision. However, our experience indicates that when effective incidents are requested first, the interviewee does not feel that the information is being obtained for a witch hunt. The purpose of this second question is to elicit information concerning specific *observable* behavior.)

● How is the incident you described an example of effective or ineffective behavior? In other words, how did this affect the task(s) the individual was performing?

Generally, an interviewee is asked to report five effective and five ineffective incidents. Attention is given to both effective and ineffective incidents because an effective incident is not necessarily the opposite of an ineffective incident. For example, setting a specific goal was found to be effective for increasing the productivity of loggers, but not setting goals by no means led to bankruptcy (Latham, 1969).

A total of 10 incidents are collected because they can usually be collected within one hour. This is the maximum time period that many employees can be away from the job without disrupting their work day. No more than 10 incidents are collected from any one individual so that the data are not biased by talkative people. In order to obtain a comprehensive sample of incidents it is recommended that at least 30 people be interviewed for a total of roughly 300 incidents.

The interviewer must be skilled in collecting information describing observable behaviors. If the interviewee says, ". . . the employee really showed initiative in solving the problem," the interviewer must ask, "what exactly did the individual do that indicated initiative?" Because the crux of the critical incident technique is obtaining examples of behavior, a brief quiz is given below. Examine these statements and determine which ones describe observable behavior. The answers are given at the end of this chapter.

1. He looked sloppy in public.

2. He wore pants covered with grease.

3. He asked who owned the wallet.

4. He was an honest man.

5. The engineer could handle any emergency as shown by his behavior last Christmas.

6. When the landing flaps failed to work the engineer replaced the cable over the drum.

7. The radar observer was weak on scope interpretation.

8. She was afraid of heights, but overcame her reluctance and became proficient in all phases of flying.

9. On the previous biology exam, the student received an A. The student got a "big head" and made a poor score on the next quiz.

Developing a BES Appraisal Instrument

The behaviorally based appraisal instrument most frequently recommended by psychologists is *behavioral expectation scales* or BES (Smith & Kendall, 1963). The BES are also referred to as behaviorally anchored rating scales (BARS), and the two terms are often used interchangeably in the scientific literature. The steps for developing a BES are as follows:

1. After incidents have been collected describing competent, average, and incompetent behavior, a group of job holders (or the job analysts) categorize the incidents into broad overall categories (e.g., technical

competence, interpersonal skill, administrative ability). Each category serves as one criterion (performance dimension) for evaluating an employee.

2. A second group of individuals is given the critical incidents and the job criteria (the categories or performance dimensions developed in step 1). This step is called the reallocation or retranslation step because the second group is asked to allocate each incident to the one criterion category or performance dimension that they believe the critical incident illustrates. Those incidents that are not assigned to the same category by more than a certain percentage (e.g., 80 percent) of this second group of judges (usually 5 or more people) are eliminated. Also, incidents falling frequently into two categories are deleted. In this way, ambiguous incidents are discarded, and independent (nonoverlapping) performance criteria for appraising employees are believed to be determined.

3. A third group of individuals, who are also familiar with the job, is given a booklet containing the performance criterion categories and the list of incidents that the previous group agreed defined each criterion. This group of individuals is asked to rate each incident, usually on a 7-point scale with a 7 representing outstanding job performance, a 4 representing average performance, and a 1 representing poor performance. Only those items for which there is a high degree of interjudge agreement (with standard deviations of less than 1.5) are retained.* These incidents are used as *anchors* or benchmarks on the rating scale, hence the term "behaviorally anchored" rating scales. The numerical value given to each of these items is the average of all the judges' ratings.

The term BES is derived from the fact that the critical incidents used as anchors are reworded from actual behaviors (e.g., works overtime) to *expected* behaviors (e.g., could be expected to work overtime). This change is made to underscore the fact that the employee does not need to demonstrate the exact behavior that is used as an anchor in order to be rated at that level. The anchors are simply illustrations to aid the rater in defining outstanding (7), average (4), or poor (1) performance. An example of a BES/BARS is shown in Table 3.7. In the blank space

---

*A standard deviation is a measure of the extent to which there is agreement among the judges. A small standard deviation indicates high agreement. See Arvey (1979) for a brief discussion of this concept.

TABLE 3.7
An Example of a BES

Motivation—the desire and willingness to work hard.

7 —— After job responsibilities are met, this employee could be expected to help other employees complete their assignments.

6 ——

5 —— Employee could be expected to do the job when the supervisor is gone.

4 ——

3 —— Employee could be expected to refuse to work overtime.

2 ——

1 —— Employee could be expected to criticize peers who work more rapidly than others.

Describe critical incidents to support your rating:

underneath the scale the appraiser is asked to record critical incidents throughout the appraisal period to substantiate the assigned rating. This documentation is crucial for good rating, effective discussion, and legal defensibility.

BES have at least two advantages. First, the anchors are behavioral in nature and are expressed in the raters' own terminology, which eliminates much of the ambiguity found in rating scales based on traits. Second, these scales may lend themselves to employee counseling/motivation by providing the employee with specific feedback on strengths and areas in need of improvement. This tendency is true to the extent that the supervisor has had the discipline to systematically record a representative sample of incidents describing the employee's behavior throughout the appraisal period. These two advantages are present because the instrument is based on the critical incident technique.

BES/BARS have several limitations, however. Among these, as Schwab, Heneman, and DeCotiis (1975) have noted, is the fact that a substantial number of critical incidents generated in the job analysis are discarded. That is, if seven job categories or performance criteria are identified as critical for appraisal purposes, the most incidents that can be used as anchors is only 49 out of a possible total of literally hundreds of different incidents that were reported in the critical incident job analysis.

> . . . . if one assumes that the original pool of incidents generated in any BARS study all represent behavior that an evaluator may see and assess in an applied setting, instruments defined and anchored by relatively few examples would create at least two problems. First, the evaluator may have difficulty assigning observed behaviors to specific dimensions. Second, the evaluator may have difficulty deciding the scale value of effectiveness of the observed behavior against the examples provided. (Schwab et al., 1975, p. 558)

A second problem, cited by the same authors, is that the subjective process used in developing the instrument, namely, judges categorizing the incidents, may result in criterion categories that are not independent. Independent categories are important for minimizing redundancy in the measurement instruments.

A third problem, pointed out by Borman (1979), is that raters often have difficulty discerning any behavioral similarity between a ratee's performance and the highly specific behavioral examples used to anchor the scales. They frequently are unable to match observed job behavior directly with the scale anchors. In many cases, they cannot even infer the overall performance dimension or criterion on which to rate the specific incidents that they have recorded.

A fourth problem is that for BES to be used properly for counseling and development purposes, the supervisor, as stated previously, must record systematically a representative sample of incidents describing each employee's behavior throughout the appraisal period. Most people lack the discipline and/or time to do this. BES advocates acknowledge this point, and make the rather dubious recommendation that each superior's manager should police each subordinate manager on the extent to which a diary is being kept on each employee (Bernardin & Buckley, 1979). This suggestion goes far beyond the need to be able to explain to an employee or a court why a person did or did not retain a job, receive a promotion, or receive a salary increase. A procedure that overcomes these and other limitations of BES/BARS, but retains their advantages is called *behavioral observation scales* or BOS (Latham & Wexley, 1977).

Developing a BOS Appraisal Instrument

The primary difference between BES and BOS is essentially the same as that which differentiates the Thurstone (1928) and Likert (1932) approaches to the development of attitude scales. The development of the BES is similar to the Thurstone approach in that judges numerically rate incidents obtained in the job analysis in terms of the extent to which each incident represents effective job behavior.

The BOS is similar to the Likert method in that: (1) a large number of behavioral statements related to the object in question (e.g., costs) are collected; (2) employees are observed and rated on a 5-point scale as to the frequency with which each of them engages in each of the behaviors; (3) a total score for each employee is determined by summing the observer's responses to all the behavioral items; and (4) a statistical analysis is conducted to identify those behaviors that most clearly differentiate effective from ineffective performers. It is the use of statistical analysis in the Likert and BOS methods to select items for building an appraisal instrument that most clearly distinguishes it from the Thurstone/BES method.

An example of one BOS criterion is shown in Table 3.8. A complete appraisal instrument for evaluating employees in a bowling lane company is shown in Appendix A. As can be seen, BOS are nothing more than summated rating scales. That is, the rater simply adds together (sums) the numbers (ratings) indicative of the frequency with which an employee has been observed engaging in specific behaviors. The term BOS is used simply to draw attention away from the "E" in BES. It connotes the necessity of both supervisors and subordinates knowing explicitly prior to an appraisal period what it is the employee is to do on the job,

TABLE 3.8

Example of One BOS Criterion or Performance Dimension for Evaluating Managers

---

I. Overcoming Resistance to Change*

  (1) Describes the details of the change to subordinates.

   Almost Never   1   2   3   4   5   Almost Always

  (2) Explains why the change is necessary.

   Almost Never   1   2   3   4   5   Almost Always

  (3) Discusses how the change will affect the employee.

   Almost Never   1   2   3   4   5   Almost Always

  (4) Listens to the employee's concerns.

   Almost Never   1   2   3   4   5   Almost Always

  (5) Asks the employee for help in making the change work.

   Almost Never   1   2   3   4   5   Almost Always

  (6) If necessary, specifies the date for a follow-up meeting to respond to the employee's concerns.

   Almost Never   1   2   3   4   5   Almost Always

Total = _____

Below Adequate	Adequate	Full	Excellent	Superior*
6–10	11–15	16–20	21–25	26–30

---

*Scores are set by management.

and what the supervisor should look for (observe) to coach, counsel, and/or develop an employee.

The specific steps required for developing BOS are as follows:

1. Critical incidents that are similar, if not identical, in context are grouped together to form one behavioral item. For example, two or more incidents concerning a foreman who compliments or rewards employees for doing a good job were used by Latham, Fay, and Saari (1979) for writing the item, "praises and/or rewards subordinates for specific things they do well."

2. Behavioral items that are similar are grouped together by job incumbents and/or analysts to form one BOS criterion. For example, the above behavioral item was grouped together with similar items (e.g., counsels employees on personal problems) to form the criterion, "Interactions with Subordinates."

It should be noted that the advantage of the job analysts categorizing the incidents is that it takes less time than training job incumbents how to write behavioral items that are observable and cluster them into meaningful criteria. The advantage of having job incumbents rather than the researchers categorize the incidents and develop the appraisal instruments, although appealing intuitively, has yet to be justified empirically.

The results of two studies (Friedman & Cornelius, 1976; Warmke & Billings, 1979) have been interpreted by some people as suggesting that user participation in developing an appraisal scale leads to a reduction in rating errors (see Chapter 5) when the scale is subsequently used to appraise people. Neither study, however, provided an adequate test of the participation hypothesis because none of the researchers addressed the issue of the value of job analysts versus job incumbents' developing the appraisal instrument. Before one considers conducting such a test we would like to point out that the requirement for every rater to physically participate in the construction of all phases of a rating scale is not technically feasible in all but very small organizations. Even there, the extent to which there is a changing work force would make the procedure impractical.

We believe that the contribution of information by raters as part of the job analysis is necessary to insure that a representative sample of critical job behaviors are included on the instrument, and that these job behaviors are written in a form that is clear and unambiguous to them; but even here, it is only necessary that a representative sample of users of the rating scale contribute this information for the job analysis rather than having every single rater who will use the scale participate in this task. This procedure, we believe, meets the spirit and intent of the 1978 Civil Service Reform Act (see Chapter 2) that requires that employees have a say in the areas on which they will be evaluated.

3. Interjudge agreement is assessed to determine whether another individual or group of individuals would have developed the same behavioral criteria from the critical incidents obtained in the job analysis. This step is similar to the reallocation step (Smith & Kendall, 1963) followed by BES advocates.

The incidents are placed in random order and given to a second individual or group who reclassifies the incidents according to the categorization system established in step 1. The ratio of interjudge agreement is calculated by counting the number of incidents that both groups agree should be placed in a given criterion divided by the combined number of incidents both groups placed in that criterion. Thus, if one group of judges classified incidents 4, 7, 8, 9, and 17 under the same criterion, the interjudge agreement would be $.60 \left[\frac{(7, 8, 9)}{(4, 7, 8, 9, 17)} = \frac{3}{5} = .6 \right]$.

An a priori decision is usually made that the ratio must be .80 or higher for a behavioral criterion to be acceptable. If the ratio is below .80, the items under the criterion are reexamined to see if they should be reclassified under a different criterion and/or if the criteria should be rewritten to increase specificity.

4. The BOS criteria (e.g., Interactions with Peers, Safety, Technical Competency) are examined regarding their relevance or content validity (Nagle, 1953). Relevance or content validity is concerned with the systematic evaluation of appraisal instruments, by people who are intimately familiar with the job, to see if they include a representative sample of the behavioral domain of interest as defined by the job analysis (Anastasi, 1976). Two tests for content validity are described below.

 a. Prior to the categorization of the critical incidents, 10 percent of the incidents are set aside. After the categorization is completed in step 1, these incidents are examined to see if any of them describe behaviors that have not yet appeared. If this examination necessitates the development of a new behavioral criterion, or the formation of two or more behavioral items under an existing criterion, the assumption that a sufficient number of incidents have been collected is rejected.

 b. The second test of content validity involves recording the increase in the number of behavioral items with the increase in the number of incidents classified. If 90 percent of the items appear after 75 percent of the incidents have been categorized, the content validity of the BOS is considered satisfactory.

5. The appraisal instrument is developed by attaching a 5-point Likert scale to each behavioral item. Only 5 numbers are placed under each behavioral item because research shows that there is little utility in adding scale values beyond 5 (Jenkins & Taber, 1977; Lissitz & Green, 1975). Observers (e.g., peers, supervisors) are asked to indicate the frequency with which they have observed a job incumbent engage in each behavior. An example of one behavioral item follows.

Immediately informs supervisor of people who need ear plugs.

Almost Never   0   1   2   3   4   Almost Always

Employees receive a 0 if they have been observed engaging in a behavior 0-64 percent of the time, 1 for 65-74 percent of the time, 2 for 75-84 percent of the time, 3 for 85-94 percent of the time, and 4 for 95-100 percent of the time.* These percentages corresponding to the 5 points on the Likert scale can change depending upon the job and organization involved.† In some cases, the behavioral items are stated in terms of ineffective behavior if that is the way the incidents were described by the interviewees during the job analysis.

6. Many items on the BOS, although critical in terms of defining highly effective or ineffective performance occur either so frequently or infrequently that they do not differentiate good from poor job incumbents. For example, of 90 supervisors rated on "Has the smell of liquor on his/her breath," Latham et al. (1979) reported that 85 received 4 (almost never), 4 received a 3 (seldom), and 1 person received a 2 (sometimes). A major purpose of a performance appraisal instrument is to

---

*Other percentages besides those discussed can be used. For example, some authors have used 20 percent intervals for the five numbers (e.g., Latham, Mitchell, and Dossett, 1978).

†The degree to which observers can actually distinguish between 0–64 percent of the time, 75–84 percent of the time, and the like is sometimes questioned. Judgment obviously affects these ratings as it does any criterion measure. This is why we strongly recommend teaching skills in observing and recording job behaviors (see Chapter 5). However, adequate measures of reliability and validity have been obtained with this procedure in the absence of rater training (e.g., Latham & Wexley, 1977; Latham, Wexley, & Rand, 1975). The expectancy charts shown in Tables 3.5 and 3.6 were developed from recorded observations of untrained raters.

differentiate between good and poor performers. The above item does not meet this requirement since almost every supervisor received the same rating. Therefore, these types of items are eliminated by conducting an item analysis. This statistical procedure involves correlating the scores on each behavioral item with the sum of *all* items so that each section on the appraisal instrument is unambiguous to the appraiser.

Latham et al. (1979) compared the frequencies of supervisors in five categories (e.g., superior, excellent, full) on an original BOS with a revised BOS (after item analysis). The effect of removing nondifferentiating items spread out the total ratings (see Table 3.9).

7. If there are approximately three to five times as many individuals to be rated as there are behavioral items, a factor analysis can be conducted. A factor analysis goups behavioral items together on the extent to which they correlate with one another to form different behavioral criteria (e.g., Interaction with Peers, Organizational Commitment). This grouping removes the need for two groups of judges to categorize the incidents into overall categories because the factor analysis performs this step for them. This is one reason why factor analysis rather than judges should be used to group the items into behavioral categories. It saves time. Further, it insures that the different behavioral criteria will be independent of one another and thus contain the minimum number of items on which the employee should be evaluated.*

Since each BOS criterion contains a different number of behavioral items the question of weighting the scales may need to be considered. A grade point average (GPA) analogy is adopted by many BOS users. For example, college students are graded from 0.0 to 4.0. A grade point average (overall performance rating) is usually computed by averaging across all courses regardless of the number of exams (items) used in each

---

*The primary concern here is the ability of behavioral items to *discriminate* between effective and ineffective job performance. Having *independent* criteria is an ideal goal for statisticians, but "it is unlikely to occur for real behaviors" (Smith, personal communication, 1979). This is because the criteria are often logically related. For example, BOS may tap different aspects of supervisory behavior as opposed to skills that are logically unrelated (e.g., physical versus cognitive abilities). Multidimensional criteria are necessary because the measures seldom overlap one another completely and, more importantly, they facilitate accountability and control by the organization, and feedback and development for the individual.

TABLE 3.9
Number and Percentage of Supervisors in Each Category

	ORIGINAL BOS	REVISED BOS
1. Below Adequate		
2. Adequate		3 (3%)
3. Full	15 (17%)	24 (27%)
4. Excellent	59 (65%)	50 (56%)
5. Superior	16 (18%)	13 (14%)

course (criterion). That is, each course grade is weighted equally. The score received on each BOS criterion can be used to compute the "GPA" for each job incumbent. Giving each criterion equal weight is compatible with research in selection (Lawshe, 1959; Trattner, 1963) that has shown that the sophisticated weighting of predictors (e.g., using multiple regression) seldom yields higher validities than simply adding up the individual predictor scores. Moreover, refraining from using a statistical weighting procedure allows the supervisor to use his or her own "expert judgment" to take into account prevailing conditions (e.g., the general economy, an organization's competitive position in the market, distribution of present skills within the organization) at the time that a decision based on an overall evaluation of the employee (e.g., promote, layoff, transfer) is required (Guion, 1961).

Advantages of BOS

The advantages of using BOS for conducting performance appraisals include the following:

1. BOS, like BES, are developed from a systematic job analysis supplied by employees for employees. Thus, understanding of and commitment to the use of the appraisal instrument are facilitated. The frequently heard complaints from both managers and subordinates that the items on the appraisal instrument are either sufficiently vague to defy understanding or completely inappropriate for the individual's appraisal are minimized. Thus, both approaches satisfy the requirement of the 1978 Civil

Service Reform Act to allow employees to participate in identifying the critical requirements of their job.

2. BOS can either serve alone or as a supplement to existing job descriptions in that they make explicit what behaviors are required of an employee in a given job. As a job description, BOS can also be used as a "job preview" for potential job candidates by showing them what they will be expected to do. Job previews are an effective means of reducing employee turnover and job dissatisfaction (Wanous, 1980). They can assist candidates in making a decision as to whether they would want to consistently demonstrate the behaviors described on the BOS.

3. BOS, unlike BES, are content valid in the sense that the behaviors differentiating the successful from the unsuccessful performer are included on the instrument. Appraisers are forced to make a thorough evaluation of an employee rather than emphasizing only what they can recall at the time of the appraisal. Again, it must be stressed that a major limitation of BES is that it requires the appraiser to have the discipline to record daily in brief essay form incidents that have been observed on the part of the employee. The typical supervisor simply does not have time to record systematically instances of adequate and inadequate behavior. Thus, the behaviors that are recorded, both effective and ineffective, are unlikely to be a representative sample of the employee's behavior (Feldman, 1979). The BOS approach specifies to both the supervisor and the employee "exactly what must be observed."

4. BOS facilitate explicit performance feedback in that they encourage meaningful discussions between the supervisor and the employee of the latter's strengths and weaknesses. Generalities are avoided in favor of specific overt behaviors for which the employee is praised, or is encouraged to demonstrate on the job. Explicit performance feedback using BOS combined with the setting of *specific* goals (see Chapters 6 and 7) has been shown repeatedly to be an effective means for bringing about and/or maintaining a positive behavior change (Dossett, Latham, & Mitchell, 1979; Latham & Yukl, 1975a; Latham, Mitchell, & Dossett, 1978). BES can facilitate feedback to the extent that the supervisor has the discipline to record a representative sampling of incidents describing the employee's behavior during the appraisal period. BOS procedures also request the supervisor to record incidents describing the employee's behavior. We have found, however, that supervisors often ignore this request, and base their feedback on the numbers that they have circled under each behavioral item. The behavioral items not only focus the supervisor's attention on what to look for during an appraisal period, but also facilitate recall in discussing the results of the appraisal with the employee.

5. BOS can satisfy EEOC Guidelines in terms of validity (relevance) and reliability. The content validity, interjudge agreement of the categorization system, and the internal consistency of the criteria (discussed next) are usually found to be satisfactory. In previous studies (Latham & Wexley, 1977; Latham, Wexley, & Rand, 1975; Ronan & Latham, 1974) the test-retest and inter-observer reliability, as well as the validity of the BOS in indicating employee attendance and productivity, were demonstrated. Rater bias is minimized because observers do not have to extrapolate from what they have observed to the placement of a checkmark beside an example on the scale that may or may not be appropriate.

Empirical comparisons between BES and BOS have yet to be made in industrial settings.* However, a rational comparison suggests that the use of BOS avoids the following problems with BES as summarized by Atkin and Conlon (1978).

1. Endorsement of an incident above the neutral point of BES implies endorsement of all other incidents between the incident checked and the neutral point. This endorsement, which may be unwarranted, is avoided with BOS because the rater is allowed to evaluate an individual on each and every item. Making several ratings, as is done with BOS, rather than one per dimension, as is done using BES, may increase the reliability of each BOS dimension score for the same reasons that adding items to a test generally increases the test's reliability—it reduces content sampling error (Borman, 1979).

2. The subjective definition of "critical" is minimized in the generation of the behavioral items for BOS. Rather, emphasis is placed on developing

---

*In a university setting Bernardin found that BOS were as good (Bernardin, 1977), if not better than BES (Bernardin, Alvares, & Cranny, 1976), in terms of reducing rating errors (see Chapter 5) or biases. Campbell et al. (1973) compared BES with a summated rating scale, but the latter were not item analyzed and thus cannot be properly referred to as BOS.

an inventory of behaviors, rating employees on the frequency with which they demonstrate each behavior, and conducting an item or a factor analysis for determining the items that should comprise each criterion on the final rating instrument.

3. In using BES, standard or normal behaviors may not be remembered in the same way as unusual or unique behaviors. Hence, at the time of the rating, raters may not have enough information about the performance of standard behaviors to use them in the BES context unless the raters recorded the incidents at the time at which they occurred. The BOS, however, serve as a checklist for both the rater and the ratee to take into account in their respective day-to-day job functions. That is, the rater knows what he or she should be alert to in observing an employee, and the employee knows explicitly what the rater is looking for. Thus, there are actually two issues here: (a) a smaller cognitive load is placed on the rater, and (b) the behaviors to be rated are more salient than is the case with BES.

4. Consistent with problems surrounding the use of judges to develop Thurstone scales, Atkin and Conlon (1978) suggest that to the degree to which supervisors believe that a particular dimension is substantially more important than others, they will define a relatively narrow range of acceptable behaviors, a relatively broad set of unacceptable behaviors, and virtually a null set of neutral behaviors. Whereas, with the BOS, all the raters are required to do is to indicate the frequency with which they observe the behavior; the behaviors that they are to observe are listed on the scale.

Essentially, the choice of BOS versus BES can be reduced to a preference for Likert versus Thurstone scales. Empirical comparisons of these two scales in the area of attitude measurement has demonstrated the superiority of the Likert scale in terms of reliability (Seiler & Hough, 1970). It is unlikely that a substantially different conclusion will be reached in the area of performance appraisal. Reliability refers to the consistency of a measurement system and is important because it can affect validity. Validity refers to the extent to which the measurement system is measuring what it is intended to measure.

RELIABILITY AND VALIDITY

Earlier in this chapter we made the important point that performance appraisal instruments should be based on a job analysis, they should be reliable, and they should be valid. Job analysis has already been discussed in the development of two types of appraisal instruments, namely, BES and BOS. Let us now turn our attention to the reliability and the validity of performance appraisal systems.

To serve the organization's purposes of appraising an employee's performance, and to satisfy the legal requirements discussed in Chapter 2, the performance appraisal criteria must provide a representative sampling of the employee's job performance. If the appraisal system is used for estimating an employee's potential for advancement, the appraisal system must provide accurate data about such potential. In other words, the appraisal system must be valid—it must measure what it professes to measure.

Reliability affects validity in that a performance measure that is extremely unreliable cannot be valid.* For example, if a supervisor rates employees solely on their mood on a particular day, the measures probably will not be consistent (reliable) from one time period to the next. Furthermore, the performance appraisal instruments will not be measuring the employees' performance but their mood swings. Thus the measure is not valid. A valid measure should yield consistent (reliable) data about what it is concerned with regardless of the time of day, week, or month the measures are taken, and regardless of who takes the measures.

The following ways can be used to determine the reliability of a performance appraisal system. Each is designed to answer a different issue.

1. The *test-retest* method assesses the reliability of a performance measure in terms of its stability. It provides a measure of the extent to which the appraisal measure is free of time sampling error. This requires measuring the performance of employees (e.g., 30 or more) on two or more occasions with the same performance appraisal instrument. As Lazer and Wikstrom (1977) point out, this procedure is analogous to taking several photographs of the same person, and determining the differences among them. The degree of similarity is the measure of reliability.

Perfect reliability yields a correlation of 1.0. A correlation simply shows the relationship between two sets of measures. A correlation of 1.0

---

*Reliability is an attribute of *one* factor, e.g., a selection test score *or* a job performance rating. Validity concerns the *relationship* between *two* factors, e.g., how a selection test score *correlates* with a job performance rating or how a performance rating in one job correlates with a performance rating in a subsequent job.

means that how a group of individuals performed at one point in time is exactly the way they performed at a second point in time. However, a test-retest reliability will never be perfect because individuals will vary in their performance due to knowledge and skill acquired over time. The reliability measure, however, should ideally be .70 or higher. To the extent that the performance measures are unstable they may reflect nothing more than random fluctuations over time due to such things as fatigue level or mood swings. When behavioral criteria are used, the random fluctuation in work or fatigue may be indigenous to the rater instead of, or in addition to, the employee. For this reason, calculating interobserver reliability is useful for determining the reliability of an appraisal.

2. Interobserver reliability is assessed by determining the agreement (consistency) between two or more raters in evaluating an employee. This procedure is analogous to comparing a number of photographs of an employee that were taken at the same point in time, but by two or more people. Perfect interobserver reliability (i.e., 1.0) is rarely obtained because two observers seldom see an employee at the same points in time. However, the correlation among different raters should be at least .60 (Osburn & Manese, 1972). When the agreement is less than .60, when the raters have had opportunities to observe the employee, and when they are capable of discerning the competent from incompetent performance, it is likely that the appraisal is not measuring the employee's performance, but rather the different attitudes and biases of the appraisers.

3. Another method for measuring reliability is often referred to as the *internal consistency* of a measuring instrument. It provides a measure of the extent to which the instrument is free of content sampling error. For example, if the appraisal instrument is designed to assess knowledge of algebra, items that do not correlate with knowledge of algebra should be discarded.

To determine internal consistency, the ratings on the odd-numbered items of the instrument are correlated with ratings on the even- numbered items. Ideally, the correlation should be at least .80. This number is higher than that for test-retest and interobserver reliability because it is under the control of the person who develops the appraisal instrument. Statistical procedures exist for developing internally consistent tests, whereas the person who develops the appraisal instrument has no control over the behavior of the employees who are being appraised, or the opportunities of the people who observe and record the behavior of employees.

One advantage of BOS over BES is that the internal consistency of each criterion or scale can be calculated. Moreover, the internal consistency correlations as well as those for test-retest and interobserver reliability have been found satisfactory for a wide variety of jobs using BOS (e.g., see Latham & Wexley, 1977).

As previously noted, the reliability of a performance appraisal criterion is important because, in general, it sets the upper limit on validity (Ryan & Smith, 1954). However, an appraisal measure may be reliable and not valid. For example, the measure may be consistently measuring the wrong thing (e.g., the prejudices of two or more supervisors year after year rather than the actual behavior of the employee). In other cases, the instrument may yield consistent ratings of the employee's behavior; but, if the observations are being used to make judgments about the employee's potential for jobs other than the current one, the appraisal may not be valid. For instance, where the requirements of the present job differ vastly from those of another job, the appraisal may be useless for estimating performance in that other job. An example of this is that the best mechanic doesn't necessarily make the best supervisor.

A discussion on validity is meaningful only in terms of the specific uses for which the appraisal will be used. An appraisal may be valid for one purpose and invalid for another. To be useful for the organization, the appraisal system must be both reliable and valid for every purpose for which it is being used.

The validity of an appraisal instrument can be assessed in three primary ways. First, the appraisal instrument itself must be *content valid.* Content validity, as previously noted, is concerned with the representativeness and relevance of the items composing the instrument in terms of the critical requirements of the job. It involves a systematic review of the instrument's content to determine whether it adequately measures the behaviors considered *critical* for effective job performance. The determination of content validity or relevance is made on the basis of judgments by experts (job incumbents, supervisors, clients) with regard to the appropriateness of the instrument's content in relation to a *job analysis* (i.e., the CIT). Both the Uniform Guidelines and the courts stress the importance of this issue. They state that the performance criteria must represent major critical work behaviors *as revealed by careful job analysis.*

Second, if one purpose of the appraisal instrument is to predict future performance of employees on a different job, *predictive validity* must be shown. Performance appraisal scores obtained on individuals in the present job are correlated with performance measures of the same individuals in a subsequent job. Predictive validity is seldom used by organizations because the validation sample requires the collection of performance measures on a large number of people (e.g., 30 or more people). It is difficult to show that there is a significant relationship between two sets of measures when the number of people on whom the measures are collected is small. Unfortunately, there are seldom 30 or more job openings in an organization for a given position *above* the entry level. The number of years over which a large number of openings for a given job or job family occur would probably be so great that the data collected earlier on the initial 10 or 15 people would be out of date by the time the data on the remaining 10 or 15 people are collected.[*] Where predictive validity is not technically possible, *construct validity* may be considered.

Construct validity is a third approach for establishing the job relatedness or validity of an appraisal system. It is used to *infer* the degree to which the persons being evaluated possess some quality or construct (i.e., employee worth to the organization) presumed to be reflected in the performance measure (Blum & Naylor, 1968). The general procedure for determining construct validity involves gathering several different performance measures that logically appear to measure the same construct (e.g., administrative skill), and then observing the relationship among these measures. For example, the construct validity of behavioral observation scales has been demonstrated by showing the correlations among BOS and cost related measures (Latham & Wexley, 1977; Latham

---

[*]Arvey (1979) describes procedures that may be used to obtain large sample sizes. First, two or more jobs that are substantially similar (e.g., clerical and secretarial jobs) might be treated as one job. Second, a job analysis can be conducted to isolate dimensions of behaviors that are common to several jobs, and the sample in those jobs can be used to validate appraisal decisions for those behavioral dimensions. This procedure is known as *synthetic validity.*

Wexley, & Rand, 1975; Ronan & Latham, 1974). The two sets of measures (behavioral and cost related) were collected independently on employees at the same point in time by different observers who were unaware of each other's appraisal of a given employee. The results were presented graphically in Tables 3.5 and 3.6.

The use of different observers can also be used in a multitrait/multirater framework (Lawler, 1967) to assess the construct validity of appraisal decisions. The use of the word trait, in light of our earlier discussion on the limitations of trait appraisals, is unfortunate. In this instance it simply refers to the use of multiple criterion dimensions (e.g., technical competence, interpersonal skill, administrative ability). Multiple raters refers to the use of different raters such as supervisors, peers, and subordinates in making appraisals of the employee. To show construct validity of the appraisals, there should be agreement among knowledgeable observers of the employee's performance on each criterion. However, how employees are evaluated on one criterion (e.g., technical competence) should not correlate highly with how they are evaluated on another criterion (e.g., interpersonal skill). A high correlation among the different criteria is traditionally interpreted as evidence of halo error (see Chapter 5). That is, it is presumed that the raters are making one overall global rating without taking into account how each employee is really doing on the different aspects or dimensions of the job. The assumption underlying this argument is that it is unrealistic to think that everyone who is outstanding on one criterion measure is equally good on all aspects of a job. People have different strengths and weaknesses. A performance appraisal system with construct validity should reflect these strengths and weaknesses. It is the requirement of a low correlation between different aspects of job performance (e.g., mechanical skill versus verbal skill) that differentiates this approach to measuring construct validity from the method of assessing interobserver reliability. However, in practice it is fallacious to assume that high intercorrelations are always indicative of halo error. Industries, like universities, strive for homogeneity by discharging individuals who perform poorly in one or more areas. Moreover, the criteria used to evaluate performance are often logically related. For example, students are evaluated on their cognitive skills. Thus, we would expect how they perform in one class would be similar to how they perform in another class. This is in fact the case. In the winter quarter of 1980, we found that the agreement among four professors regarding the grades of 26 students in four different classes at the University of Washington was .76. There was no significant difference in the mean grades given among the four classes. Since the professors in the four different classes were unaware of the grades given to those students by their fellow professors, this agreement can hardly be considered halo error.

In closing this discussion on reliability and validity, it is important to understand that neither reliability nor validity refers to a specific procedure, but rather to the inferences that are made from the use of one or more procedures. The key consideration in reliability and validity is whether these inferences are appropriate. Further, the categories of content validity, predictive validity and construct validity are three inseparable aspects of validity, not discrete types of validity. The classification was made for convenience and clarity for discussion purposes only. For example, we emphasized that the appraisal instrument must contain a representative sampling of critical job behaviors if it is to be considered content valid. But, what good is this requirement if the recorded observations of people fulfilling these requirements are biased or incomplete? "The emphasis, therefore, should be on validation as a total process of investigation, leading to information bearing on the appropriateness of inferences about individuals" (Division of Industrial-Organizational Psychology, *American Psychological Association,* 1980, p. 3).

PRACTICALITY AND STANDARDIZATION

Related to the issue of validity are the issues of practicality and standardization. An appraisal instrument must be understandable, plausible, and acceptable to those who will be using it (Smith, 1976). If the users perceive the instrument as difficult and cumbersome to administer, it cannot serve the purposes for which it was established. This requirement from an organization's standpoint is obvious, but it relates to legal requirements as well.

If an appraisal system is shown to be affected by the race or sex of employees, the courts may require that its continued use be justified by its *business necessity.* That is, an organization would have to show that the system is essential to the safe and efficient conduct of the business. A system that is not practical cannot be serving important organizational purposes. The danger here, of course, is that in attempting to be practical, organizations are often very impractical in trying to develop simple, easily administered appraisal system containing seven or eight traits (see Tables 3.1 and 3.2) that can be used for all employees.

Fay and Latham (1980) investigated the practicality of BOS, BES, and trait scales using a 12-item practicality questionnaire. The questions focused on the users' judgment of content validity (e.g., the rating form forces me to rate things that don't seem relevant; the rating form omits relevant aspects of performance) as well as their perceptions of the ease and convenience of using the scale for making personnel decisions (e.g., the rating scale is a helpful tool in counseling an employee on how to improve performance; the rating scale makes it easy to explain to an individual how a decision was made; it is easy to differentiate high, low, and medium performance using this scale). Each question was answered on a 5-point scale ranging from strongly agree to strongly disagree. Users of BOS rated the scale significantly higher than did users of BES or trait scales. There was no significant difference between the users of BES and trait scales on their respective judgments of practicality.

Standardization refers to minimizing differences in administering and scoring the appraisal instrument. The issue of standardization is important because as the Conference Board pointed out:

> Appraisal data are used to make comparisons among employees who may or may not be in the same unit of the organization. A system that is not standardized in its administration, that uses different forms or procedures from place to place or time to time, raises the probability that at least some differences in the performance measures of different employees are in fact the result of the appraisal system and its administration, rather than of real differences in employee performance. (Lazer & Wikstrom, 1977, p. 5)

COMPOSITE VERSUS MULTIPLE CRITERIA: A RECURRENT TOPIC IN DEVELOPING APPRAISAL INSTRUMENTS

The final issue reviewed in this chapter is the controversy over whether composite or multiple measures should be used to determine an employee's job performance. This issue concerns when and how to *combine* various measures of an employee's performance. Advocates of the composite position believe that the method for combining criteria (e.g., appraisals of technical competency, administrative ability, adaptability) should be specified prior to implementing the appraisal system in the organization. At least three different methods can be used to combine job performance criteria.

First, each criterion may be weighted equally (as was done earlier using the grade point analogy with the BOS). This practice assumes that each criterion is equally important for defining overall success on the job. While this assumption may be erroneous, the argument can be made that in the long run we can only guess at the correct weighting anyway. Consequently, we will make less error if all the criteria are treated as equally important.

Second, the criteria can be subjectively weighted (Toops, 1944; Nagle, 1953; Schmidt & Kaplan, 1971) by "experts" (e.g., supervisors or jobholders themselves). The problem with this approach is that the experts frequently disagree with one another.

Third, the criteria can be weighted in terms of their dollar value for the organization (Brogden & Taylor, 1950). The problem here is that most measures of job effectiveness are not expressible in monetary terms for each individual worker.

The position of those who advocate the use of multiple criteria (e.g., Ghiselli, 1956) is that most measures of job performance (e.g., manual dexterity, ability to make oral presentations, budget preparation) are relatively independent of one another. Thus, there is no way to combine the scores on the different measures into a single value, unless a dollar value can be calculated. This argument is akin to saying you can't add together apples and oranges. If criterion elements display low or zero correlations with one another, then they are obviously measuring different variables, and weighting them into a composite results in scores that are so ambiguous as to be uninterpretable. Nevertheless, a decision often needs to be made regarding the status of an employee (e.g., for a pay raise or a promotion). Guion's (1965) position is that the decision makers should refrain from combining the scores until a decision is necessary. The scores should then be subjectively weighted by the decision makers to take into account the prevailing needs and market conditions of the organization.

CLOSING REMARKS

Guidelines for developing and using performance appraisal instruments can be followed on the basis of the 1980 *Principles for the Validation and Use of Personnel Selection Procedures* prepared by Division 14 (Industrial-Organizational Psychology) of the American Psychological Association, and the 1978 Civil Service Reform Act. The latter was discussed in Chapter 2.

1. The appraisal instrument must be based on a systematic examination of the job and the context in which it is performed.

2. The job analysis should be conducted at a time when the job is reasonably stable and not in a period of rapid evolution. The logic of the job analysis is that it is undertaken under conditions as comparable as possible to those which will exist when the appraisal instrument will be used.

3. The job analysis information should be obtained from a sample of individuals who are representative of the populations of people and jobs to which the results are to be generalized.

4. The appraisal instrument should contain criteria that represent important work behaviors or behavioral outcomes as indicated by the job analysis. There is no virtue in measuring ability to handle trivial aspects of work.

5. The possibility of bias or other contamination should be considered. For example, economic measures may be excessive and/or deficient. Behavioral measures may be affected adversely by rater biases or an inadequate opportunity to observe the individual on the job.

6. The criterion measures must be reliable. Criterion reliability can place a ceiling on validity.

7. If several criteria or scales that make up the appraisal instrument are to be combined to obtain a single score, there should be a rationale to support the rules of combination.

8. The appraisal criteria should be subjected to pretesting and an analysis of the procedures in terms of the means, variances, and intercorrelations of its parts. Parts that do not contribute to the total variance should be eliminated. The appraisal instrument should enable the appraiser to differentiate good from poor performers.

9. Concerns over high intercorrelations among criteria on the appraisal form should be dealt with judiciously. Extreme redundancy of measurement should be avoided. However, a certain amount of redundancy provides adequate reliability of measurement. Discarding different items with high intercorrelations may reduce accountability and control by the organization, and impede feedback to and development of the individual. For example, just because the grades a student receives often intercorrelate highly, that is no reason to suggest that the student should be graded in only one class.

10. Persons who provide the appraisal information must be clearly qualified to do so (see Chapter 4). That is, they must have thorough knowledge of the job, ample opportunity to see the individual on the job, and expertise in interpretation of what is seen. Furthermore, individuals who conduct appraisals should be thoroughly trained with regard to recording accurately what is seen (see Chapter 5), and in reporting what was seen to the employee (see Chapter 7).

11. Reports on the appraisal system should enable a person competent in personnel assessment to know precisely what was done. The reports should be worded to communicate as clearly and accurately as possible the information readers need to know to complete appraisal forms completely and faithfully.

12. The appraisal instruments should be reviewed periodically and revised as needed. New appraisal instruments may be necessary whenever there is a substantial change in the organization's goals, technology, procedures, or workflow.

13. Reports should be written that warn readers against common misuses of appraisal information (e.g., using present assessments for determining managerial potential in the absence of valid data). The appraisal system must be valid for every purpose for which it is being used.

14. The procedures manual for persons who conduct appraisals should specify the procedures to be followed and emphasize the necessity for standardization of scoring and interpretation.

15. People should be evaluated on the extent to which they fulfill the requirements of the job rather than on how well they perform relative to other employees.

SUMMARY

This chapter has been concerned with the development of performance appraisal instruments. Three critical requirements of appraisal instruments are that they be based on a *job analysis* and that, once developed, they provide *reliable* and *valid* measures of an employee's performance. In addition, performance appraisal instruments must be practical and standardized.

A job analysis identifies the behaviors critical to fulfilling responsibilities, duties, and task requirements. Reliability refers to consistency in measurement. Three ways of determining the reliability of performance appraisals are test-retest, inter-observer, and internal consistency. Reliability is important because it can set the upper limit on validity. Validity refers to the extent to which the appraisal provides an accurate measure of what it was designed to measure. Three aspects of validity are content, predictive, and construct validity.

Practicality refers to the ease of administering the appraisal instrument. Standardization refers to minimizing differences in administering and scoring the appraisal instruments.

Trait-based appraisal instruments are seldom developed from a job analysis and, more important, do not specify to employees what is explicitly required behaviorally of them on the job. For this reason trait-based instruments are generally frowned upon by the courts. A job analysis approach that makes explicit the behaviors that employees must engage in to be effective on the job is the critical incident technique.

Two appraisal instruments that can be developed from the critical incident technique are BES and BOS. The BOS have been shown to be reliable as measured by interobserver, test-retest, and internal consistency methods. The instrument itself has been shown to be content valid, and the appraisal ratings have been shown to possess construct validity. The value of this instrument is that it serves as an employment contract in the sense that it specifies that the employee should behave in a certain manner, a manner that will influence positively the bottom line. The employer has a legitimate concern with those behaviors in this contract because they contribute to the productive aspects of the job (e.g., the speed at which the job is performed, the regularity with which the employee is in attendance at work, and the thoroughness or quality of the work performed). A good performance appraisal instrument serves as an employment contract in that it specifies critical or important measures of job performance. BOS procedures address these activities directly without attempting to alter underlying personality traits of employees (see Appendix A).

Because the BOS serve as a contract that increases accountability, some employees may resist the procedure out of fear that they will receive a negative evaluation unjustly. Experience has shown that once the system is in operation and employees have experienced an appraisal on BOS, these same employees become supporters of the system. This support occurs because many employees have worked for years in an environment in which their performance was evaluated subjectively with no measurement of what was actually done, no stated levels or goals of expected performance, and no perceived consequences for the achievement of high levels of performance. Feedback and praise that lead to the setting of specific goals, which in turn lead to more feedback and praise, contribute most to productivity and job satisfaction. BOS facilitate the use of these motivation principles (see Chapter 6).

Economic measures or performance outcomes such as production rate may be used without a full job analysis where a review of information about the job shows that these criteria are important to the employment situation of the user. Because such measures are obtainable only when the employee produces a distinguishable output, they are generally of value when dealing with blue-collar workers only. Even here, they can only be used when the individual's productivity is largely unaffected by situational factors beyond the control of the individual or by the performance of fellow workers. The primary problem with these measures from a counseling and development standpoint is that they do not inform the employee what to start doing, stop doing, or continue doing on the job.

A recurring issue in the appraisal literature is whether scores on each appraisal scale measuring performance in one area of the job should be combined with performance assessments on other areas of the job. Our position is that the scores in most instances should be subjectively weighted by the decision makers to take into account the prevailing needs and market conditions of the organization at the time the decision must be made.

ANSWERS TO QUIZ*

1. No. What is meant by "sloppy"?

2. Yes.

3. Yes.

4. No. Explain what was done to indicate honesty.

5. No. Describe the emergency. Describe the behavior.

6. Almost. Specify the type of cable and the drum.

7. No. Define weak. Define scope interpretation.

8. No. Define reluctance, proficient, and "all phases."

9. No. Define "big head" and poor score.

---

*Adapted from Latham and Beach (1974).

Sources of Performance Appraisals

INTRODUCTION

Once the performance appraisal instrument has been developed, the next step is to determine who will perform the assessment function. There are at least six alternatives: (1) the supervisor, (2) the employee, (3) peers, (4) subordinates, (5) a person or persons outside the employee's immediate work environment, or (6) some combination of the above.

The key criteria for qualifying as a source for appraising an employee's performance are being aware of the objectives of the employee's job, frequently observing the employee on the job, *and* being capable of determining whether the observed behavior is satisfactory. People need to be aware of the objectives of a job to know what behaviors are critical to fulfilling job requirements. They must frequently observe people *on the job* to insure that their appraisals are based on a representative sampling of the person's performance.* They must be capable of ascertaining whether the behavior is effective in order to draw correct conclusions about the employee's value to the organization. For example, we are aware of the aims and objectives of shipyard supervisors because we have developed BOS for them. We could have completed a quarterly evaluation

---

*The italics in the above sentence stress that it is relevancy rather than frequency of contact per se that is critical for obtaining valid ratings. Appraisers who interact with ratees in a situation relevant to the dimension being rated are more valid in their evaluations than are appraisers who interact with ratees in a nonrelevant situation (Landy & Farr, 1980).

of them because we practically lived in the shipyards for three months. However, neither of us would qualify as a person to complete the appraisal because neither of us have the ability to ascertain whether the items on the BOS are being performed properly.

SUPERVISOR APPRAISAL

Table 4.1 shows that 95 percent of the appraisals conducted at lower and middle management levels are performed by the individual's immediate supervisor. There are several reasons for this trend.

First, the management hierarchy of most organizations reinforces the right of the supervisor to make both evaluative and developmental decisions concerning subordinates. Second, the supervisor generally controls the magnitude and scheduling of the rewards and punishments that can be administered to subordinates. Since performance is enhanced when rewards are based on performance, it is logical that the appraisal be conducted by the person who normally administers the rewards. If this were not the case, it is likely that in many organizations the employee might view the appraisal process as having little or no importance. Third, it is commonly felt that of all the various sources of evaluation, the immediate supervisor is in the best position to observe a subordinate's behavior, and judge the relevance of that behavior to job objectives and organizational goals.

Despite this logic, performance appraisals conducted by supervisors have a drawback. In a study of middle managers and merchandising executives, Barrett (1966) concluded that an employee's evaluation depends heavily on how each supervisor *thinks* the work should be performed rather than how well it is *actually* performed by the employee. This finding simply confirms what most employees already know, namely, that managerial evaluations are frequently loaded with subjectivity and bias. They are neither as reliable nor as valid as peer ratings. Alternative sources to supervisory appraisals are especially needed when the supervisor seldom sees the employee on the job.

SELF-APPRAISAL

Bassett and Meyer (1968) investigated a self-rating appraisal process at General Electric Company (GE) in which only the employee completed

TABLE 4.1
Sources of Performance Appraisal

Appraiser	Lower Management (217 Companies)		Middle Management (208 Companies)		Top Management (160 Companies)	
	Number of Companies	Percent of Companies	Number of Companies	Percent of Companies	Number of Companies	Percent of Companies
Immediate supervisor	106	95%	198	95%	138	86%
Self	25	12	27	13	23	14
Peers or coworkers	0	—	0	—	1	a
Subordinates	0	—	0	—	0	—
Group or committee	11	5	9	4	14	9
Representative from the divisional personnel department	6	3	4	2	3	2
Representative from the corporate personnel department	7	3	10	5	7	4
Internal staff consultant	0	—	0	—	0	—
External management consultant	1	a	1	a	1	a
Other	7	3	7	3	5	3

[1] Some companies report that more than one person has the responsibility for doing the appraisal; therefore, the percentages do not add to 100.

[a] Less than one percent

Source: Reprinted from *Appraising managerial performance: Current practices and future directions*, by R. I. Lazer and W. S. Wikstrom, by permission of the Conference Board. ©1977.

the appraisal form. The subsequent discussion between the manager and the employee was based solely on the employee's comments. This approach was compared with the traditional managerial appraisals conducted at GE. The results indicated that: (1) the self-appraisals were rated as more satisfying and constructive by the managers than the traditional supervisory-prepared appraisals; (2) there was less defensiveness on the part of subordinates regarding the appraisal; (3) the discussions based on self-ratings more often resulted in superior on-the-job performance than did the traditional appraisal; and (4) low-rated employees were especially likely to show an improvement in performance, as rated by managers, after a self-review discussion.

Other benefits of a self-appraisal include the following:

1. Given that the employee has a structured appraisal instrument (e.g., BOS), the self-appraisal process forces the individual to focus on *what is expected* in that job.

2. The supervisor learns how the employee perceives the job responsibilities, performance on the job, and problems encountered in carrying out job responsibilities (Hall, 1951).

3. Self-appraisals help clarify, if not resolve, differences of opinion between the employee and the manager regarding job requirements and job performance (Bassett & Meyer, 1968).

4. It is an effective tool for stimulating self-development in that employees are encouraged to think about their strengths, and to set specific goals for future improvement (Wexley & Yukl, 1977).

5. Self-appraisals are especially appropriate where employees are working in isolation or possess a rare skill, because such employees may have more information about their own behavior than does anyone else.

6. Self-ratings often contain less halo error than supervisory ratings, and thus are more discriminating across different performance dimensions (Heneman, 1974; Parker, Taylor, Barrett, & Martens, 1959). Halo error refers to inappropriate generalizations regarding an individual's performance. For example, a person who does exceedingly well (or poorly) on one aspect of the job may be rated erroneously as outstanding (or poor) on all aspects of the job.

The advantages of self-rating must be weighed against the following disadvantages. First, employees who have experienced few supervisory appraisals (e.g., new employees) or employees who are low in their need for independence express greater satisfaction with the traditional supervisory appraisal than a self-rating procedure (Bassett & Meyer, 1968; Hillery & Wexley, 1974). Thus individual differences must be taken into account when deciding whether to use self-appraisals.

Second, several studies have found low agreement between self-appraisals and supervisory appraisals. However, the research is not consistent as to the direction of the disagreement. Three studies (Beatty, Schneier, & Beatty, 1977; Parker et al., 1959; Thornton, 1968) found self-ratings to exceed those given by managers, whereas two other studies (Heneman, 1974; Teel, 1978) reported that self-appraisals are lower than ratings made by superiors.

Teel (1978) recommends combining self-appraisals and managerial appraisals. The procedure is as follows: One or two weeks before the performance appraisal is to take place, the employee and the manager independently complete the performance appraisal form. At the appraisal interview, the manager and the subordinate compare their evaluations. Differences of one point in the ratings are recorded on the official appraisal form at the higher rating, regardless of who assigned the higher rating. For those areas on which ratings differ by two or more points, the manager and the employee have an in-depth discussion to identify and clarify the reasons for the differences (see Chapters 6 and 7).

The advantage of this procedure over traditional supervisory based appraisals is that employees ask more questions and volunteer more comments and suggestions during the appraisal interview (Teel, 1978). However, at this time, no data have been systematically collected to evaluate the effects of this approach on subsequent job performance.

Given this state of the science, we are guardedly optimistic in recommending the use of self-appraisals. In a recent literature review Thornton (1980) concluded that self-appraisals frequently lead to inflated ratings, show little agreement with other sources, and are less reliable than ratings by supervisors and peers. However, in no case was BOS used. What makes us guardedly optimistic about self-assessments when BOS are used are the results of a study involving over 1000 people in 50 different factories in Great Britain. The employees were asked to appraise their overt behavior.

In that study Downs, Farr, and Colbeck (1978) hypothesized on the basis of Bem's (1972) theory of self-perception* that in making inferences about their own beliefs individuals use the same cues that would be available to an *external observer of one's behavior.* Specifically, they argued that the theory could be usefully extended to cover self-influence concerning one's own ability to engage in specific job behaviors. The results supported the hypothesis. Employees in a training course, who were unaware of their tests scores or trainer ratings of them, evaluated their performance the same way as the employing organization that used the test scores and trainer ratings. Thus, on the basis of Bem's theory and this one study, it would appear that employees are capable of arriving at reasonably realistic self-appraisals when the self-appraisal "is confined to essentially behavioural-type tests which take place within the visual field of the testee . . . , i.e., the testee is visually able to observe her own performance" (Downs et al., 1978, p. 276).

PEER APPRAISAL

Peer appraisals, unlike supervisory or self-appraisals, have been shown consistently to meet acceptable standards of reliability (Wherry & Fryer, 1949; Gordon & Medland, 1965). For example, DeJung and Kaplan (1962), Fiske and Cox (1960), Hollander (1957), and Kubany (1957) reported test-retest reliability coefficients of .60 to .70 for periods ranging up to one year, and interobserver reliability coefficients of .80 to .90.† Moreover, appraisals made by peers after a short period of acquaintance have been shown to be as good as those made after longer periods of time (Hollander, 1965). Peer evaluations are even reliable when the person is transferred from one group to another within the same organization (Gordon & Medland, 1965).

The high reliability of peer appraisals is a function of at least two factors. First, reliability is affected positively by the daily interactions

---

*According to Bem, just as we may often infer other people's attitudes by observing their actions, we determine our own attitudes by observing our own actions.

†Test-retest reliability refers to a correlation between appraisal scores on a group of people at one point in time with appraisal scores of the same people at a later point in time. Interobserver reliability refers to a correlation between two or more observers' appraisals of the same group of employees.

among peers. They not only see how an employee interacts with them, but also see how that employee interacts with subordinates as well as the boss. In short, peers have a comprehensive view of an employee's job performance. Consequently, they have more job relevant information than do other sources upon which to make an evaluation.

Second, the use of peers as raters makes it possible to get a number of independent judgments. The average of several ratings is often more reliable than a single rating (Bayroff, Haggerty, & Rundquist, 1954). Such ratings frequently provide a stable measure relatively free of the bias and idiosyncrasies of a single rater. For this reason, the training to be discussed in the next chapter for minimizing rating errors may not be as critical if peer ratings are used for performance appraisal purposes rather than self-ratings or supervisory ratings.

In addition to being reliable, peer appraisals are valid predictors of job performance. In fact, they have higher predictive validities than supervisory appraisals (Wherry & Fryer, 1949; Williams & Leavitt, 1947). Korman (1968), after reviewing the literature, concluded that peer ratings are among the best predicators of performance in subsequent jobs. These are significant findings, particularly when the appraisal is used as a basis for making promotions.

The validity of peer ratings as predictors of both objective and subjective performance criteria has been investigated extensively in military settings (Amir, Kovarsky, & Sharan, 1970; Hollander, 1954a, 1954b, 1965; Wherry & Fryer, 1949; Williams & Leavitt, 1947). Peer ratings have also been shown to be valid for predicting success in such jobs as industrial managers (Roadman, 1964), insurance agents (Weitz, 1958; Mayfield, 1970), salespeople (Waters & Waters, 1970; Mayfield, 1972), medical students (Kubany, 1957), and police officers (Landy, Farr, Saal, & Freytag, 1976). The time elapsed in these studies, from the time of the initial rating until job performance was measured, varied from several months (Wherry & Fryer, 1949) to two years (Hollander, 1965). The validity coefficients are typically around .40.*

Several studies have compared peer ratings with supervisory and self-appraisals. There is clear evidence of differences between ratings assigned

---

*Validity here refers to the correlation between the peer ratings and the measures of performance taken two years later.

by peers versus superiors (Campbell et al., 1970). Peers and supervisors perceive differently aspects of an employee's behavior in large part because individuals often behave differently when the boss is present (Wexley, 1979). Similarly, self-ratings and peer ratings have low agreement (Kavanagh, MacKinney, & Wolins, 1971; Lawler, 1967). Compared to peer ratings, self-appraisals are typically inflated and may be distored by self-serving biases.

DeNisi and Mitchell (1978) argue that friendship may bias peer evaluations. However, the empirical research (Hollander, 1956; Waters & Waters, 1970; Wherry & Fryer, 1949) shows that this bias does not exist.

Related to the issue of friendship is the extent to which racial differences affect validity. Cox and Krumholtz (1958) and DeJung and Kaplan (1962) found that raters gave significantly higher ratings to ratees of their own race. However, Schmidt and Johnson (1973) found that when the number of blacks and whites in peer groups are approximately the same, no racial effects on peer evaluations are present.

A potential problem with peer appraisals is the unwillingness of peers to evaluate each other (Roadman, 1964). For example, in implementing the BOS shown in Appendix A, the president and general manager encountered strong resistance from employees. The employees viewed peer appraisals as a way for the organization to encourage snitching on one another.

The president overcame the problem by first stressing the concept of fairness: "Jim [the manager] and I see you only some of the time that you are on the job. Your peers see you all the time. This means your appraisals are presently based on the very limited observations of two people, Jim and me. Peer ratings minimize biases because they are averaged together. If one or two people are unfairly critical, the rating will be offset by those people who are evaluating you objectively."

Second, the President asked for their cooperation: "I need your help in order to make sure that I am rewarding people fairly. You people are aware of the aims and objectives of each other's job. You see each other working almost every day. Most importantly, you are far more skilled than I am in recognizing effective as well as ineffective behavior."

Third, he addressed the issue of snitching by pointing out that the appraisals were to be completed *anonymously,* and that the results were to be used primarily for counseling and development purposes: "Every week each of you voices a complaint to Jim or me regarding work that has not been accomplished by a colleague. It has been difficult for us to take action without letting that person know that you discussed the problem with us. Through peer ratings that are anonymous, I can sit down with each of you three times a year and express my appreciation for areas that you are doing well. Where there are areas that you have been rated poorly, I can take steps to immediately provide you with training, remove obstacles that are getting in the way of you doing your job, or discuss with you ways of minimizing the 'erroneous' perceptions of peers who gave you a poor rating."

Finally, the President stressed to the employees that BOS completed by peers was as valuable to them as it was to him. "You will have a copy of each evaluation for your personal files. This document ensures that you will always be treated fairly by management. If Jim and I should play favorites regarding salary increases, promotions, or terminations that adversely affect you, you will have a document of your performance that will stand up before a labor relations board or a court of law."

Peer appraisals are now completed willingly three times a year by the employees. The President reported a sharp sustained increase in productive employee behavior within the first three months.

The major drawback of peer evaluations is that in order for them to be valid, group members must have close contact with one another (Hollander, 1954a, b). Some organizations may have difficulty finding peers who have first-hand knowledge of one another's behavior. Furthermore, the interaction among peers must be relevant to the performance dimensions being evaluated. For example, it is not enough for salespersons who work in different geographical areas to meet once a month for a staff meeting; they must frequently observe one another on the job if the ratings are to be reliable and valid. Where the above issues do not present a problem, our recommendation is for peers to complete the appraisal document anonymously, and for the managers to use these ratings in a counseling and developmental manner (see Chapter 7). This procedure takes the manager out of the role of judge and into the role of helper. To our knowledge, no one has systematically tested the effectiveness of this developmental approach relative to the other approaches discussed in this chapter. This is surprising in light of the consistency with which peer ratings have been shown to be both reliable and valid.[*]

---

[*]See Kane and Lawler (1978) and Lewin and Zwany (1976) for exhaustive reviews of the literature on peer appraisals.

Another problem of peer appraisals is the time required in large departments for one person to complete the appraisal document on all employees. This problem can be minimized by randomly selecting among those people who frequently observe one another, so no one person has to complete more than five or six appraisals.

In doing peer appraisals, one can choose among three basic procedures, namely: (1) peer nomination, (2) peer rating, and (3) peer ranking. The three methods differ primarily in terms of their ability to discriminate among members of a work group on job effectiveness (Kane & Lawler, 1978). The three procedures are described in increasing order of discriminability.

Peer Nomination consists of having each employee in a work group designate a specified number of coworkers as being the highest or best in the group on some particular dimension of job performance (e.g., credit management, community relations, or inventory control). Often, each employee is asked also to nominate others in the group who are lowest or worst on each performance dimension. Employees are usually told to exclude themselves from the nominations given.

Peer Rating entails having each employee rate all others in the work group on a given set of performance dimensions. This method lends itself easily to the use of BOS.

Peer Ranking consists of having each employee rank order all others in the work group from best to worst on one or more performance dimensions. This method is the most discriminating of all the peer appraisal methods since the average rank received by each employee will likely differ from that received by others.

What can be said about the relative strengths and weaknesses of these methods? According to Kane and Lawler (1978), the three different procedures appear to be applicable to different appraisal needs. Peer nominations are best used for identifying employees whose performance is extremely good or bad. This would be especially important as a basis for making decisions regarding promotions, layoffs, separations, and transfers. The major limitation of this method is that it is virtually useless in providing appraisal feedback to employees, because it furnishes no explanatory behavioral information about each employee's score, and it provides no meaningful information to those employees who received no nominations.

Peer rating is most useful for appraisal feedback, since the employees can be evaluated in terms of specific behaviors describing the actual way each individual performed. The information fed back to a person is strictly behavioral information about the individual, and not merely a comparison of the person to some extreme or nonextreme subgroup as is done with peer nomination. A potential problem with this method is its reliability. Unless the raters are trained to minimize rating errors (see Chapter 5), this method is susceptible to rater bias. Assuming careful rating scale construction and the training of raters, we recommend that this appraisal method be used.

At this time there is insufficient research data to permit definitive conclusions regarding the validity of peer rankings. It is likely that this approach violates the 1978 Civil Service Reform Act where ranking is prohibited (see Chapter 2).

SUBORDINATE APPRAISAL

There are circumstances when subordinate appraisals can be valuable to an employee and to the organization. For example, Maloney and Hinrichs (1959) instituted a program at Exxon (known then as Esso) called "Rate Your Supervisor." The program provided each supervisor with a computer printout showing the average of anonymous subordinate ratings, and how the manager was rated relative to other supervisors. As a result of this program: (1) 25 percent of the subordinates said they had seen lasting changes in their supervisors, (2) 88 percent of the supervisors said they had tried to change their behavior after receiving the report, and (3) 60 percent of the supervisors and the subordinates agreed that productivity had increased as a result of the program.

A division of the Weyerhaeuser Company has taken this program a step further. The foremen and superintendents receive a computer printout showing how they were rated by both a superior and subordinates on each overall performance dimension or criterion that was identified through a job analysis (Latham et al., 1979) as critical to job success. The printout also shows the superior's ratings and the average of the subordinate ratings on each behavioral item of each BOS, as well as the person's standing relative to peers. Peer appraisals are not used because the superintendents seldom see one another on the job. Similarly, foremen seldom interact with other foremen.

The appraisal score is the composite of the superior's rating *and* employee ratings across four BOS. This procedure was implemented primarily to assure employees that their voices were not only being heard by management, but that their foreman was taking action based on their input as well as that of the superintendent.

Table 4.2 shows a performance appraisal printout that each foreman receives. The foremen in this organization are evaluated on four BOS, namely, interaction with subordinates, safety, work habits, and organizational commitment. The maximum number of points on interaction with subordinates that this particular foreman could have received from the superintendent is 60 (5-point scale times 12 items). Under the raw score column it can be seen that this particular foreman received a 31. The rating given by the foreman's supervisor for each behavioral item is shown on the bottom left side of the printout.

Similarly, the maximum number of points on interaction with subordinates that the foreman could have received from subordinates is 70 (5-point scale times 14 items). The total number of items rated by the foreman's supervisor on this criterion is different from the total number of items rated by subordinates because of the item analysis procedure discussed in Chapter 3. This analysis indicated that there were some items that subordinates were more capable of observing than supervisors.

This organization uses the words superior, excellent, full, adequate, and below adequate to describe the performance of foremen. This is similar to the five grades used in educational institutions, namely A (4.0), B (3.0), C (2.0), D (1.0), and E (0.0). The raw scores from supervisor and subordinates are listed as a 2.0 (full) and a 3.0 (excellent) under interaction with subordinates. Relative to other foremen, this foreman fell in the bottom sixth percentile on this criterion as viewed by superiors and in the fifty-second percentile in the eyes of subordinates with an overall average percentile rank of 18. This means that in terms of combined scores on interaction with subordinates, 82 percent of the foremen received higher scores than the individual shown in Table 4.2.

Where there is a large discrepancy between superior and subordinate ratings, management can investigate the reasons. Frequently, the cause is a personality conflict between the individual and the supervisor. It is for this reason that individuals in this organization value subordinate appraisals.

TABLE 4.2
Performance Appraisal–Computer Printout

| | Performance Appraisal Summary Report | | | | | | | | |
| | Raw Score | | | G.P.A. | | | % Rank | | |
	Sup.	Sub.	Mean	Sup.	Sub.	Mean	Sup.	Sub.	Mean
I. Interaction with Subordinates	31	52	41.5	2.0	3.0	2.5	6	52	18.0
II. Safety	19	21	20.0	2.0	3.0	2.5	9	68	33.0
III. Work Habits	37	59	48.0	2.0	3.0	2.5	2	36	8.0
IV. Organization Commitment	5	23	14.0	0.0	3.0	1.5	2	44	4.0
Total	92	155	123.5	1.5	3.0	2.3	2	45	12.0

Ratings by Superior					Ratings by Subordinates					
I	1.2		5.4	2.2	I	1.4		3.4		14.3
	2.2		6.1	3.1		2.3		4.5		15.4
	3.4	III	1.3	4.1		3.4		5.4	IV	1.4
	4.2		2.2			4.4	III	1.4		2.4
	5.4		3.3			5.4		2.4		3.4
	6.1		4.2			6.4		3.4		4.3
	7.2		5.4			7.3		4.4		5.4
	8.3		6.4			8.4		5.4		6.4
	9.2		7.5			9.4		6.4		
	10.3		8.2			10.4		7.5		
	11.3		9.2			11.4		8.4		
	12.3		10.2			12.3		9.4		
II	1.3		11.2			13.3		10.3		
	2.3		12.4			14.4		11.4		
	3.4		13.2		II	1.4		12.4		
	4.4	IV	1.1			2.4		13.4		

The use of these multiple appraisals reduces the effects of an unfair appraisal from one person—the boss.

Foremen are allowed to keep the results of the subordinate ratings confidential for three months before showing them to their superior. The foremen are trained to conduct team-building sessions with their subordinates (French & Bell, 1978), and they are allowed to use consultants for the team-building process to assist them in resolving concerns that were highlighted by the subordinate appraisals. The words *team building* refer to subordinates and their foreman discussing and resolving problems of mutual concern, and thus building a productive work team. Typically, the supervisor categorizes areas where the subordinate ratings were low into three areas: (a) areas that I can't change; here is the rationale; (b) areas that I can change immediately; and (c) areas that through discussion and help from you (subordinates) we can change together.

Through this process subordinates begin to view problems through the eyes of their supervisor, and equally important, the supervisor begins to see concerns from the perspective of subordinates. The result can be an increase in group productivity and job satisfaction within two or three months. The supervisor can then take the subordinate ratings to his or her superior and explain what has been done to maintain or improve the ratings. An additional value of subordinate ratings is that they can aid management in identifying individuals who are promotable because of their skill in managing people.

There are, however, potential problems with subordinate appraisals. Some subordinates may perceive the process as threatening. They may feel that their supervisor will reprimand them for an honest, unfavorable appraisal. This is why anonymity is critical for increasing the likelihood of accurate ratings. As a rule of thumb, we recommend avoiding subordinate ratings where there are too few subordinates (e.g., less than four).

Research on the effectiveness of subordinate evaluations is limited at this time. Questions concerning their reliability and validity have yet to be answered. However, it seems likely from a counseling and development standpoint that subordinate ratings, particularly when used as a basis for team building, have far more advantages than disadvantages.

APPRAISAL BY OUTSIDERS

Some organizations use persons outside the immediate work environment to conduct performance appraisals. These sources include: (1) assessors in an assessment center, (2) field reviews conducted by people in the personnel department, and (3) evaluations from trainers.*

---

*The president of the bowling lanes referred to earlier in this chapter has the BOS shown in Appendix A completed by customers as well as peers.

The term *assessment center* refers to a standardized off-the-job method for assessing managerial effectiveness. Although no two programs in industry are exactly alike, they all place heavy emphasis on the use of multiple methods of assessment as well as the observation of behavior in simulated situations (Moses & Byham, 1977). The exercises generally include, but are not limited to, in-basket tests, business problems, and the leaderless group discussion.

In-basket tests are exercises consisting of letters and memoranda. The employees being appraised are asked to pretend that these materials have accumulated in their in-baskets. They are instructed to do as much as they can to solve the problems that the materials present. This technique is an excellent measure of an individual's administrative skills regarding organization planning and decision making.

Business problems are games in which groups of employees are given capital with which to establish themselves in business. Their task as a group is to organize their business, manufacture a product, or perform a service so as to make as much profit as possible in the time allotted. During this game, each employee's skills in such areas as human relations, resistance to stress, and energy are assessed.

A leaderless group discussion (LGD) is a conference among several persons in which no formal leader has been assigned. The discussion is often of a competitive nature in that each individual takes a position and tries to win its adoption by the group. For example, each individual might be asked to assume that he or she is a member of a school board vying for funds. Sometimes the LGD is of a cooperative nature in which each person is assigned a role and told to help the group arrive at an important decision (e.g., whether to sell one of its subsidiary companies). During this exercise, employees are assessed in terms of such qualities as oral communication, personal impact, and behavioral flexibility.

The assessors are typically line managers two or more organization levels above the people who are being assessed. The assessors administer the individual exercises and observe the employees. The ratio of assessors to employees is usually about 1:2 or 1:3. The employees are assessed on criteria identified through a job analysis as relevant to success in management.

The advantage of performance appraisals conducted in an assessment center is that it allows the assessors to see five to seven employees doing the same thing at the same point in time under standardized conditions.

Some psychologists feel (e.g., Wallace, 1965; McCall & DeVries, 1976) that the only hope for evaluating people objectively is to establish simulated criteria in which their performance can be compared to known standards under controlled, standardized conditions.

A drawback of assessment centers for performance appraisal is that the performance being evaluated is based on simulated exercises rather than actual job performance. Thus, employees may resent its use for appraising their present performance. However, the reliability of this procedure is high, and its validity for predicting success in higher level jobs is impressive. (See Wanous, 1980, for a discussion of both the selection and recruitment functions of the assessment center.) Where the purpose of the performance appraisal is to assess promotion potential, the assessment center is highly effective.

The *field review* derives its name from the fact that a representative of the personnel department goes into the field to interview managers and supervisors about the performance of each subordinate. The personnel representative then writes evaluation reports, which are sent to the manager who modifies them, if need be, and then signs them to indicate approval. The strengths of this method are that it provides line managers with professional assistance in making appraisals, it cuts down on the amount of time they normally have to spend in writing appraisals, and it increases the standardization of the evaluation process throughout the total organization.

On the other hand, almost nothing is known about the reliability or validity of this performance appraisal technique. Also, in some organizations where the procedure does not have the support of high level management, it is used as an excuse by supervisors and managers to avoid their responsibility for seriously evaluating their subordinates (Wexley & Yukl, 1977).

Another type of outside evaluation is that given by training staff. When individuals receive training, the training staff can give ratings based on what they have seen the employee do during the training program. In several studies on military personnel (Gordon & Medland, 1965; Williams & Leavitt, 1947) trainer evaluations were found to agree substantially, indicating acceptable interobserver reliability. However, it was also found that training staff appraisals were less reliable and had lower predictive validity than peer evaluations by fellow trainees. Again, this may be because peers have more information on which to make an appraisal than do trainers.

Saari & Latham (1980) examined the validity of assessments made by two trainers immediately after training 64 foremen who had attended nine two-hour leadership training sessions. The pooled judgments of both trainers correlated significantly with supervisory and subordinate performance appraisals of the trainees conducted one year after training.

One potential advantage of the use of outside appraisers is that it may reduce the randomness in evaluations that is due to appraisers using different standards in evaluating performance. As mentioned previously, Barrett (1966) found that supervisory appraisals depend heavily on how the supervisor thinks the work should be done, and supervisors often differ widely on their requirements. Barrett concluded that evaluations done by outsiders can be based on a common frame of reference and are thus more likely than evaluations by supervisors to be consistent across the organization. However, this advantage can be offset through the use of BOS (see Chapter 3) and the training of supervisors to minimize rating errors (see Chapter 5).

There are several disadvantages with using outside appraisals. As Cummings and Schwab (1973) point out, it is not known whether meaningful conversations take place between a manager and a subordinate about performance when the appraisal is based on input from someone outside the work unit. Furthermore, outside appraisals may sometimes be inefficient in that they can require significantly more time and manpower than other types of appraisals. Finally, the appraisals are often not based on direct observations by the appraiser of the employee on the job. When the appraisals are based on direct observations, and there are no other sources (e.g., peers, manager) available, they can, of course, be valuable. This was the case in the series of studies on loggers discussed in Chapter 3 (Latham & Wexley, 1977; Latham, Wexley, & Rand, 1975; Ronan & Latham, 1974). The logging supervisors were independent businessmen. They seldom, if ever, interacted with other supervisors on job sites. Many of their subordinates were illiterate and could not complete the BOS. The subordinates were reluctant to be interviewed on the performance of their boss. Consequently, the appraisal information was collected from two sources, namely, the dealers to whom the logging supervisors sold their wood and company foresters on whose land they were cutting timber. Wood dealers and company employed foresters are aware of the aims and objectives of the logging supervisor's job, they frequently see the loggers on the job, and they are capable of discussing competent behavior.

CLOSING REMARKS

The usual practice in most organizations is for an employee to be evaluated by an immediate superior. In recent years, many progressive organizations have come to realize that other sources besides an employee's boss can provide appraisals. These sources include the employee, peers of the employee, subordinates reporting to the employee, and appraisers outside the employee's work unit.

What can be said about the use of appraisals from sources other than the individual's manager or supervisor? We believe that the use of multiple sources increases the probability of obtaining a comprehensive picture of an employee's total contribution to the organization. Quite often, the performance ratings of an individual from appraisers at different organizational levels do not agree highly with one another. Often this is because the appraisers see different aspects of an employee's behavior. Employees behave differently with their boss, peers, and subordinates. It is for this reason that we recommend the systematic collection of input from supervisors, peers, subordinates, and the individual themselves when making a performance appraisal. We are not enthusiastic at the present time with the use of outsiders unless the outsiders base their conclusions on first-hand observations. If only one procedure is to be used, we would recommend the use of peer ratings with the feedback and counseling being conducted by the supervisor, and the employee participating with the supervisor in setting specific performance goals (see Chapters 6, 7 and 8) based on this information.

The underlying issue of this chapter is the necessity for maximizing direct (first-hand) observations of an employee's performance through the use of all relevant sources of information, namely, peers, supervisors, and subordinates. Only in this way can appraisals have what Locke (1976) calls logical validity. That is, an appraisal must be integrated in a noncontradictory fashion with all pertinent information relevant to the phenomenon being measured. Logical validity requires, in the case of BOS, that the contradictions among different appraiser responses to the scale be resolved.

This is done by pointing out contradictions to the appraisers and by discussing with them explanations for the contradictions. When such a procedure is followed, Locke points out that it will usually be found that in responding to the different items or scales, an appraiser may have used a different frame of reference or interpreted one or more items idiosyncratically. Note that this procedure validates the appraisers, not the appraisal instrument. The construct validity of appraisals was discussed in Chapter 3. Logical validity supplements this discussion.

SUMMARY

In this chapter we discussed the important question of who should provide the information for the performance appraisal. The assessment of an employee's performance may be based on the observations of supervisors, employees themselves, peers, subordinates, people from outside the department or plant, or some combination of the above.

Most appraisals are based on observations by the employee's immediate supervisor because that individual has the responsibility for developing subordinates. Observer bias, however, is frequently a problem with this method.

Self-appraisals are especially appropriate where the employee is working alone or possesses a rare skill. Moreover, the self-appraisals can force the individual to focus on what is expected in that job and clarify differences of opinion between the employee and the supervisor regarding job requirements, job performance, and developmental needs.

Peer appraisals are the best single source of information from the standpoint of reliability and validity. They are not only a valid way for assessing present performance, but also an accurate predictor of future performance. The primary disadvantage of peer ratings is that they are limited to jobs where the peers frequently interact with one another on the job.

Subordinate appraisals can facilitate team building where the supervisor and the subordinates discuss and resolve problems of mutual concern and thus build a productive work team. Subordinate ratings can assist management in identifying individuals who are promotable because of their skill in managing people. A drawback of subordinate ratings is that there is little knowledge regarding their reliability and validity.

Appraisals from outsiders are of dubious value unless the evaluations are based on first-hand observations. An excellent method for assessing promotability is a series of job simulation exercises known as the assessment center. Employees, however, may question its use for assessing their present performance.

The ideal approach to making appraisals is to collect observations from multiple sources such as peers, subordinates, and the supervisor. Logical validity requires that contradictions among the different resources be pointed out and resolved. This procedure is analogous to the discussion of construct validity in the previous chapter.

Minimizing Rating Errors in Observing and Evaluating Performance

5

INTRODUCTION

No combination of raters will result in accurate decisions if the appraisals are affected by employee characteristics that are irrelevant to the job. Thus, regardless of whether evaluations are obtained from multiple appraisers or from only the employee's immediate superior, all raters should be trained to reduce errors of judgment that occur when one person evaluates another. This training is necessary because to the degree a performance appraisal is biased, distorted, or inaccurate, the probability of stimulating the productivity of the employee is greatly decreased. Moreover, wrong decisions will be made regarding whom to promote, retain, or replace, which in turn will penalize the organization's bottom line. In addition, when a performance appraisal is affected by rating errors, the employee may be justified in filing a discrimination charge (*Watkins* v. *Scott Paper Co.*, 1976). Without admitting guilt, AT&T agreed in court to compensate women and minority employees with payments that are estimated to run between $12 to $15 million. The payments are intended as retroactive compensation to those who in the past may have been victims of discrimination in promotions, transfers, and salary administration (Miner, 1974).

At the present time, few organizations incorporate training that will reduce rating errors in their performance appraisal system. They assume incorrectly that the careful construction of the appraisal instrument will obviate the need for training raters. This type of thinking is a mistake!

Despite attempts to build sophisticated appraisal instruments that both lend themselves to counseling and development and are resistant to rating errors (e.g., Berkshire & Highland, 1953; Blanz & Ghiselli, 1972; Smith & Kendall, 1963), evaluators continue to make errors when observing and evaluating employees.

This chapter describes common rating errors that people typically make when observing and evaluating others. In addition, it includes a review of training programs that have been used to help people minimize rating errors.

RATING ERRORS

Rating errors are errors in judgment that occur in a systematic manner when an individual observes and evaluates another. Rating errors may be defined technically as a difference between the output of a human judgment process and that of an objective, accurate assessment uncolored by bias, prejudice, or other subjective, extraneous influences (Blum & Naylor, 1968; Feldman, 1979). What makes these errors so difficult to correct is that the observers are usually unaware that they are making them. In those instances when they are aware of errors, they are frequently unable to correct them themselves (Wexley, Sanders, & Yukl, 1973). The unfortunate result can be an employee who is inappropriately retained, promoted, demoted, transferred, or terminated. The most common rating errors include contrast effects, first impressions, halo, similar-to-me, central tendency, and positive and negative leniency.

The *contrast effects* error is the tendency for a rater to evaluate a person relative to other individuals rather than on the requirements of the job (Wexley, Yukl, Kovacs, & Sanders, 1972). For example, think of the best looking man or woman you have known. Rate this individual on a 9-point scale with 9 representing outstanding in terms of physical attractiveness. Now, think of your favorite glamorous movie star. Rate that person on the same criteria by which you rated the previous individual. Now, rerate the first individual. If you are tempted to give that person a lower rating, you are on the verge of making a contrast error. The rating should be given on the basis of the attractiveness criteria that you established prior to the rating, *not* on the basis of a comparison with another individual. Similarly, employees should be rated on the degree to which they fulfill predetermined job requirements, not on how they compare with others.

Contrast effects occur most frequently in selection when a person interviews one or more highly qualified candidates for a job opening and then interviews one who is only average; or conversely, when a person interviews one or more very underqualified candidates followed by an interview with an average candidate. In the first case, the average applicant may be rejected only for looking bad relative to the two previous candidates. The candidate may very well have met the requirements of the job. If there were several job openings in the company, the rejection was the organization's loss and possibly a competitor's gain. In the second instance of contrast effects, the average candidate may get a higher rating than would be deserved simply due to the favorable comparison to much weaker candidates.

Contrast effects are particularly troublesome in performance appraisals because of the deeply imbedded assumption by many personnel people that the distribution of ratings should resemble a normal or bell-shaped curve. To automatically rate on a curve is not only in violation of the 1978 Civil Service Reform Act (see Chapter 2), but it is also absurd.

For example, work units that have experienced a series of economic recessions that resulted in layoffs may have only excellent employees remaining. It is unethical for a personnel officer to insist that at least some of them be given low ratings on the performance appraisal form. People should be evaluated on the degree to which they fulfill the requirements of their jobs, not on how well they do relative to other people. This point is especially true if the other people are doing different jobs. To do otherwise not only invites a possible lawsuit, but also can create havoc within the organization.

Consider the following incident. An individual in one department appeared to be outstanding relative to (in contrast with) the other people in the department. Consequently, the individual was promoted to a higher paying job in another work unit. The individual is presently a failure in the new job. This person has been promoted into incompetence. Why? Because no one asked whether that person could fulfill the requirements of the new job, let alone how well the requirements of the original job were being performed. Instead, everyone was impressed with how well the person was doing relative to the poor performers in that original department.

Another example of contrast effects that is dangerous from the standpoint of reducing an organization's productivity and increasing the chances of a lawsuit occurred when a company was recently experiencing the results of an economic recession. An average manager working in an exceptionally good department was laid off. An equally average manager doing the same exact job, but in a poor department, was given additional responsibility and subsequently promoted. Thus, even though these two individuals were comparable in terms of their job performance, one benefited from the mediocrity of peers while the other one suffered because the peers were exceptional. The moral for employees, as far as contrast effect errors are concerned, is to practice what we all can recall from school, namely, "be the smartest kid in the stupid class."

First-impression error refers to the tendency for a manager to make an initial favorable or unfavorable judgment about an employee, and then ignore (or perceptually distort) subsequent information, so as to support the initial impression. For example, the first month on the job one individual did outstanding work. For the next five months the person did at best average work. The manager committed first-impression error by continuing to give the individual a high rating despite the fact that once the employee knew that a good impression had been created, he decided to coast on the job. Conversely, another individual initially experienced difficulties on the job for a variety of nonjob-related (e.g., divorce) reasons. After three months this individual was doing extremely well, but the manager continued to assign mediocre ratings. The unfortunate result was that the challenging assignments were given to the first individual who was no longer performing the job well.

The *halo effect* refers to inappropriate generalizations from one aspect of a person's performance on the job to all aspects of a person's job performance. For example, a person who is outstanding on only one area of the job (e.g., inventory control) may be rated inaccurately as outstanding on all areas of the job (credit management, customer relations, community relations). Conversely, if a person is rated as deficient in one area of the job, that person may be rated incorrectly as doing poorly on all aspects of the job. The point here is that people have both strengths and weaknesses, and each needs to be evaluated independently.

Now consider a different rater error. Suppose that you could find the perfect person for the job in terms of background, aptitude, knowledge, and experience. Would you rate the person lower if that individual had twelve brothers and sisters, if the father drove a bus, and if the mother was a maid? Most people would give an emphatic no to this question. And if we persisted by asking whether such variables would influence their ratings in any way, they might wonder if we had lost our senses.

Managers who had several years of experience in conducting performance appraisals were given a detailed job description for a position in their unit. They then observed a videotape of a person who met all the requirements of the job. However, one group of predominantly middle class managers heard the applicant say that he had two brothers, a father with a Ph.D. in physics, and a mother with a Masters degree in social work. A second group of middle class managers received the exact same job description. They then saw the same videotape. The only difference was that the tape was spliced so that the managers heard the applicant say that he had 12 brothers and sisters, his father was a bus driver, and his mother was a maid. The first group rated the person a 9 on a 9-point scale indicating that he was outstanding. The second group gave this same person 5s and 6s.

The error these managers made is known as the *similar-to-me effect* (Rand & Wexley, 1975; Wexley & Nemeroff, 1974). This error is a tendency on the part of raters to judge more favorably those people whom they perceive as similar to themselves. That is, the more closely an employee resembles the rater in attitudes or background, the stronger the tendency of the rater to judge that individual favorably. Why does this effect occur? We all tend to like and to think more highly of others whom we perceive as like us rather than unlike us because it is flattering and reinforcing. This effect may be acceptable in social situations, but it is an error when making appraisals on the job because it can lead to charges of discrimination, not to mention the assignment of tasks to the wrong people.

Central tendency error is committed by the person who wants to play it safe. This error refers to people who consistently rate an employee on or close to the midpoint of a scale when the employee's performance clearly warrants a substantially higher or lower rating. If the manager rates the individual as average, and the individual subsequently does extremely well, the manager can say, "See, I told you the employee wasn't bad." On the other hand, if the employee does poorly, the manager can say, "What did you expect? I told you that individual wasn't all that good."

Negative and *positive leniency* errors are committed by the manager who is either too hard or too easy in rating employees. In the performance appraisal process, positive leniency may raise unwarranted expectations of the employee for raises, promotions, or challenging job assignments. With negative leniency or toughness, the employee may get tired of banging his or her head against the wall, because no matter how hard the individual tries, the boss cannot be satisfied. In both instances, the result can be the same: the employee stops working hard. It is interesting to note from anecdotal evidence that workers generally do not like supervisors who are tough unfairly, and they do not *respect* supervisors who are too lenient in their ratings. In the latter case it is demotivating to see someone who is lazy receive the same high rating as someone who is a hard worker.

TRAINING APPROACHES TO MINIMIZING RATER ERRORS

For years, psychologists have stressed the importance of providing training to improve objectivity and accuracy in evaluating an employee's performance. But, it is only recently that training programs for reducing rater errors have appeared.

Stockford & Bissell (1949) and Levine and Butler (1952) can be credited with some of the first known attempts at improving the rating practices of supervisors. Levine and Butler, for example, worked with 29 supervisors in a large manufacturing plant where it had been determined that the supervisors overrated those working in the higher job grades and underrated those in the lower grades. This evaluation was most unfair because the supervisors were obviously not rating the individual's performance as much as they were the job that individual held.

Consequently, these supervisors were randomly assigned to a control, a lecture, or a discussion group. Supervisors in the control condition were given no training or information. Supervisors in a second group were given a detailed lecture on the theory and technique of performance ratings. The lecturer explained to the supervisors the problem caused by their previous ratings, and what each supervisor needed to do to correct the problem. In the discussion group, the supervisors met together to discuss the nature of the problem and how it could be solved. The discussion leader merely acted as a moderator, avoiding interjection of his own opinions. After generating a number of ideas, the group arrived at one solution acceptable to all, namely, to focus solely on the extent to which the person is fulfilling the requirements of the job.

The results showed that the lecture method had practically no influence on changing the supervisor's method of rating. The same was true for the control group who had received no training. Only the group discussion method, in which the members participated in arriving at solutions to the problem, was successful in overcoming the rating errors.

Two limitations of this study were that it dealt with only one rating error, and the effects of the training were not assessed over time. Nevertheless, a major conclusion of this research was that *knowledge alone* (i.e., lecturing) *is not sufficient to change rating behavior.*

Similarly, in a university setting, Wexley, Sanders, and Yukl (1973) found that warning individuals to recognize and avoid contrast effects did not reduce this error. Only an intensive workshop resulted in a behavior change. The workshop was based on psychological principles of learning, namely, active participation, knowledge of results or feedback, and practice. Specifically, the workshop gave trainees a chance to practice observing and rating actual videotaped individuals. In addition, the trainees were given immediate feedback regarding the accuracy of their ratings.

A recent review of the literature by Spool (1978) indicated that the majority of the approaches to reducing rating errors suffer from one or more methodological problems. For example, many training programs do *not* provide trainees an opportunity to practice the skills learned, nor do they provide them feedback on how well they are performing (Bernardin, 1978; Bernardin & Walter, 1977). Other studies fail to include a control group (Borman, 1975), while others do not evaluate the effects of training at all (Burnaska, 1976).

What is worse, is that many training programs have taught trainees inappropriate behaviors. For example, in the training programs developed by Bernardin (1978) trainees are shown rating distributions such as those shown in Table 5.1.

He tells the trainees that the ratings provided by Rater 1 probably contain halo error while those provided by Rater 2 probably do not. Explicit in Bernardin's programs is that certain rating distributions are desirable. As another example, skewed distributions are said to be an indication of leniency error. Raters are encouraged to conform more closely to a normal distribution across ratees. This training is inappropriate

TABLE 5.1
Performance Criteria

Rater/	Technical Ability	Human Relations Skills	Organizational Commitment	Safety	Overall
1	5	6	5	5	5
2	5	3	6	3	4

because it teaches people to use the entire range of the scale when evaluating people, when the advice may be unwarranted; and, to give low rather than high ratings (Bernardin & Pence, 1980). It is therefore not surprising that rater reliability and accuracy (validity) does not improve as a result of this approach to training.

Bernardin and his colleagues (Bernardin & Buckley, 1979; Bernardin & Pence, 1980) concluded correctly that rater training programs, if they are to be effective, should concentrate on enhancing the accuracy of ratings through discussion of the multidimensionality of work performance, the importance of recording objectively what is seen, and the development of specific examples of effective and ineffective employees. This is an advantage of using BOS. BOS specifies standards of what is meant by effective/ineffective performance for the observer. Finally, Bernardin (Bernardin & Buckley, 1979) concluded that only training programs similar to that used by Wexley, Sanders and Yukl (1973) are likely to be effective in improving rating accuracy.

On the basis of Wexley's work, Latham, Wexley and Pursell (1975) developed a performance training program to help people minimize rating errors when observing and evaluating others. In addition they developed a group discussion method similar to that used by Levine and Butler. Both methods were selected because each one had previously been effective in reducing at least one type of rating error. They have subsequently turned out to be the only two programs that have been shown to systematically reduce rating errors and increase rate accuracy in organizational settings. In fact, they have been described as "the most advanced rater training programs related to rating job performance." (Borman, 1979, p. 412).*

*The results of the workshop approach have been successfully replicated by Bernardin and Pence (1980).

In a study to evaluate the effectiveness of this training program, sixty personnel people and line managers were randomly assigned to one of three conditions: a workshop, a group discussion, or a control group that was not to receive training until it was certain that at least one of the two training methods could attain the objectives for which it was designed, namely to reduce rating errors. The training required six to eight hours of instruction depending on the amount of discussion generated among the trainees. Note the marked contrast with previous training programs that lasted from five minutes to an hour (e.g., Bernardin, 1978; Bernardin & Walter, 1977) and did not bring about a lasting behavioral change.

WORKSHOP

The workshop consisted of videotapes of job candidates being evaluated. The trainees gave a rating on a 9-point scale according to how they thought the manager in the videotape rated the candidate; they also rated the candidate. Group discussions concerning the reasons for each trainee's rating of the job candidate followed. In this way, the trainees had an opportunity to *observe* other managers making errors, to *actively partici-pate* in discovering the degree to which they were or were not prone to making the error, to receive *knowledge of results* regarding their own rating behavior, and to *practice* job-related tasks to reduce the errors that they were making. The relationship between the training content and the actual job was similar in principle so as to facilitate *transfer of learning* back to the job.

The first exercise focused on the similar-to-me effect. The trainees were given a job description and a list of the job requirements for a loan officer's position. They were then shown a videotape of an interview. The content of the interview revealed a strong attitudinal and biographical similarity between the manager and the applicant. Relatively little job-related information from this below average applicant was elicited by the manager. When the tape ended, the trainees were asked to give two ratings: (1) How would you rate the applicant? (2) How do you think the manager rated the applicant? Their ratings were then discussed in relation to the similar-to-me effect. Possible ways of minimizing this error in performance appraisal situations were discussed by the trainees. Typical of the many solutions brainstormed by the trainees for minimizing this error in performance appraisals are as follows:

1. Establish the standards of performance expected on all jobs before rating employees.

2. Make certain that all criteria on which employees are evaluated are clearly job related.

3. Rate employees solely in relation to the job responsibilities, not in terms of how similar they are to oneself.

4. Have employees evaluated by mutiple raters with different backgrounds and attitudes from one another.

The second exercise focused on the halo effect. The trainees were again show a videotaped situation and they rated how the manager and they themselves would rate an individual who was outstanding in only one area of the job.

As with the similar-to-me error, the trainees were asked to brainstorm solutions to halo error in performance evaluation settings. The solutions suggested most frequently by the workshop participants are as follows:

1. Do not listen to comments about a person until you have made your own evaluation.

2. When an individual is to be evaluated by multiple raters, be certain that the raters assign their ratings independently; group discussion about the employee should come after everyone has had an opportunity to observe and evaluate the individual. The discussion should not take place before the ratings are assigned.

3. Rate the individual solely on the behavioral items that define a given criterion (e.g., safety). Recognize that different performance measures are not always related. A person can do well on one criterion and perform poorly on another (e.g., a professor may be a good researcher and a poor teacher).

The third exercise dealt with contrast effects. The trainees were given a job description and a list of the job requirements for an accountant's job. Trainees were then given a resumé of a highly qualified applicant and were asked to make a rating. The procedure was repeated with a second highly qualified applicant and then with an average applicant. The fact that evaluations of job applicants can be affected by the suitability of immediately preceding applicants, and that subordinates are often evaluated in comparison to other subordinates rather than on established standards was discussed. The necessity of basing ratings on predetermined job standards was then emphasized.

Solutions to contrast effect are:

1. Appraise a large number of people at the same point in time; the error is more frequent when only a few individuals are interviewed or appraised.
2. Base your performance evaluations on specific *predetermined* job requirements or standards.
3. Do not rate people in any particular order (i.e., don't rate the best or the worst people first.)
4. Rate people on the extent to which they fulfill the requirements of the job; compare people after, rather than before, an evaluation. For example, Kim received an A in Algebra while Pat received a B. Kim's score was compared with Pat's after each test was graded in accordance with predefined standards, namely, the answer key. The two students were not rated on a curve.

The final exercise was a demonstration of the effects of *first impression.* The trainees were given a job description and a listing of the specific job requirements for an insurance rater. They were then shown a videotape of an interview. The interview began with the applicant presenting a poor impression by her answers, actions, and appearance. The remainder of the interview showed that the applicant was acceptable for the job; however, the interviewer continued to act according to the initial impressions. Again, the trainees gave two types of ratings: (1) How would you rate the applicant? and (2) How do you think the interviewer rated the applicant? The trainees discussed their individual ratings as well as ways to reduce the rating error in the performance appraisal. Among the solutions mentioned by the trainees were:

1. Reserve all judgments about an employee until the end of the time period for which the appraisal is scheduled.
2. Be a note taker rather than an evaluator during the interval between performance appraisals. Ideally, supervisors should record daily a subordinate's behavior that they observed lead to adequate or inadequate

performance on job assignments. The incidents should be reviewed later by the manager when it is time to assign ratings. Read the incidents in an order other than the recorded sequence. For example, first read the incidents that occurred during the middle of the appraisal period, then read those that occurred toward the beginning of the appraisal period. The recording of incidents should be done regardless of whether BOS or BES are used. The advantage of using BOS is that where the incidents have not been recorded daily, the items on the BOS can facilitate recall of incidents.

The final exercise dealt with positive and negative leniency. Again, raters were trained to record exactly what they saw, and to compare what they recorded with critical job behaviors/standards required in a job description or contained in the appraisal instrument.

GROUP DISCUSSION

In the group discussion method each error was defined by the trainer. An example of each error was given in the context of a performance appraisal, a selection interview, and an off-the-job situation. This procedure was followed to insure that the trainees thoroughly understood the error. The trainees were then divided into groups to discuss personal examples that they had experienced in these three situations. Following this, the trainees generated solutions to the problem. These solutions were identical to those given in the workshop.

The advantage of the group discussion procedure over the workshop method was that it was less formal. Thus the trainees could be more relaxed. In addition, the expense of preparing the videotapes and the renting of equipment was not necessary.

The disadvantage of this method compared to the workshop was that the trainees did not have an opportunity to experience the errors or to practice solutions to the errors. Thus, they were able to obtain knowledge from the trainer and from each other about their understanding of the problem, but not about their own specific behavior with regard to the problem. Note that in neither the workshop nor the group discussion procedure were examples given of good/bad rating distributions or intercorrelations among ratings. Instead, training focused solely on the necessity for recording exactly what was said or done by the person on the videotape so as to be able to justify a given rating in terms of the job description/responsibilities the trainees received prior to viewing the videotape.

TRAINING RESULTS AND IMPLICATIONS

A critical limitation of many training programs is that no attempts are made to assess their long-term effectiveness. That is, managers may know that the training program was or was not effective in modifying an individual's behavior immediately after training; however, they have no measure of its effectiveness once the person has returned to the job. There is a danger that many concepts and principles taught in training are forgotten or are discarded soon after the trainee returns to the daily pressures of the job. For this reason the long-term effects of training programs must be evaluated to see if they bring about a relatively permanent change in trainee behavior.

The results regarding an actual change in rating behavior immediately after training were disappointing. In general the trainees in the two training conditions continued to make rating errors as did the trainees in the control group. Rating errors, as previously noted, are well-established habits that are highly resistant to change.

The results of the two training programs were evaluated again six months after training on the basis of two criteria, namely reaction measures and actual behavioral samples. The reaction measures consisted of the trainees' opinion on a 9-point rating scale of the extent to which they believed that they benefited from the program after they returned to their job. The mean ratings given to the workshop and the group discussion methods were 8.8 and 6.3, respectively.

These results were surprising in that the researchers had predicted that the greater freedom in the group discussion method to participate in informal evaluations of their own and their peers' understanding of each rating error would result in trainees being more satisfied with the training than those in a highly structured workshop. Furthermore, it was felt that the workshop trainees might become embarrassed and defensive after committing rating errors in the presence of fellow trainees.

The actual results, however, are congruent with studies done in other settings that show that participation in itself is not always desirable. For example, Hillery and Wexley (1974) compared trainee satisfaction in a program that permitted trainees a great deal of participation in evaluating their own performance versus one in which they were allowed comparatively little participation. Results of the study indicate that in a training setting, people generally want to be told how they are doing; employee participation in this situation is not highly valued.

The second group of measures for assessing the effectiveness of the two training programs were behavioral samples. Trainees were given the requirements for a specific job. They were then shown videotapes, which none of them had previously seen, of a job candidate being interviewed for that job. The trainees were given the following instructions prior to viewing the videotapes.

You are going to see some applicants. Please rate each person in terms of the degree to which you feel that he or she is acceptable for the job. There are no tricks. For example, if you see someone who obviously does not fulfill the requirements of the job, don't say to yourself that this is obviously a trick so I will rate the individual as acceptable. If the individual is unacceptable, rate the individual as unacceptable. Similarly, if you see someone who is obviously terrific, don't fool yourself by saying, "There must be something wrong somewhere." Rate each individual on the basis of what the individual actually says or does."

The results showed that the control group committed the following errors: similar-to-me, halo, and contrast effects. The group discussion trainees committed only one error. Rather than exhibiting a first-impression error, the individuals displayed a sizable recency or last-impression error. The trainees in the workshop did not commit any rating error. It would appear that managers need an opportunity (e.g., six months) to practice on the job the skills that are taught in these training programs before the beneficial effects of the training become evident.

That the workshop appears to be more effective than the group discussion method in eliminating rating errors could be a result of one or more factors. First, the trainees in the group discussion were able to obtain *knowledge of results* from the trainer and from each other about their personal understanding of the errors and their solutions; but, unlike the trainees in the workshop, they did not receive feedback about their own specific *behavior* in committing an error.

Second, the trainees in the workshop reported that the highly structured format of their program made them feel that the time taken away from their jobs was being used wisely, which was not always the case with the trainees in the group discussion. Although this group was given greater freedom to participate in the structuring of the training content, they wanted more feedback from the trainer than from each other. Consequently, some of them expressed a lack of interest in the program.

The primary disadvantage of the workshop approach is that it can be costly and time consuming to develop. On the other hand, once the materials are developed, the training of the trainers is relatively easy compared to the training required for the group discussion leaders, because a major part of the workshop program includes the use of the videotapes. In light of the rating errors eliminated, and trainees' reaction to the program, a workshop procedure would appear to be the more effective training approach. When the cost and time for developing a structured training program is prohibitive, the group discussion method appears to be a beneficial technique for minimizing these errors.

TRAINING AND RATING SCALES

As stated in the introduction to this chapter, psychologists have spent years attempting to develop the ideal rating scale that would be resistant to rating errors. Suggestions have ranged from using a 2-point scale to a 22-point scale, using BOS versus BES, or a ranking system versus a forced-choice format in which the rater has to select from equally favorable and unfavorable alternative statements in describing an individual. But comparatively little has been accomplished toward solving the problem of rating errors. Why? Because as we have pointed out, people must be *trained* to minimize these errors. Rating errors are well-entrenched habits that are difficult to break.

In a study by Fay and Latham (1980) it was found that rating errors are made regardless of whether BOS, BES, or trait scales are used. Once raters are properly trained, however, the rating format or scale is important for reducing rating errors.

For example, there was no difference between BOS and BES with regard to rating errors after the raters had received the training described by Latham, Wexley, and Pursell (1975). Both BOS and BES were superior in this regard to trait scales. This finding contradicts the conclusions of Borman (1979) and Warmke and Billings (1979) regarding the effectiveness of the training procedures described in this system.

For example, using the same structured videotaped program as Latham, Wexley, and Pursell (1975), Borman (1979) found that training had little effect on rating errors. Similarly, Warmke and Billings reached the same conclusion after using the group-discussion approach to training that had originally been found effective by Latham et al. (1975). Despite the fact that different trainers and different rating formats were used in those three studies, the most parsimonious explanation for the differences in conclusions is based on the motivation level of the subjects and the time devoted to training. Where training has been shown to be effective, the trainees were either managers (Latham, Wexley, & Pursell, 1975), foremen (Pursell, Dossett, & Latham, 1980), or business students (Fay & Latham, 1980). They had the knowledge and/or experience prior to receiving training to appreciate the relevance of the program to them personally. In Borman's study, the subjects were drawn primarily from a liberal arts college. They may not have seen the necessity of acquiring the knowledge and principles taught during training. Moreover, these liberal arts students, unlike the managers, foremen, and business students in the previous studies, did not appear to understand or comprehend some of the performance dimensions on which they were to rate people (Borman, 1979).

A second factor that may explain the differences in conclusions is training time. It took Wexley, Sanders, and Yukl (1973) two hours to eliminate only one rating error. Latham et al. (1975) exposed the trainees to six to eight hours of training to minimize four rating errors. The same time length was used in the Pursell et al. (1980) study to be described later. In the Fay and Latham (1980) study the trainees received four hours of training to reduce three rating errors.

In the two studies where training was not found to be effective, the trainees received only two to three hours of training (Warmke & Billings, 1979; Borman, 1979, respectively) to reduce three to four rating errors (Borman, 1979; Warmke & Billings, respectively.) Remember, rating errors are well-ingrained habits that are difficult to break. The extra hours of training that trainees received in studies where training proved to be effective may have been critical for allowing the trainees to practice those skills necessary to minimize these different rating errors.

A third explanation for the discrepancy in findings on the value of training may be that Borman did not spend sufficient time teaching the trainees to focus on behavioral observation skills. Similarly, Warmke and Billings reported difficulty in keeping the discussion of their trainees on the subject matter. In the studies where the training has proved effective, the one question that is asked over and over again is: "What did the individual *do* to deserve the rating that you made?" The trainer stresses again and again the necessity of focusing on observable job behavior and ignoring all non job-related factors so as to maximize productivity and minimize legal challenges to these decisions. This emphasis on productivity and legal challenges is well accepted by business students, foremen, and managers; it has been greeted with derision by people in our introductory psychology classes whom we suspect are similar in attitude to the people trained by Borman.

A final explanation was reported by Bernardin and Pence (1980). These two authors allege that both Borman and Warmke and Billings made the mistake of including in their training program the teaching of inappropriate response sets discussed earlier (e.g., "never give one person the same ratings on different criteria; use the entire scale in evaluating a person").

A limitation of the Latham et al. (1975), Borman (1979), and Fay and Latham (1980) studies is that all three were conducted in a laboratory setting or involved managers using simulated criterion measures. A fourth study of the effectiveness of the structured videotape-based training was conducted in the field. The purpose of that study was to validate a selection system for hiring electricians.

For years, psychologists have worked on the development of reliable and valid selection systems (e.g., reference checks, interviews, weighted application blanks, aptitude tests, personality inventories). In many instances the results have proved to be reliable, but not valid. Why? Because the selection tests were not good? Not necessarily. The tests may have been quite good; the criterion against which they were evaluated may have been quite poor. In general, psychologists have ignored the criterion problem (Ronan & Prien, 1971).*

---

*The criterion problem refers to the failure to take into account the reliability of performance measures, reliability in the observation of performance, the multi-dimensionality of performance, and situational factors affecting performance. Traditionally, psychologists have focussed their attention primarily on the predictor side of the predictor-criterion equation. In this particular study, the problem had to do with the observation/recording of performance.

Pursell, Dossett, and Latham (1980) correlated the results of a selection battery with performance appraisals of journeyman electricians. The relationship was essentially zero. Rather than concluding that the tests were poor, and going through the costly and time-consuming procedure of choosing and/or developing new tests plus retesting the applicants, Pursell et al. concluded, on the basis of their job analysis, that both the selection and performance appraisal instruments were satisfactory. The problem, they believed, was with the supervisors who used the appraisal instrument. The researchers felt that the performance ratings were contaminated by such rating errors as contrast effects, halo, first impressions, and similar-to-me.

Consequently, the supervisors, who were unaware of the employee test scores or that the validation study was a failure, received the training workshop described by Latham et al. (1975). They were then asked to reevaluate the employees' performance. This time four of the five test scores correlated with the performance measures. The result was a validated selection process that predicted employee performance. Thus, it would appear that the training described in this chapter not only reduces rater bias, but also improves rater accuracy or validity as well.

CLOSING REMARKS

A major problem that must be overcome in developing measures of a person's job performance is the elimination of bias in the observation and appraisal of behavior (Ronan & Prien, 1966, 1971). Observer bias in performance appraisals can be largely attributed to well-known rating errors such as first impressions, halo, similar-to-me, and contrast effects. Rating errors are errors in judgment that occur in a systematic manner when an individual observes and evaluates another. They lie at the core of decisions that adversely affect women and minorities. In order to minimize the occurrence of rating errors and costly litigation battles, the observer must be trained. For this reason, organizations, regardless of the appraisal instrument that they use, are well advised to expose people who evaluate employees to a training program to minimize rating errors.

The probability that a training program will bring about a relatively permanent change in behavior can be estimated prior to training by looking at three factors: (1) the extent to which the trainees actively participate (as opposed to passively recording notes) in applying the principles during the training; (2) the degree to which they receive knowledge of results about the extent to which they are performing the skills correctly; and (3) the opportunity they are given to practice the new skills.

Training programs designed to reduce rating errors must refrain from telling trainees: "Don't give too many high ratings; don't rate a person high or low on all factors." Trainees must be taught the necessity of defining effective/ineffective employee behavior on the basis of a job analysis. They must record the frequency with which they see an employee engage in these behaviors. This is the advantage of using BOS. BOS define explicitly what it is the observer is to look for on the part of an employee. The observer's task is reduced to that of a recorder.

SUMMARY

Raters should be trained to reduce rating errors regardless of the appraisal scale that is used. Human judgment enters into every criterion regardless of whether the performance measure consists of economic variables, traits, or BOS. Rating errors may be defined technically as a difference between the output of a human judgment process and that of an objective accurate assessment uncolored by bias, prejudice, or other subjective extraneous influences. Among the most common rating errors are contrast effects, first impressions, halo, similar-to-me, central tendency, and positive and negative leniency.

Contrast effects is the tendency for a rater to evaluate a person relative to other individuals rather than on the extent to which the individual is fulfilling the requirements of the job.

First-impression error refers to the tendency of a rater to make an initial favorable/unfavorable judgment about an employee that is not justified by the employee's subsequent job behavior.

The halo effect refers to inappropriate generalization from one aspect of a person's performance to all aspects of the person's job performance.

The similar-to-me effect is a tendency for people to be judged more favorably who are similar rather than dissimilar to the rater in attitudes and background even if the latter are not job related.

Central tendency refers to consistently rating people at the midpoint of a scale.

Negative and positive leniency refers to consistently rating people at the low or high end of the scale.

A training program that is to bring about a relatively permanent change in behavior must incorporate the following principles of learning: active participation, knowledge of results, and practice. In addition, a training program that is designed to teach people how to avoid rating errors should teach people how to define effective/ineffective behavior in specific overt terms. Most importantly, it should teach people to accurately record the frequency with which they see an employee demonstrate these behaviors.

Employee Motivation

6

INTRODUCTION

Motivating employees through performance appraisal involves five basic steps. First, a supervisor must determine what it is the employee is required to do on the job. That is, the supervisor must answer the question, "What is truly critical for the individual to perform effectively on the job?" This is why BOS developed from a systematic job analysis are so useful. They identify the strategies that employees must follow to fulfill the requirements of the job.

Second, a supervisor must be sure that the people responsible for completing the BOS are able to recognize effective performance when they see it. Inaccurate appraisals can lead to discouragement and apathy on the part of employees. So care must be taken to select observers who are aware of the aims and objectives of an employee's job, who frequently observe the employee on the job, and who are capable of discerning competent performance. Further, training must be given to insure that the observations are recorded accurately.

Third, a supervisor must engage in the setting of specific performance goals with the employee. Specific goals that are difficult, but attainable, have been shown to consistently lead to effective performance.

Fourth, a supervisor must take steps to insure that the consequences of goal attainment are positive or the goals will not be accepted. If the immediate consequences of behavior are positive, the probability that the behaviors will be repeated is increased.

Finally, employees must be allowed to participate in solving problems that are of concern to both them and their supervisors. In this way, effective work teams are formed.

Chapters 2 through 5 were concerned with steps 1 and 2. That is, they dealt with the performance appraisal *system* of rules, regulations, procedures, and training that exist for people who conduct appraisals. Steps 3 through 5 are concerned with the performance appraisal *process* whereby the person who conducts and the person who receives the appraisal communicate and attempt to influence one another. The purpose of this chapter is to discuss the theories underlying these latter three steps. Chapter 7 explains how these steps can be applied.

GOAL SETTING

Goal setting is a technique that has received a great deal of attention in the scientific literature within the past ten years. This is because it is a fundamental concept indigenous to most, if not all, motivation theory (Locke, 1978; Latham & Locke, 1979). Nevertheless, many people in industry have down played its importance because they believe there is nothing new in the concept, and that almost everyone sets goals. They are right in asserting that there is little that is novel in this approach. They are wrong in assuming that the concepts are systematically applied throughout most organizations. Whenever one group of employees is required to have specific production goals, they invariably increase their productivity substantially over that of groups who allegedly set goals, but actually do not. This is true regardless of whether the employees are engineers, typists, or loggers.

The Theory

The theory underlying goal setting began in a laboratory. In a series of experiments (Locke, 1968), individuals were assigned different types of goals on a variety of simple tasks (e.g., addition, brainstorming, assembling toys). It was found repeatedly that individuals who were assigned *hard* goals performed better than individuals who were assigned moderate or easy goals. Furthermore, individuals who had *specific* challenging goals outperformed individuals who were trying to do their best. Finally, it was found that *incentives* such as praise, feedback, participation, and money lead to an improvement in performance only if they cause the individual to set specific hard goals.

There are three related reasons why goal setting affects performance. Primarily, the setting of goals has a *directive* effect on what people think and do. Goals focus activity in one particular direction rather than others. Simultaneously, goals regulate energy expenditure, since people typically put forth *effort* in proportion to the difficulty of the goal, given that the goal is accepted. Finally, difficult goals lead to more *persistence* (which can be viewed as directed effort over time) than easy goals. These three dimensions, namely, direction (choice), effort, and persistence are three central aspects of the motivation/appraisal process.

The Evidence

The following studies illustrate the value of setting specific goals. Ronan, Latham, and Kinne (1973) identified three supervisory styles used by independent logging supervisors in the South; (1) staying on the job with the crew, (2) setting specific production goals, but not staying with the crew, and (3) setting a specific production goal *and* staying on the job with the crew. The productivity of crews whose supervisors exhibited the first style was mediocre. Turnover was a problem in the crews whose supervisors set goals, but left the crew unsupervised. Productivity was highest and injury rates were lowest when the supervisor set a specific goal and closely supervised the crew.

Latham and Kinne (1974) located 20 independent logging crews who were all but identical in crew size, mechanization level, terrain on which they worked, productivity, and attendance. The logging supervisors of these crews were in the habit of staying on the job with their men, but they did not set production goals. Half of the crews were randomly selected to receive training in goal setting. In this way no one could be accused of only teaching goal setting to those supervisors who were already high performers.

The logging supervisors who were to set goals were told that a way had been found to increase their productivity at no financial expense to anyone. They were given production tables that had been developed through time and motion techniques by the company's industrial engineers.

The tables enabled the supervisor to determine how much wood should be harvested in a given number of man-hours. The 10 supervisors in the training group were asked to use these tables as a guide for determining a specific production goal to assign to their employees. In addition, each sawhand was given a tally-meter (counter) that he could wear on his belt. The sawhand was asked to punch the counter each time he felled a tree. Permission was requested from the supervisor to measure the crew's performance on a weekly basis.

The 10 supervisors in the control group (the people who were not asked to set goals) were told that the researchers were interested in learning the extent to which productivity is affected by absenteeism and injuries. Therefore, they were urged to do their best to maximize their productivity and crew attendance, and to minimize injuries. It was explained that the data would be used to find ways to increase productivity at little or no cost to the wood harvester.

To avoid the Hawthorne Effect (improvements due merely to attention received) the control group was visited as frequently as the training group. Performance was measured for 12 weeks. For all 12 weeks the productivity of the goal-setting group was significantly higher than that of the control group. Moreover, absenteeism was significantly lower in the groups that set specific goals than in the groups who were simply urged to do their best. Injury and turnover rates were low in both groups. These were important findings because these people were considered marginal workers (Porter, 1973) in that their attendance, turnover, and productivity is unacceptable by conventional industry standards. They may work three days one week, one day a second week, and no days a third week. Many have little or no education beyond elementary school. They were not employed by pulp and paper companies; however, they were people on whom these companies in the South were largely dependent for their wood supply.

Why should anything so simple and inexpensive as goal setting affect the work of these people so significantly? Anecdotal evidence from conversations with both the loggers and the company woods managers who visited them suggested several reasons.

Harvesting timber can be a monotonous, tiring job with little or no meaning for most woods workers in the South. By introducing a goal that is difficult but attainable, a challenge is provided. Moreover, a specific goal makes it clear to the worker what is required. Goal feedback via the tally-meter, and weekly record keeping provides the worker with a sense of achievement, recognition, and accomplishment. The employee can see how well he is doing now versus how well he has done in the past, and, in some cases, how well he is doing in comparison with others. Thus, the employee may not only expend greater effort, but may also devise better or more creative tactics for attaining the goal than he was previously using.

In a third study (Latham & Baldes, 1975), the problem that confronted the organization was the loading of logging trucks. If the trucks were overloaded, the unionized drivers could be fined by the Highway Department and ultimately lose their jobs. If the trucks were underloaded, the company lost money. The drivers decided to underload the trucks.

For three months management tried to solve this problem by (1) urging the drivers to try harder to fill the truck to its legal net weight, and (2) developing weighing scales that could be attached to the truck. The latter approach was not cost effective. The scales were unreliable and continually broke down due to the rough terrain on which the trucks travelled. The drivers all but ignored the first approach. For the three months in which the problem was being examined, the trucks were seldom loaded in excess of 60 percent of the truck's capacity.

At the end of the three month period, the results of previous goal setting studies were explained to the union. They were told (1) that the company would like to set a specific net weight goal for the drivers, (2) that no monetary reward or fringe benefits other than verbal praise could be expected for improved performance, and (3) that no one would be criticized for failing to attain the goal. The idea that simply setting a specific goal would solve a production problem seemed too incredible to be taken seriously—by the union. Nevertheless, agreement was reached that a difficult but attainable goal of 94 percent of truck net weight would be assigned to the drivers providing that no one would be reprimanded for failing to attain the goal. This latter point was emphasized to the company's supervisors.

Within the first month performance improved to 80 percent of the truck legal net weight. After the second month, however, performance decreased to 70 percent. Interviews with the drivers revealed that they were testing management's statement that no punitive steps would be taken against them if their performance suddenly dropped. Fortunately, no such steps were taken by supervisors; and, performance exceeded 90 percent of the truck's net weight after the third month. Their performance has remained at this level for six years.

The results over the nine month period in which this study was conducted saved the company $250,000. This figure, determined by the company's accountants, is based on the purchase of the extra trucks that would have been required to deliver the same quantity of logs to the mill if goal setting had not been implemented. This figure would have been even higher if it included the cost for the additional diesel fuel that would have been consumed, and the expenses that would have been necessary for recruiting and hiring the additional truck drivers.

Why could this procedure work without the union demanding an increase in hourly wages? First, the drivers did not feel that they were really doing anything differently, which in a sense was true. They were not working harder; but they were working more efficiently than they had in the past. Moreover, the men began to record their truck weight in a pocket notebook, *and* they began to brag about their accomplishments to their peers. They viewed the goal setting as a challenging game, "It is great to beat the other guy."

Competition was a crucial variable for bringing about goal commitment.* However, the hypothesis that the improvement in performance was due only to the competition can be rejected because no special prizes or formal recognition programs were provided for those individuals who came closest to or exceeded the goal. No effort was made by the company to single out one winner. More important, the opportunity for competition to occur prior to goal setting had always existed for the drivers through *their knowledge* of their truck's weight, and the truck weight of each of the 36 other drivers every time they hauled wood into the wood yard. In short, competition affected productivity in that it led to the acceptance of and commitment to the goal; but, it was the setting of the goal, and the working toward it that brought about the increase in performance and the decrease in costs.

Several investigators have examined the benefit of involving the

---

*A word of caution: We do not recommend setting up formal competition. As Latham and Locke (1979) noted, competition may lead employees to place individual goals ahead of company goals. The emphasis should be on accomplishing the task, getting the job done, not necessarily "beating" the other person.

employees in setting specific performance goals. At General Electric, Meyer (Meyer, Kay, & French, 1965) examined the results of allowing middle level managers to participate in setting specific performance goals during their performance appraisal. Meyer found that goals were attained more often when the employee had a say in the goals that were set than when the goals were assigned by a supervisor. However, this was true only for employees with a supervisor whose managerial style throughout the year encouraged employee participation in decision making. Employees with a supervisor who did not normally encourage participation performed better when the goals were assigned to them. Meyer concluded that the way a goal is set is not as important as it is to set a specific goal.

At Weyerhaeuser Company, Latham (Latham, Mitchell, & Dossett, 1978) examined the results of involving engineers and scientists in the setting of goals during the performance appraisal. BOS were used. The major finding of this study was that participation in goal setting is important to the extent that it leads to higher goals being set than is the case where the goals are assigned unilaterally by a supervisor. And yet, employee perception of goal difficulty was the same among those with assigned and participatively set goals. Only individuals with participatively set goals performed significantly better than individuals who were either urged to do their best or received no feedback at all. Finally, as the theory states, giving employees specific feedback without setting specific goals on the basis of their feedback had little or no impact on employee performance.

In a subsequent study at Weyerhaeuser (Dossett, Latham, & Mitchell, 1979), female clerical personnel were randomly assigned to participative, assigned, or do-your-best goal conditions on a clerical test. With goal difficulty held constant, goal attainment in terms of test scores was higher in the assigned than it was in the participative condition. The performance appraisal results of these same people on BOS showed that assigned goals resulted in higher performance and greater goal acceptance than did participatively set goals.

In reviewing these results, Likert (personal communication, August 1977) commented that when assigned goals have been effective, the supervisor had always behaved in a highly supportive manner. Three key aspects of modern organizational theory (Likert, 1967) are supportive relationships with employees, participative decision making, and goal setting. Latham and Saari (1979b) tested this assumption in a laboratory setting where students were given a brainstorming task.

Goal difficulty was held constant between the participative and assigned goal setting groups. The supportiveness of the experimenter was varied by having him behave in either a supportive or a hostile manner. Supportiveness led to higher goals being set than was the case when the experimenter was nonsupportive. The setting of specific goals led to higher performance than urging people to do their best. Finally, participation increased performance by increasing the individual's understanding of how to attain the goals.

In summary, goal setting is effective because it clarifies exactly what is expected of an individual. As several employees have commented, "by receiving a specific goal from the supervisor we are able to determine for the first time what that S.O.B. really expects from us." Moreover, the process of working for an explicit goal injects interest into the task. It provides challenge and meaning to a job. Through goal attainment, feelings of accomplishment and recognition (from self and/or supervisor) occur.

Effective goal setting in performance appraisal should take into account the following points:

1. Setting specific goals leads to higher performance than adopting an attitude of do your best. That is, a specific score on BOS should be specified along with the key behaviors that the employee needs to work on to improve or maintain the score.

2. Participation in goal setting is important to the extent that it leads to the setting of higher goals than those that are assigned unilaterally by superiors. Participation does not necessarily lead to greater goal acceptance than when goals are assigned by a supportive manager. However, employee understanding of how to attain them may be increased as a result of participating in the goal setting process.

3. Given goal acceptance and ability, the higher the goal, the higher the performance. However, the goal should be reasonable. If the goals are unreasonable, employees will not accept them. Nor will employees get a sense of accomplishment from pursuing goals that are never attained. People with low self-confidence or ability should be given more easily attainable goals than those with high self-confidence and ability.

4. Performance feedback is critical for showing employees how they are doing relative to the goals, maintaining the employees' interest in the goals, revising goals, and prolonging effort to attain the goals.

5. If employees are evaluated on overall level of performance rather than goal attainment, they will continue to set high goals regardless of whether the goals are attained. High goals lead to higher performance levels than easy goals. If employees are evaluated on goal attainment regardless of the difficulty of the goal, they are likely to set low goals or reject hard goals imposed by supervisors.

6. There must be some latitude for the individual to influence performance. Where performance is rigidly controlled by technology or work flow (such as the typical assembly line) goal setting may have little effect on performance.

7. Workers must not feel threatened that they will lose their jobs if they increase their performance under the goal setting procedure. Most people have enough sense not to put themselves out of work by being too productive. Goal setting is most effective when the supervisor behaves in a supportive manner when interacting with subordinates.

These principles are basic to most programs. The primary difference between the thesis of this book and that of MBO advocates is that the latter emphasize the use of cost-related measures (e.g., number of sales) for performance appraisal purposes whereas we argue for the use of behavioral measures for counseling and development. We have no objection to the use of MBO as a vehicle for planning where the organization, department, or individual should focus attention and efforts over the next three months, six months, one year, or five years. Nor do we have any objection to the inclusion of these objectives on the performance appraisal instrument. Cost-related objectives can clarify the context or situation where the employee's behavior will be appraised. The BOS clarify how the employee is to behave when attempting to attain those objectives. It is for this reason that we agree with Kearney (1979) that the missing link in MBO is *behavior.**

---

*Campbell (1977) has made a similar argument regarding the use of cost-related measures of performance in the field of leadership. In fact, he cited the use of these measures as a major factor impeding the development of useful information in this area: "We should not be using 'objective' organizational measures of subordinate performance, such as the amount of productivity, total sales, etc. We should not be

In general, there will be close agreement between the employee's performance and performance outcomes (e.g., costs, profits). As we have repeatedly stated, good cost-related outcomes generally come about because someone did something correctly. The purpose of BOS is to specify what it is the person did correctly. Where there is disagreement between the BOS scores and performance outcome measures, there are four possible explanations.

First, the BOS may not be comprehensive. This is why the importance of a systematic job analysis was stressed in Chapters 2 and 3.

Second, BOS may be contaminated by rating errors, which is why the careful selection and training of raters were discussed in Chapters 4 and 5.

Third, the cost-related measures may be contaminated by judgmental errors. A problem inherent in MBO programs is that the employee is likely to get systematically more credit (or blame) than is actually deserved, because people are seen as more "causal" than they in fact are for performance outcomes (Feldman, 1979). Thus, the observing supervisor is likely to overstate the contribution of the employee for any positive or negative outcomes. This problem is especially troublesome when the employee belongs to a group not prevalent in the organization (e.g., women/blacks). To the extent the supervisor is pleased or displeased with the cost-related outcomes, the probability increases that attributions of causality will be assigned incorrectly to the person rather than to the situation (Feldman, 1979). If the employee is well liked or highly disliked by the supervisor, biases in the causal attribution of behavior will benefit the liked employee and harm the disliked person. There is no question as to how many products were produced or sold. But, one person will receive undeserved credit for good outcomes; the other person will receive undeserved blame for poor outcomes. The use of comprehensive BOS are helpful here because they alert the manager to look elsewhere for situational factors that may account for the good/bad outcomes when the BOS scores are incongruent with the outcome measures.

---

using summary indices of work group performance (e.g., total absenteeism). All of these are measures that are determined by many factors besides the influence of a leader and, even in the best of all possible worlds, the leadership factor may account for only a small portion of the total variability in these criteria" (Campbell, 1977, p. 233).

Finally, it is sometimes the case that the BOS scores are low and the cost-related measures are high because the employee is engaging in unethical behavior or in behavior that has at best a short-term positive effect on performance outcomes. For example, Likert (1967) has shown that highly autocratic managers who behave in a nonsupportive manner may achieve performance outcomes superior to those of managers who do not behave in this manner. The superiority is short lived as peers, subordinates, and/or clients respond adversely to this conduct.

Thus we believe the setting of specific behavioral goals are as important as establishing cost-related targets. They specify appropriate behaviors for attaining cost-related targets. BOS lend themselves to the setting of specific behavioral goals.

CHANGING BEHAVIOR BY CHANGING THE CONSEQUENCES

A straightforward approach to understanding why a goal is or is not accepted is to examine the consequences for the employee of accepting/rejecting the goal. Behavior is in part a function of its consequences. If the consequences are positive, the probability that the behavior will be repeated is increased. The reverse is true if the consequences are aversive for the employee.

The importance of these statements for managers is that they can more easily understand employees by examining the environment, that is, the consequence(s) of employee behavior rather than looking "inside" employees for causes such as their attitudes, drives, or feelings.* In short,

---

*This statement is not intended as an endorsement of the philosophy of behaviorism. No attempt is made in this chapter to adhere to the vocabulary of the behaviorists. Moreover, the statement does not deny the value of asking why people value given consequences. The statement is an endorsement of an operant analysis that incorporates two simple but powerful ideas, namely, that the reward value of an outcome can be known only through its effects on behavior; and, the behavior to be influenced must be described carefully in concrete observable terms. For example, the performance appraisal process must deal with the observable behaviors the person should exhibit during the subsequent appraisal period, rather than making generalized arguments for being more aggressive, committed, etc. The power of the operant model lies in the descriptive analysis of behavior that it forces upon the user (Campbell, 1977). Even knowledgeable behaviorists (e.g., Bandura, 1977) acknowledge that consequences affect a person's thought processes. Consequences change behavior

a supervisor can better motivate an employee by setting goals and concentrating on observables (i.e., overt behavior and its consequences) rather than by armchair speculation about what makes the employee "tick."

Behavioral consequences consist of neutral events, punishers, and reinforcers. A neutral event neither increases nor decreases the probability that a behavior will be repeated. A punisher always decreases the probability that a behavior will be repeated. A reinforcer is any behavioral consequence that increases the frequency with which a behavior is repeated. Reinforcers can be either positive or negative.

A *positive reinforcer* is a consequence of behavior that increases the probability that the behavior (e.g., coming to work, completing a report on time, being courteous to a subordinate) will be repeated. Examples of positive reinforcers for most people include food, a smile, and praise. Performance feedback in the form of graphs can often improve employees' performance because people usually find it satisfying to be able to observe the effect of their efforts on the attainment of a specific goal. Note that informative feedback in itself is not inherently reinforcing. Rather, knowledge of performance assumes significance in relation to the employee's goals, and thus provides the basis for self-evaluative reinforcement (Bandura, 1977). "Hence, correctness feedback on tasks that are personally devalued or regarded as trifling will, if anything, reduce the amount of effort expended on them" (Bandura, 1977, p. 163). Thus the importance of BOS—they emphasize critical job behaviors reported as important by job incumbents. Informative feedback indicating that an employee's performance matches the goals that were set will sustain effort by creating self-satisfaction with subgoal achievements, and by raising goals for subsequent performance.

A *negative reinforcer* is a consequence (nagging) whose termination immediately after a behavior (taking out the garbage) has occurred increases the probability that the response (taking out the garbage) will be repeated. Negative reinforcers are *not* to be confused with punishers.

---

by affecting goals. Most managers, however, are not cognitive psychologists; they will be more effective as managers if they restrict themselves to *describing* employee behavior and the consequences in observable objective terminology that can be corroborated easily by other observers. It is true that the effectiveness of various consequences is affected by a person's values; but it is also true that what a person values is generally the result of a history of behavioral consequences. Moreover, determining a given person's values often exceeds the abilities of most people.

As previously noted, reinforcers (positive or negative) *increase* response strength. Punishers and the absence of reinforcers *decrease* response strength.

Consequences affect behavior largely through their informative and incentive value (Bandura, 1977). That is, consequences affect behavior antecedently by creating expectations in the employee of similar outcomes on future occasions. Thus the likelihood of an employee engaging in particular actions is increased by anticipated reward, and reduced by anticipated punishment. The only way to determine whether a given consequence is a reinforcer or a punisher is to *present* or *withdraw* it after the behavior occurs, and then observe whether the behavior subsequently increases or decreases in frequency. If the presentation of a variable (a smile) following a behavior (saying hello) increases the response frequency (saying hello), the variable (smile) is by definition a reinforcer. If the immediate consequence of a response (saying hello) is the *withdrawal* of the variable (a smile), and the response (saying hello) decreases, the variable (withdrawing a smile) is by definition a punisher. Table 6.1 shows the effects of reinforcers and punishers on behavior.

TABLE 6.1

Definitions of Positive Reinforcer, Negative Reinforcer, and Punisher

	Variable *Presented* Immediately After the Behavior	Variable *Withdrawn* Immediately After the Behavior
Increases Frequency of Behavior	Positive Reinforcer Example: Turn in a report on time (behavior) then receive praise (positive reinforcer)	Negative Reinforcer Example: Take out the garbage (behavior) then nagging withdrawn (negative reinforcer)
Decreases Frequency of Behavior	Punisher Example: Walk across middle of street (behavior) then receive jaywalking ticket (punisher)	Punisher Example: Say hello (behavior) then smile withdrawn (punisher)

The principle of reinforcement can be broken down into four basic subprinciples when applied to performance appraisal. First, the reinforcer must be made contingent upon the desired or appropriate behavior. If the presentation of a reward is not a consequence of a given behavior, the behavior may not increase in frequency.

Second, in performance appraisal, the employee must clearly perceive the relationship between the desired behavior and the reinforcer. This point is particularly true when money is administered by a manager with the expectation that it will reinforce high performance. Many behavioral scientists (e.g., Herzberg, 1968) have reported that salary increases do not motivate employees to increase their productivity. The reason for this is that salaries are not made contingent upon performance. Money is often given as a function of the employee's hours on the job, tenure with the company, or negotiations on behalf of a union, rather than as a result of the quantity or quality of work that the individual accomplishes.

Third, the reinforcer must be administered soon after the desired behavior has been emitted. In theories that recognize only the role of external consequences, and contend that consequences shape behavior automatically, it is asserted that reinforcers must be administered immediately after a desired behavior occurs where the intent is to increase the probability that the behavior will recur. Research involving human beings as opposed to rats and pigeons does not support this view. People are able to process and synthesize feedback information from sequences of events over periods of time regarding the conditions necessary for reinforcement, as well as the pattern and rate with which actions produce outcomes (Bandura, 1977). However, it is true that to the extent that a reinforcer is delayed, its effectiveness is sometimes decreased. This occurs because the worker may not clearly see the connection between the reinforcer and the behavior. Even worse, delayed reinforcers may inadvertently reinforce inappropriate behaviors. For example, a new superintendent in a start-up operation initially may perform at a high level. The manager may attempt to reward the superintendent with a salary increase. Unfortunately, the salary increases may not be approved by the vice president until months later. By this time, the superintendent's high level of performance may have diminished as a result of numerous frustrations. When the salary increase finally occurs, the superintendent is, in effect, being reinforced for mediocre performance.

Fourth, the reinforcer must be a valued outcome for the employee. Thus, if recognition for fasting for a cause is valued by an individual, food will not be a reinforcer, but attention from others may be effective in maintaining abstinence. Similarly, it has been found that many workers set self-imposed limits on the amount of work they do, and anyone who tries to exceed the limit becomes a rate buster in the eyes of coworkers. Here, social factors may be far more valuable (reinforcing) than money. However, in organizations where workers have initiated self-imposed limits, it is interesting to note that the money is almost always given after a considerable amount of time has elapsed since the occurrence of the desired behavior. In other words, the reinforcer is *not* immediately presented after the desired behavior occurs. In addition, the money is usually given on a continuous schedule of reinforcement.

Reinforcement Schedules

A schedule of reinforcement refers to the plan or pattern for giving a reinforcer. A plan that calls for a reinforcer to be given every time a desired behavior or response occurs is called a *continuous* schedule of reinforcement. A *variable ratio* schedule is one in which reinforcers are given for only some of the responses, and the ratio of reinforced responses changes within the same schedule from time to time. For example, a reinforcer might be administered after one response, then after three more responses, then after six, then after five, then again after one. Some mean (average) number of responses for reinforcement is chosen. A variable ratio 4 (VR-4) schedule means that a behavior is reinforced, on the average, only one out of four times.

A most intriguing finding by psychologists is that a variable ratio (sometimes called intermittent) schedule of reinforcement can lead to higher performance levels than a continuous schedule. This finding is thought provoking in that it runs counter to common sense. It would seem that a person would always work harder for a "sure thing." However, numerous studies have demonstrated the superiority of variable ratio schedules.

For example, Yukl, Wexley, and Seymore (1972) studied three groups of clerical workers who were paid $1.50 an hour for grading multiple choice examinations. They found that immediately paying each individual in one group, after grading an examination, a bonus of 50 cents contingent upon correctly guessing the outcome of a coin toss (VR-2) led to a greater increase in productivity than paying individuals in another group a 25 cent bonus every time (a continuous schedule) they finished grading an examination. And yet, the total amount of money received by the employees in the two groups was exactly the same over the long run. Even more interesting was the finding that paying employees a 25 cent bonus contingent upon grading an exam and correctly guessing the outcome of a coin toss (a VR-2 schedule) was as effective in increasing performance as paying the previous group a 25 cent bonus every time (a continuous schedule) they graded an examination. In essence, one group of workers was producing the same amount of work for 50 percent less money than another group.

It is still not clear *why* the variable ratio schedule often results in higher performance than the continuous reinforcement schedule. One possible explanation is that being on a variable ratio schedule is like going to a Las Vegas casino; it generates excitement and interest precisely because the person cannot predict when the reinforcer will occur. This explanation may be particularly true for explaining the effectiveness of variable ratio schedules for administering money to people with jobs that are repetitive or dull.

A second explanation is based on the principle of reinforcement itself. This principle states that the behavior occurring at the time of reinforcement increases in strength. For example, if planting trees were the reinforced behavior, that behavior should increase in strength. Common sense would argue that tree planting should therefore increase at a faster rate if the response of planting each tree is reinforced every time it occurs, rather than just some of the time. A close analysis of the situation, however, may render this conclusion invalid. After a worker has planted a tree and has received the first reinforcement on a variable ratio schedule, the tree planting response is strengthened. This means that the second and third responses will occur fairly rapidly, and the faster and more stable that the worker makes these responses, the higher the probability that the reinforcer will occur on a variable ratio schedule. The reinforcements thus coincide not only with planting a tree, but also with a fast, consistent rate of planting. If, however, the schedule is a continuous one, a reinforcer will be administered every time a tree is planted regardless of whether the rate is fast or slow. Thus, a fast, stable rate of responding will not be reinforced by a continuous schedule.

A third explanation for the relatively greater effectiveness of variable ratio schedules of reinforcement is that an individual who is on a continuous schedule may become satiated with the reinforcer. For example, a person who is always complimented for each and every meal (providing that the cooking is indeed satisfactory) may not work as fast or as hard in preparing subsequent meals as the person who is intermittently reinforced for the way in which a meal tastes. Similarly, a letter of commendation from a vice president in which an employee is recognized and appreciated may be much more reinforcing if it is sent once in a while rather than every single time the employee demonstrates outstanding behavior.

Latham and Dossett (1978) investigated the relative effectiveness of incentive plans administered on continuous and VR-4 schedules of reinforcement with unionized employees. The workers were paid $5.00 an hour to trap mountain beaver that destroy young trees. The trappers were randomly assigned to one of two groups. In one group the trappers received $1.00 for every beaver they trapped. At the end of four weeks, they were switched to a VR-4 schedule. They then received $4.00 after trapping a beaver and correctly guessing the color of one of four marbles prior to drawing it from a bag held by the supervisor. In the other group, the order of the schedules was reversed.

The results showed that employee productivity increased and company costs decreased. Both the experienced and the inexperienced workers preferred the VR-4 schedule over the continuous schedule. Inexperienced workers, however, performed better on the continuous rather than the VR-4 schedule while the opposite was true for the experienced workers. This finding is in agreement with laboratory studies on learning which show that a continuous reinforcement schedule results in more rapid response acquisition than variable schedules for inexperienced people who have yet to master the task. However, once a behavior is learned, the response rate is higher on a variable than on a continuous schedule.

An important inference that can be drawn on the basis of reinforcement principles is that performance appraisals should be given on a continuous basis to new employees, and on an intermittent (or variable) basis for experienced employees. It is doubtful that the traditional practice of conducting a formal performance appraisal once a year for every employee has any positive effect on anyone's behavior. A performance appraisal does not have to consist of a 45 minute behind-closed-doors discussion. The discussion may last five minutes or less; it can take place on a shop floor or in a corridor (see Chapter 7).

Now put yourself in the role of a supervisor. A straightforward approach to attempting to understand why an employee does or does not accept a goal is to draw the following diagram:

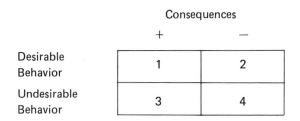

First, list in cell 1 all the positive consequences that an employee receives as a result of engaging in a desirable behavior (e.g., a mechanic working ten rather than six hours).

Second, list in cell 2 all the aversive consequences or punishers for engaging in this desirable behavior (e.g., fatigue, arriving home late for dinner).

Repeat the above steps regarding the consequences of engaging in undesirable behavior. For an in-depth analysis, repeat these steps by discussing them with the employees themselves. This approach can provide a rational way for understanding why people behave the way they do. More importantly, it provides a basis for motivating them to do what you want them to do by indicating the consequences that need to be changed in order to change their behavior. The approach is straightforward and costs little; however, the cost of changing the consequences sometimes exceeds the benefits of changing the behavior. The advantage of this approach is that people can estimate the costs knowing, with a high degree of certainty, that if the consequences ar changed, the behavior will change.

This approach was used successfully by Emery Air Freight. Emery found that efficiency was reduced by 45 percent because people on airport loading docks shipped items in the wrong containers. This inefficiency was costing the company over $1,000,000 annually. Rather than implementing a training program, they examined the positive consequences to the employee of loading containers properly. This analysis revealed that there were few, if any, consequences of any kind (i.e., positive or aversive). Moreover, most employees believed they were performing efficiently.

Emery instituted a goal-setting program. The program requires each employee to fill out a behavioral checklist similar in concept to BOS. All employee improvements in performance are reinforced with praise by a supervisor, regardless of whether the goals are attained. Failure to attain a goal is reinforced by praise for honesty in reporting that failure. In this way, behavior is shaped toward desired objectives through praise. Criticism and blame can lead to defensiveness and discouragement on the part of employees, and dishonest behavior. Dishonest behavior occurs when the honest behavior of reporting failure is punished; the dishonest behavior of exaggerating success is inadvertently praised.

Providing feedback about the consequences of behavior gives workers a feeling of task accomplishment because it lets them know how they are doing on the job. It increases acceptance of present goals and encourages the probability of setting more difficult goals. Feedback on performance is important because many employees only know how well they are getting along with their supervisor.

The keys to the design of effective feedback systems are threefold. First, feedback must be based on behaviors over which the employee has control. Second, feedback must be provided on a frequent basis. Immediate feedback, as previously stated, is more effective than either delayed or infrequent feedback. Third, *specific goals* must be set in relation to the feedback.

The goal-setting program at Emery increased productivity from 45 percent to 90 percent *within one day.* The cost of the program was $5,000. Travel costs amounted to $4900 for one person to travel from Emery's Corporate headquarters to explain the approach to key people in each facility. Approximately $100 was spent on developing BOS for providing feedback to the employee.

We have now discussed two key ways of motivating individuals to increase their performance—setting goals with regard to emitting critical job behaviors; and, insuring that the consequences of those behaviors are perceived by the employee as positive, so as to insure that the goals are accepted, and desired behaviors are repeated. In this vein, we now examine a recurring issue in the performance appraisal literature: Should money be tied to performance?

Linking Pay to Performance Appraisal

The 1978 Civil Service Reform Act mandates tying pay to performance for federal employees who are managers covered by the Act, that is, managers and senior executives. It may be only a matter of time before a series of violations of the Equal Pay Act by organizations in the private sector results in a similar requirement for them.

The arguments for linking money with performance include the following issues outlined by Lawler (1971) and Mobley (1974).

First, linking money to a performance appraisal is a relatively objective and logical way to allocate financial rewards. One of the strengths of BOS is its emphasis on specifying job requirements in measurable terms. Thus, BOS provide a basis for relatively more objective (especially with rater training) performance evaluation than traditional approaches. A natural corollary is to use the performance evaluations, rather than undefined or unrelated reasons, for making merit compensation decisions.

Second, it establishes a performance-reward contingency for the employee. To the extent that pay is a valued reward, linking it, along with other desirable rewards (e.g., praise), to performance enhances employee motivation.*

Third, it helps insure that these two management processes do not work at cross purposes. Separating pay from performance can only raise questions among employees as to the importance of an appraisal and the equity of pay decisions.

Fourth, while praise from others is a powerful source of feedback, money tells employees how well they are truly valued by the organization.

---

*It is interesting to note that in a recent interview with *Time Magazine* editors, Castro blamed Cuba's economic problems in part on the failure to use monetary incentives: "For a long time we based all production efforts exclusively on moral incentives while disregarding the material ones. We used to pay everybody the same, whether they produced two or three times what they should. We were not encouraging production. . . . It seemed as if enthusiasm could solve everything, but it's not enough." (Grunwald & Duncan, 1980, p. 48)

Fifth, most managers want their pay to be based on performance. (Andrews & Henry, 1963; Lawler, 1971)

There is, however, no lack of arguments *against* linking pay to performance appraisals. Among the leading advocates of this position are Meyer (1975) and Deci (1972). These arguments are as follows:

1. Tying pay to performance appraisal may encourage people to avoid difficult goals, which is a problem with many MBO programs. The problem can be overcome by always evaluating performance rather than goal attainment. For example, one student's goal may be to get an A. Another student's goal may be to get a C. The first student may receive an 86 and get a B+ as a grade. The second student may get a 72 and receive a C as a grade. If goal attainment were rewarded, only the second individual would be eligible for a reward. But, if performance were rewarded, both individuals might be eligible for a reward.

2. It may fail to reflect total performance by emphasizing the measurable to the exclusion of more subjective, yet important, aspects of the job. This argument poses a problem for MBO programs that emphasize cost-related measures, but the argument is not an issue with BOS that are content valid.

3. It may place undue emphasis on individual as opposed to team performance. But, this problem is almost always overcome with content valid BOS that specify cooperative behaviors that are required of each employee.

4. Installing an incentive plan with workers as opposed to managers is difficult because considerable effort is required to build a trusting relationship between management and workers. Many employees feel they cannot trust an organization to administer incentive schemes properly. But, the issue of trust needs to be resolved regardless of whether pay is tied to performance. Team building is an excellent way of increasing trust. In fact, team building has led to the development of effective incentive plans (Hinrichs, N., 1978b), which in turn increases trust among supervisors and employees. (Team building is discussed in the subsequent section in this chapter.)

5. It introduces conflict into the appraisal. It makes the appraiser a judge as well as a counselor. However, this conflicting role always exists in relationship between managers and employees. It is a naive employee who believes that management is not evaluating performance on a regular basis. It is even more naive for an employee to believe that during the appraisal the manager will suddenly stop being an evaluator and become a counselor only (see Fig. 6.1).

6. It is difficult to measure performance. This is an issue where cost-related measures are used. But, the advantage of the BOS is that they are

Figure 6.1

"Barkley, I perceive my role in this institution not as a judge but merely as an observer and recorder. I have observed you to be a prize boob and have so recorded it.'

Source: Reprinted by permission of Chicago Tribune-New York News Syndicate, Inc.

based on observable behavior and, hence, are measurable. Employee input is used as the raw data for developing BOS so that everyone understands and agrees on the performance measures. The appraiser is trained to minimize rating errors so that objectivity is increased and observer bias is decreased. This helps to increase trust and reduce conflict between the supervisor and employee.

7. Large amounts of money must be given to the good performers if employees are to place a high value on good performance and the raises to which it leads (Lawler, 1971). This is true; but performance should and must be rewarded if productivity is to improve significantly.

8. Money can diminish interest in a task. It detracts from the feeling of doing a job well for its own sake. This argument is nonsense. As Bandura (1977) notes, monetary incentives can increase performance, decrease performance, or have no effect whatsoever depending upon the way in which the rewards are used and the activities involved.

For example, decreases in performance may reflect employee reactions to how the incentives are presented rather than to the incentives themselves. Incentives can be used in a coercive manner: "Sam, you will not receive the bonus unless you do . . . ; do you hear me!" Coercive contingencies may evoke oppositional behavior. Incentives can also be presented in a supportive, appreciative manner: "Sam, this is in recognition of your achieving . . . . " Alternatively, incentives can convey evaluative reactions: "Sam, this is what we think your performance is worth." As Bandura noted, "it is unlikely that concert pianists lose interest in the keyboard because they are offered high performance fees. Indeed, they would feel devalued and insulted by low fees" (Bandura, 1977, p. 111).

In summary, tying money to performance can bring about large increases in performance (Yukl & Latham, 1975; Latham & Dossett, 1978). However, the process is actually more complicated then it may first appear.

1. Money must be valued. That is, it must be desired by the worker. There are many employees for whom money beyond a set amount has little or no impact. Thus, systematic interviews and/or questionnaires must be given to ascertain the extent to which money is perceived as reinforcing by employees.

2. The money must be tied to all important facets of the job. For example, quantity is often achieved at the expense of quality in many incentive programs because the incentive is tied to a piece-rate system only. BOS measures based on a job analysis, however, take into account both the quality and the quantity involved in work.

3. The employees must perceive that money is tied to performance. In other words, the incentive program must be easy to understand. This is a crucial requirement. Programs that employees do not understand seldom motivate them.

4. The amount of money must be seen by the workers as worthy of their efforts. Again, systematic interviews and/or questionnaires are critical to determining what constitutes a perceived equitable bonus.

5. The money must be given soon after the desired behavior and/or outcome has taken place. In this way, money has, as anyone who has been to Las Vegas knows, its greatest impact on behavior.

6. The employees must trust management to dispense the rewards equitably.

In closing this discussion, it is appropriate to summarize the results of a survey administered to all exempt managerial and professional employees of a large manufacturing organization (Landy, Barnes, & Murphy, 1978). Performance appraisals are considered fair and accurate by employees when supervisors evaluate performance frequently, are familiar with the employee's actual performance levels, are in agreement with the subordinate on what constitute the important job duties, and set specific plans or goals with the employee for eliminating performance weaknesses. The process of goal setting in a performance appraisal has positive effects on the credibility and acceptability of the entire performance appraisal system. Thus, it would appear that frequent feedback and the setting of goals in relation to the feedback are two primary ways of increasing the performance of employees. Landy et al. found that discussing salary during the evaluation does not negatively affect perceptions of the appraisal as was thought earlier by some researchers (Meyer, Kay, & French, 1965).

EMPLOYEE PARTICIPATION IN PROBLEM SOLVING: BUILDING A TEAM

The assumption underlying this approach is that when people work together to solve problems of concern to one another, an effective work group or team is formed—hence the term team building. Allowing employees to participate in solving problems is a useful device for increasing the manager's knowledge, and thereby improves decision quality. It can lead to better decisions through input from subordinates. This is important because employees often avoid informing their supervisors about the obstacles and problems they encounter in doing their job (Likert, 1961). Further, it allows employees to begin seeing things from a supervisor's perspective; it allows a supervisor to begin seeing things from the employee's perspective.

Team building is especially applicable to performance appraisal when the appraisals are completed anonymously by an employee's peers and/or subordinates. The employee can categorize the feedback from peers and/or subordinates into the following three areas:

1. Things that I can change immediately.

2. Things that I can't change (e.g., organizational policies) even if my life depended upon it. Let me explain why.

3. Here are things that I think *we* as a group can change with your help.

The group then sets priorities for the specific issues it wants to resolve over a given time period (typically 3 months). The meetings generally last one to three hours, twice a month. The key question that is answered at the end of each meeting is *"who* is going to do *what* by *when?"* This question is the crucial goal setting step.

An approach similar to this was used effectively to reduce turnover (Krackhardt, McKenna, Porter, & Steers, 1978). Managers in 25 branches of a West Coast bank were trained to discuss possible solutions for reducing turnover with the tellers as a group. They then met with each of their tellers individually. Together they set specific goals about ways to resolve issues of employee concern. The results showed that, for those branches where goals were implemented, turnover was reduced significantly compared to the turnover in branches where this goal-setting process was not implemented.

When team building is conducted with hourly employees, the supervisor generally works with five employees who have been nominated by the group to represent their viewpoint. The advantage of using five employees is that it increases the probability that everyone's voice will be heard (Slater, 1958). When there are less than five people present, group members are frequently too tense, tactful, and constrained. The fear of alienating one another seems to prevent them from expressing their ideas freely. To the extent that the number is larger than five, team members are often seen as too competitive and inconsiderate of one another.

It is explicitly understood prior to team building that the function of the team is to make proposals; management makes the final decisions. However, when a proposal is rejected, management must explain why the proposal is rejected in words that the employees can understand.

Team building is a straightforward process. The approach has been received unfavorably by some managers who believe that it will raise employee expectations to levels that management cannot meet. This fear is seldom warranted. The fear is justified only when the team building is allowed to drift to issues peripheral to productivity. The approach has proved effective in the aerospace industry where product quality increased appreciably, at General Motors where absenteeism and grievances decreased significantly, and at the Valspar Corporation (a paint manufacturing plant) where there was not only a significant improvement in product quality, but employee turnover was reduced from 187 percent a year to a negligible amount (Hinrichs, 1978b).

Related to team building is role clarity (French & Bell, 1978). The purpose of role clarity is to clarify role expectations and obligations of group members to improve effectiveness. Often, people do not have a clear idea of the behaviors expected of them by others. And equally often, what they can expect from others to help them fulfill their own role is neither understood by them or by other people with whom they work. Agreement on role requirements can lead to productive behavior. The steps are as follows:

1. Individuals write down their views of the rationale for the existence of their job, the specific duties, and its contribution to the goals of the unit division, and/or organization.

2. The specific duties and behaviors are listed on a chalkboard and are discussed by the entire team (e.g., maintenance people and production people).

3. Behaviors are added and deleted until the group is satisfied that they have defined the role completely.

4. Individuals list their expectations of the other roles in the group that most affect their own role performance.

5. These expectations are discussed, modified, or added to, and agreed upon by the entire group.

6. The members of the group decide what they want from and expect from the person in that role (e.g., maintenance supervisor).

7. The person in each job makes a written summary of the role as it has been defined by the group. This is the role profile. It is derived from the above steps. It provides a comprehensive understanding of what is expected of each individual.

8. The written profile or job design is reviewed again at a following meeting before another role is analyzed.

This intervention can be a nonthreatening activity with a high payoff for productivity. Often the mutual demands, expectations, and obligations of interdependent team members have never been publicly examined. Individuals wonder why the other employees are "not doing what they are supposed to do" while in reality they are performing as they think the job requires. Collaborative problem solving by the team members not only clarifies who is to do what, but it insures commitment to the role once it has been clarified, and this, in turn, insures the likelihood of positive performance appraisals for individuals as well as the group as a whole.

BOS can play an integral role in team building/role clarity so as to bring about a lasting behavior change among the team members. The following approach has been used successfully by the authors in a wide variety of organizational settings.

1. The division vice president and the staff defined broad objectives about where the division ought to be in five years.

2. BOS were developed (see Appendix B). The BOS made explicit what was required of each manager to influence the attainment of these objectives.

3. The BOS were completed quarterly by the vice president and the managers on one another anonymously. This was done to give each person periodic feedback as to the appropriateness of behaviors in influencing the broad division targets.

4. The mean rating for each item on the BOS was calculated.

5. The group met together for an entire day. Participants identified items where they felt they had been rated too low.

6. The peers were asked what a given participant must *do* in the subsequent appraisal period to receive a higher score. Discussion was always on the future. Specific examples of past behavior were not allowed. There is no way to undo the past. Peers had to provide specific examples of what constitutes acceptable behavior for each individual.

7. The specific action steps for each individual were recorded. Specific goals for each individual were set in relation to the feedback from peers. A copy of each person's goals was subsequently distributed to each person in the group.

Immediate changes in behavior occurred. There is nothing "magical" inherent in the explanation. The employees knew what was expected of them. The BOS served as a communication tool for facilitating explicit feedback about how the employee was perceived by peers in doing what was expected. The employee could either reject the feedback and risk peer condemnation, or accept the feedback and win peer approval that is contingent upon engaging in specific job behaviors critical to attaining organizational objectives.

CLOSING REMARKS

A systematic approach for increasing or maintaining desirable employee behavior includes the following steps:

1. Define performance behaviorally: The manager must identify and define specific behavior or behaviors that are required of the employee on the job. The behavior must be pinpointed to the extent that it can be reliably observed and rewarded. "Showing initiative" is not pinpointed. "Calling on a customer without being asked by anyone" is. The ability to specify behavior in observable terms is the first skill managers must acquire before they can change or maintain an employee's performance. Moreover, it forces managers who are unsatisfied with an employee's performance to analyze the source of their dissatisfaction to the point of identifying the specific behavior they would like to see changed (Miller, 1978). By pinpointing these behaviors, feedback and the setting of specific goals in relation to this feedback can bring about a rapid sustained change in employee behavior. The development of BOS facilitate the pinpointing process.

2. Set specific goals: The advantage of involving the employee in goal setting is that it not only can increase an employee's understanding of what is required of the job, but it also can lead to the setting of higher goals than is the case where a supervisor sets them unilaterally. The higher the goal, the higher the performance. Feedback is necessary so employees can see how well they are performing in relation to the goals.

3. Examine consequences of behavior: In order for goals to be accepted, the employee must perceive goal attainment leading to positive consequences. Given that the employee has been adequately trained, positive consequences that occur on an intermittent basis not only minimize satiation, but also frequently lead to a higher rate with which behaviors are emitted than is the case when the consequences occur on a continuous basis.

4. Involve employees in problem solving: Team building occurs when the supervisor and the employees together analyze the consequences of given behaviors, agree on alternative actions that are acceptable to both parties, and agree on the consequences that will occur if these alternative actions are or are not implemented. Performance evaluations can be threatening for some people; but, anxiety is not heightened by the clarity of an issue, but rather by its fuzziness. When the desired behavior (goals) and the consequences are well known to both the supervisor and the employee, and when the measurement (e.g., BOS) is discussed openly, anxiety is reduced, and the relationship between the manager and the employee can be both candid and comfortable.

SUMMARY

The performance appraisal *system* involves the laws concerning performance appraisal, the construction and testing of the appraisal instrument, and the selection and training of observers. The performance appraisal *process* is concerned with the counseling and development of an employee based on the appraisal information.

The purpose of counseling and development is to sustain a high level of performance or bring about a desirable behavior change. The first and most important step in this process is to set specific goals that are difficult, yet attainable. The setting of goals has a direct effect on what people think and do. In addition, goals affect effort and persistence. Allowing employees to participate in the setting of goals frequently leads to higher goals being set than when the goals are set unilaterally by a supervisor.

Second, the consequence of setting goals and working toward their attainment needs to be examined. Consequences may be neutral, positive, or negative. Given that the employee has been trained, positive consequences that occur on an intermittent basis can lead to higher performance levels than consequences which always occur after a desirable behavior has been demonstrated.

A primary reason for tying money to performance is that it establishes a performance-reward linkage for the employee. To the extent that money is a valued outcome for the employee, the motivation to engage in critical job behaviors increases.

Team building is the involvement of employees and the supervisor working together to solve problems of mutual concern to one another. The combination of BOS, anonymous peer ratings, feedback, and goal setting can help form effective work groups and bring about long lasting desired behavior changes among team members.

Conducting Formal and Informal Performance Appraisals

7

INTRODUCTION

Despite the importance of performance appraisals for both maximizing employee productivity and minimizing the probability of litigation suits, many supervisors avoid giving the results to employees. Giving feedback is avoided because in many instances the appraisal is tantamount to a "bad joke" for both the person who gives and the person who receives the appraisal. It is a bad joke because the appraisal is often based on the wrong instrument (e.g., trait scales). Thus the employee argues that the appraisal does not provide a thorough assessment of what is actually required of the job. In essence, the employee is attacking the content validity of the appraisal instrument (see Chapter 3). The result is that the employee discredits the measuring instrument and the person who used it (Meyer, 1977).

The performance appraisal is often ineffective because, even if a content valid instrument is used, the wrong person or persons often make the appraisal. The appraisers are frequently unaware of the aims and objectives of the person's job, they seldom see the person performing on the job, and they are incapable of discerning competent behavior. It is for this reason that the use of multiple raters, particularly peers, was stressed in Chapter 4.

The performance appraisal is frequently avoided because it often fosters feelings of inequity among employees due to different supervisors using different standards. Two employees who do exactly the same things are often rated differently by two different supervisors. Uniformity and objectivity are necessary to insure feelings of equity among employees. They are particularly necessary when monetary rewards are tied to performance. This is why a training program (described in Chapter 5) to increase observer accuracy in recording what is seen is so important for insuring effective appraisals.

Finally, performance appraisals are disliked by both supervisors and employers because the employee's performance can drop to a level below where it was prior to conducting the appraisal (Meyer et al., 1965). This drop occurs because the motivational principles described in Chapter 6 are not followed. If the appraisal is to bring about a behavior change or sustain a high level of output, it must be conducted frequently, explicit feedback must be provided, specific goals must be set on the basis of this feedback, and criticism must be minimized. For example, giving golfers feedback for 30 to 45 minutes once a year is not going to improve their performance. Similarly, telling employees once a year to "keep up the good work" or "try harder" is going to have little impact on their behavior. What an employee needs to start doing, stop doing, and/or continue doing must be specified in terms of explicit goals on an ongoing basis. In this chapter we will discuss six characteristics of effective appraisals conducted by supervisors, three ways of conducting formal appraisals, and seven ways of conducting informal day-to-day appraisals. The emphasis in this chapter is on supervisors because, as pointed out in Chapter 4, supervisors conduct most appraisals.

SIX CHARACTERISTICS OF EFFECTIVE APPRAISALS

Burke, Weitzel, and Weir (1978) summarized six major characteristics of effective performance appraisals based on their review of the literature. Their findings were as follows:

1. High levels of subordinate participation in the performance appraisal result in employees being satisfied with both the appraisal process and the supervisor who conducted it (Nemeroff & Wexley, 1977; Wexley, Singh, & Yukl, 1973). The importance of this statement is that subordinate *participation* in the appraisal interview appears to increase acceptance of the supervisor's observations.

2. Employee acceptance of the appraisal, and satisfaction with the supervisor increases to the extent that the supervisor is supportive of the employee (Latham & Saari, 1979b; Nemeroff & Wexley, 1977).

3. The setting of specific *goals* to be achieved by the subordinate results in up to twice as much improvement in performance than does a discussion of general goals (Bassett & Meyer, 1968; Meyer, Kay, & French, 1965; Latham & Yukl, 1975a).

4. *Discussing problems* that may be hampering the subordinate's current job performance and working toward solutions has an immediate effect on productivity (Maier, 1958; Meyer & Kay, 1964).

5. The number of *criticisms* in an appraisal interview correlates positively with the number of defensive reactions shown by the employee. Those areas of job performance that are most criticized are least likely to show an improvement. There appears to be a chain reaction between criticisms made by the supervisor and defensive reactions shown by the subordinate, with little or no change in the subordinate's behavior (Kay, Meyer, & French, 1965; Nemeroff & Wexley, 1977).

6. The more subordinates are allowed to voice *opinions* during the appraisal, the more satisfied they will feel with the appraisal (Greller, 1975; Nemeroff & Wexley, 1977; Wexley, Singh & Yukl, 1973).

Research in a large hospital in the Midwest confirmed and expanded these conclusions (Burke et al., 1978). Both the participation and the job related items (i.e., solving job problems; setting specific goals) correlated with the employee's satisfaction with the appraisal process. However, only the job-related items correlated with an improvement in the employee's performance. Setting specific goals clarifies the behavioral paths or strategies that the subordinate can take to fulfill job requirements. Resolving job problems removes present or potential obstacles in the paths of these requirements.

In addition, Burke and his colleagues found that the amount of thought and preparation subordinates spent analyzing (1) their job responsibilities, (2) problems encountered in the job, and (3) the quality of their work correlated positively with improved performance. The employees who took this time were those who perceived that *organizational rewards are contingent on the results of one's performance.* "These data suggest that managers in organizations would get better mileage from their appraisal system if they made the appraisal of performance a priority managerial activity and overtly utilized appraisal results for distributing discretionary 'rewards'" (Burke et al., 1978, p. 917).

THREE APPROACHES TO PERFORMANCE APPRAISAL

Maier (1958) suggested three approaches to conducting performance appraisals, (1) tell and sell, (2) tell and listen, and (3) problem solving. The purpose of tell and sell is to let employees know how well they are doing (tell) and to persuade the employees to set specific goals for improvement (sell). Thus, the approach maximizes points 3 (goal setting) and 5 (criticism) discussed by Burke et al. (1978). The approach is effective for increasing the performance of trainees (Hillery & Wexley, 1974) as well as experienced employees who have been socialized to accept authoritarian leadership (Dossett et al., 1979). In addition, the approach is efficient in that it takes less time to conduct than allowing employees to participate in the appraisal process (Latham & Saari, 1979b.)

The problem with the tell-and-sell approach is that it can do more harm than good with many employees. When subordinates think that their interests and the supervisor's are no longer compatible, performance can, and often does, deteriorate (Maier, 1958). The day-to-day relationship between the supervisor and the subordinate may become strained, and job satisfaction often decreases for both of them. Finally, the approach can encourage a "yes man" in that the underlying philosophy of the approach is that the boss knows best. The boss sets the goals and dispenses the rewards and punishments. Thus, when the method works it is likely to develop dependent, docile behavior; when it fails, the result can be a rebellious employee.

The purpose of the tell-and-listen method is to communicate the supervisor's perception of the employee's strengths and weaknesses, and to let the employee respond to these statements. The approach maximizes employee satisfaction with the process. The supervisor actively listens to the employee's attitudes and feelings, makes effective use of pauses to encourage the subordinate to speak, paraphrases the employee's statements to insure understanding, and summarizes the employee's feelings at the end of the interview. Unfortunately, no *specific* goals are set; thus there is little subsequent change in the employee's performance.

The problem-solving approach maximizes the principles of allowing employee participation in the appraisal, discussing and solving employee problems, and setting specific goals. As such, the approach combines the steps outlined in the tell-and-sell, and tell-and-listen methods. The steps to conducting an effective appraisal follow.

1. Explain the purpose of the meeting, namely, that it is to provide recognition for areas in which the employee is doing well and to discuss any problems that the employee may be experiencing on the job. The employee should be given sufficient notice of the meeting so that the discussion is not one-sided.

2. At the beginning of the meeting, clearly describe to the employee what was done that deserves recognition and why it deserves recognition. Be specific so the employee knows exactly what needs to be done to maintain this appreciation. If blanket praise is given, the employee may be inadvertently reinforced for mediocre as well as excellent behavior.

3. Ask the employee if there are areas on the job where you can provide assistance. In this way you are showing that you truly want to help the employee.

4. If the employee fails to mention areas that you feel are important, discuss no more than two where you feel improvement is needed. Focusing on more than two broad criteria (e.g., technical competence and interaction with subordinates on BOS) can overwhelm an employee and increase defensiveness. Focus strictly on problems and not personalities. Simply explain what you have seen and why it concerns you.

There is no question that any evaluative process can be threatening to some employees. This anxiety is heightened not by the clarity of an issue, but by its fuzziness. When the appropriate behaviors are well known to both the employee and the supervisor, and when the measurement of these behaviors is discussed openly, anxiety is reduced and the relationship between the employee and the supervisor may be more frank and comfortable (Miller, 1978). This is another reason why BOS are so important as appraisal instruments. They make clear to all parties what is required of an employee.

5. Ask for and listen openly to the employee's concerns. It may well be the case that your initial concerns are not justified.

6. Come to agreement on steps to be taken by each of you. This is the crucial goal setting step.

7. If BOS are used, mutually agree upon a specific score that the employee will strive to attain on the subsequent appraisal.

8. Finally, agree on a follow-up date, to determine the extent to which the employee's and supervisor's concerns have been eliminated and progress has been made on the goals that have been set.

The problem-solving method is particularly appropriate for peer ratings because it minimizes the role of the supervisor as a judge, and increases the supervisor's role as counselor. The supervisor simply feeds back the information provided anonymously by the employee's peers (see Chapter 4.) If an employee becomes defensive because of a specific rating, the supervisor, rather than being required to defend the rating, can discuss with the employee what is being done or not done to give peers the "erroneous perception." More important, the two of them can discuss the specific action plans that the employee can implement to change these perceptions. Thus, the supervisor can emphasize the role of helper rather than critic.

If a content valid appraisal instrument is used, it is unlikely that peers will fail to point out an area that is of concern to a supervisor. What makes this process so effective is that by using peer ratings a supervisor can focus attention during an appraisal interview on ways of helping the employee correct the problem rather than jeopardizing the success of the interview by defending his or her own appraisal of the employee, and providing criticism after criticism to justify that appraisal.

INFORMAL DAY-TO-DAY APPRAISALS

As has been mentioned throughout this book, the results of performance appraisals must be given frequently to an employee if they are to bring about a change in an employee's behavior or maintain a high standard of excellence. Employees need feedback on how well they are doing. They must accurately perceive the consequences of their efforts and be able to set goals on the basis of this feedback. This does not mean that formal appraisals must be conducted on a daily basis. If formal appraisals were always necessary, a supervisor with eight or more employees would do nothing but conduct performance appraisals. But, on an informal basis, this is exactly what managers do each and every day, they evaluate people. There is no reason why a manager cannot feed back this information informally to employees.

Through a systematic job analysis similar to that discussed in Chapter 3, Sorcher (Goldstein & Sorcher, 1974) identified supervisory behaviors critical to the day-to-day appraisals of people. These behaviors are those that should be exhibited by a manager on an ongoing basis so that employees are knowledgeable of the consequences of their actions, and can set appropriate *goals* to increase or maintain their effectiveness in an organization. Because these behaviors may appear dogmatic to some readers, we will first present research evidence for their overall effectiveness.

Behavior Modeling Training

Latham and Saari (1979c) examined the effects of a training program developed by Sorcher (Goldstein & Sorcher, 1974) to increase effectiveness of supervisors in dealing with subordinates. The program is referred to as modeling because the trainees see a model on film demonstrate key behaviors in responding to a specific situation. They then attempt to model these behaviors in situations that are similar for them, during training, and more important, on the job. The behaviors demonstrate the principles of Maier's problem-solving approach for formal performance appraisals.*

Since it was impossible to train all supervisors simultaneously, Latham and Saari randomly selected 40 individuals and randomly assigned them to either a training or a control group. However, the people assigned to these two groups did not know that they had been labelled as a control or an experimental group. They assumed that for logistical reasons they

---

*Modeling falls in the same category as feedback in that both are sources of information. Since, as noted in Chapter 6, it has been found that feedback alone does not motivate performance, there is no reason to believe that modeling would do so. As with feedback, however, modeling facilitates the effects of goal setting when employees do not possess sufficient knowledge of how to reach the goal (Locke, 1980).

were either among the first or the last to receive the training. The mean age of these supervisors was 43 years. The mean number of years they had worked in a supervisory capacity was five. All of them were males.

The training group was divided into two groups of ten to facilitate individualized instruction. Each group met for two hours each week. The sessions included instruction on orienting a new employee, giving recognition, motivating a poor performer, discussing poor work habits, discussing potential disciplinary action, handling a complaining employee, and overcoming resistance to change. Each of these sessions is critical for learning how to conduct appraisals effectively.

Each training session followed the same format: (1) introduction of the topic by the trainers; (2) presentation of a film that depicts a supervisor model effectively handling a situation by following a set of three to eight learning points that were shown in the film immediately before and after the model was presented; (3) group discussion of the effectiveness of the model in demonstrating the desired behaviors; (4) practice in role playing the desired behaviors in front of the entire class; and (5) feedback from the class on the effectiveness of each trainee in demonstrating the desired behaviors.

In each practice session, one trainee took the role of supervisor and another trainee assumed the role of an employee. No prepared scripts were used. The two trainees were simply asked to recreate an incident relevant to the film topic for that week that had occurred to at least one of them within the past 12 months. The spontaneity of each practice session was designed to parallel what occurs on the job.

The learning points shown in the film were posted in front of the trainee playing the role of supervisor. This person had no idea what the "employee" was going to say to him. He responded as well as he could using the learning points as goals or guidelines. The rest of the group provided feedback on his effectiveness in using the learning points to deal with the situation.

The primary function of one trainer was to select and supervise the practice session of each pair of trainees. The primary function of the second trainer was to supervise the feedback given by the peers so as to maintain and/or enhance the confidence and self-esteem of the person receiving the feedback. This was done by coaching individuals how to make evaluative comments that were constructive rather than critical, namely, by having the trainee restate negative comments in a positive manner (e.g., "encourage the employee to talk" rather than "you talk too much").

At the conclusion of each training session, the supervisors were given copies of the learning points for that session. They were instructed to use the supervisory skills they had learned in class with one or more employees on the job within a one-week time period. In this way, transfer of learning from the classroom to the job was facilitated. The supervisors were asked to report their successes and/or failures to the class the following week. In instances where a supervisor reported difficulty in demonstrating one or more behaviors, he was asked to explain the situation to the class, to select one individual from the class to assume the role of an employee, and to show exactly what took place. The other trainees then gave him feedback. He then practiced the desired behavior(s) a second time. In rare instances where a supervisor said that he was absolutely stuck, another trainee was asked to show the group how he would handle that supervisor's situation.

In several instances the learning points developed by Sorcher were not rigidly followed. Where there was group consensus among the trainees that a learning point from one session should be added to another session, the learning points were rewritten. In only one instance were the learning points deleted, namely, for overcoming resistance to change. The trainees agreed on the appropriateness of the model's behavior, but not on the learning points that described his behavior. Again, the learning points were rewritten by the supervisors to fit their own organizational setting.

To further insure that the supervisors would be reinforced for demonstrating the behaviors that were taught in class on the job, their managers attended an accelerated program of two training sessions per week for four weeks. For the role plays in each of these training sessions, one superintendent assumed the role of a subordinate while a second manager played himself. This training emphasized the importance of praising a supervisor, regardless of whether he was in the training or control group, whenever they saw him demonstrate a desired behavior on the job.

The results of the training program were evaluated in terms of four different measures, (1) employee reactions to the training, (2) learning measures, (3) behavioral samples, and (4) supervisory appraisals. Initially, many people were unreceptive to the program. The trainee who was asked to take the role of an employee frequently behaved in an extremely uncooperative manner to show the trainers "the way things really are," and why this program was a waste of their time. By the third session, however, this behavior had changed. Supervisors playing the role of an employee announced publicly to the group that "this program really works; there is no way I can outmaneuver him when he sticks to those damn learning points." Concerns initially expressed to the effect that the Company was trying to get everyone to act exactly the same way gave way to such comments as, "Did you notice that none of us are doing the same thing and yet we are all following these key points?" Other representative comments included, ". . . . most training isn't worth a damn; it works in the classroom, but not on the job. With this program, it is just the opposite. It is much easier to do on the job what we learned here than it is to do it in front of all of you."

Other people simply thanked the trainers privately for giving them the confidence to do their job. These individuals included people who had been supervisors for 20 years. Still other supervisors reported how the program had helped them improve relationships with their wives and/or children. This latter information suggests the generalizability of the training to interpersonal effectiveness off the job.

The reaction questionnaire given immediately after the final training session contained five questions each with a 5-point Likert-type scale. The questions dealt with the extent to which the training (1) helped them to do the job better; (2) helped them interact more effectively with employees; (3) peers; (4) supervisors; and (5) the degree to which they would recommend this training to other foremen. The mean response for the five items was 4.15. These attitudes were supported behaviorally by the fact that six of the twenty trainees were on vacation during one or more of the nine weeks that the training was conducted. All six individuals voluntarily attended the training class held during their vacation.

The reaction questionnaire was administered again eight months later. All the questionnaires were returned. The mean response for the five items was 4.29 indicating that the initial positive reactions to the program were sustained over time.

The learning measures consisted of a test containing 85 situational questions. The questions were developed from critical incidents obtained in a job analyais (Latham et al., 1979) of supervisory behavior. The incidents were turned into questions by asking "How would you handle the following situation?" Prior to administering the test, managers behaviorally anchored 1 (poor), 3 (mediocre), and 5 (excellent) answers for each question so that the trainees' responses could be objectively scored from 85 to 425 points. An example of a question with its benchmarked answers follows.

You have spoken with this worker several times about the fact that he doesn't keep his long hair confined under his hard hat. This constitutes a safety violation. You are walking through the plant and you just noticed that he *again* does not have his hair properly confined. What would you do? The benchmarks (not shown to the trainees) were "send the worker home (1); call the shop steward and give the worker a written warning (3); or explain the rationale as to why the behavior cannot continue, and ask for his ideas on how to solve the problem (5)."

The test was completed on the job, under uniform conditions, with a personnel representative present as a monitor. Code numbers were used for identification purposes so that superintendents who scored each test could not be biased by knowledge of a respondent's identity, or whether he had received the training.

The mean score ($\overline{X}$ = 301) of the training group was significantly higher than that of the control group ($\overline{X}$ = 273). Note that the learning test did not contain questions restricted solely to the areas covered in the training, but examined all possible interpersonal situations that had been identified in the job analysis. The results indicated that the trainees had acquired the knowledge necessary to transfer the principles learned in class to different types of job-related problems.

The behavioral measures consisted of tape recorded role plays of supervisors resolving supervisor-employee problems. For these role plays, brief scripts were developed for each of the training modules. For example, the scripts for dealing with poor work habits were as follows: "You have just called in the employee sitting in front of you to inform him that you are dissatisfied with the report on environmental issues. It is incomplete. This is a consistent problem. You have never confronted the employee because you suspect that he prides himself on attention to detail. Show how you would handle this situation;" and, "Your supervisor has just called you into his office. You have heard that he has criticized your work to others. You resent this very much. Show how you would handle this situation."

The scripts were randomly assigned to the supervisors. None of these situations had been previously described to the supervisors during training and none of them were the same as the training films. The individuals who played the employee's role were people who had been through the training program. However, they did not role play with supervisors from their own training class. This was done to prevent them from knowing whether the person in the role of supervisor was from another training class or had yet to receive training. The pairing of role players was randomly determined.

The twenty supervisors in the training group were given the appropriate set of learning points to use during the role play. This is because the trainees were encouraged to keep the learning points with them at all times on the job.

Of the twenty foremen in the control group, ten were given the learning points. This step was taken in order to determine whether knowledge alone of what one is "supposed to do" is sufficient to elicit the desired behavior. If giving the supervisors the learning points as guidelines to follow was as effective as requiring them to attend training sessions, considerable time and expense would be saved for the Company.

The tape recordings were evaluated by fifteen managers who worked in groups of three. The managers did not know the identity of each supervisor not whether the supervisor had received training. To eliminate the possibility of judges recognizing a person's voice on a tape, managers in one area of the company evaluated the tape recordings of supervisors from another area of the company.

The rating scale consisted of the learning points taught in class, each with a 5-point scale on which the judge rated the quality of the performance. In addition, the individual playing the role of the hourly worker was rated on eight five-point bipolar adjectives (e.g., helpful-frustrating), which was designed to determine whether the role plays of hourly workers were significantly different among the three conditions in terms of difficulty level. No significant difference was found among the ratings of the hourly workers in the training group, the control group who received the learning points, or the control group who did not receive the learning points.

The evaluation of the trained group ($\overline{X}$ = 4.11) was significantly higher than those of the control groups with ($\overline{X}$ = 2.70), and without the learning points ($\overline{X}$ = 2.84). There was no significant difference in the performance of the two control groups.

These measures only assessed skill levels in performing the specific behaviors for which the training program was designed to teach. The critical question was whether the training program brought about a relatively permanent change in supervisory behavior on the job.

Managers evaluated the supervisors on behavioral observation scales one month before and one year after the training. Because the superintendents knew who had received training, they received intensive instruction on minimizing rating errors (see Chapter 5) when appraising others.

The results were conclusive in showing that the supervisors who received the training program performed far better on the job one year later than did peers who did not receive the training. The content of the training is described next.

Orienting a New Employee

If one accepts the premise that a fundamental purpose of a performance appraisal is to counsel and develop an employee, performance appraisal begins with orientation.*

The key points to follow are:

1. Give the employee a friendly welcome to your area. The two days an employee will recall vividly about an organization are the first day on the job and the last day. Performance appraisal is a two-way process. It is on the first day that the employee forms initial impressions of you and the organization. This is the time to start building interest in and commitment to the job.

2. Make the employee comfortable through casual conversation about the employee's background and interests. Most employees are nervous and unsure of themselves when they first report to a new supervisor. In the process of appraising you, they do not always hear everything you are saying. Consequently, they often do things contrary to what was explained to them during orientation. In the interest of productivity and safety, it is imperative that the employee feels relaxed enough to listen to you.

It is appropriate to inquire about difficulties the employee may be

---

*See Wanous (1980) for an in-depth discussion on the "organizational entry" of new employees.

experiencing in settling into the community. Again, the issue is productivity and safety. If the employee is thinking about housing, plumbing, financing, barbershops and the myriad of the important and not-so-important factors that affect a person who moves to a new community, he or she is not thinking about the job. Related to this suggestion is to pair a new employee with another individual who is relatively new to the department or company (Porter & Steers, 1973). This second individual can relate to the problems that the new employee is either currently facing or will be facing in the near future, and can suggest ways of alleviating or minimizing these concerns.

3. Express your desire to help the employee on the job by telling the person to feel free to see you for help, questions, or suggestions.

4. Stress the importance of safety when there are hazards on the job. Explain and then show the employee what needs to be done to avoid danger. Finally, ask the employee to show you what needs to be done to avoid danger. In this way you can be certain that the employee understands your instructions.

5. Make it clear that you feel that the employee will do a good job, which can be done by relating any previous work the employee has experienced which is similar in principle to requirements of the present job. Then give the employee recognition for the areas that are performed well.

Giving Recognition

The employees who receive recognition for their work are generally the outstanding workers and the poor performers. The poor performers often get recognition in terms of attention from others, which may take the form of reprimands from supervisors and approval from colleagues. The outstanding employees frequently receive recognition in terms of awards, promotions, and stock options.

The majority of employees are neither poor performers nor outstanding workers. They do an adequate job in that their work habits seldom warrant criticism. In short, they do what is expected of them. They come to work every day; they are seldom, if ever, late; they get along with others; and, they cause little or no problem for anyone. Typically, no recognition is given to these people for the work that they are doing. They are average employees. Yet, the job of their manager would increase in difficulty if these employees suddenly stopped doing what was expected of them, and became poor performers. To prevent such an occurrence they must be given positive feedback from a supervisor for those things usually taken for granted. To borrow academic phraseology, the primary objective here is to keep a C student from becoming a D or an F student. In some instances, the outcome of giving recognition may be a B, or an A student. The key learning points to follow are:

1. Clearly describe to the employee *specifically* what was done to deserve recognition. The word *specifically* is emphasized because telling an employee, "you are doing a good job" doesn't let the employee or the employee's colleagues know exactly what was done to deserve the compliment. Moreover, blanket praise may inadvertently reinforce mediocre behavior on the part of the employee. Blanket praise may increase the employee's job satisfaction, but specific praise can increase both job satisfaction and productivity. A second reason for making the praise specific is that it increases the probability that the employee will perceive it as sincere. Blanket praise sometimes generates skepticism as to motives behind the comment.

An advantage of using BOS is that it specifies the behaviors that a manager should look for to praise the employee. Many managers have no problem noticing and commenting upon ineffective behavior. These same managers often appear to be either blind or tongue-tied with regard to effective behavior on the part of their subordinates.

2. Express your personal appreciation to the employee. It may amount to nothing more than saying thank you. The rationale behind points 1 and 2 is simply to let the employee know that you both *notice* and *appreciate* what is being done on the job. This conversation does not need to take place in an office. It can occur anywhere the two of you meet. Preferably the conversation should occur *immediately* after the desired behavior on the part of the employee takes place.

3. Ask the employee if there is anything you can do to be of assistance regarding job-related problems. Many managers are reluctant to follow this step because they are afraid of being "hit with a laundry list" of complaints. In the literally hundreds of cases where we have trained people to follow this step, this fear has never materialized. In most cases the employee simply looks at the supervisor in awe. In other cases the employee has said thank you and later commented that it was the first time in literally years that anyone had commented in this fashion. As most motivational theorists hypothesize, and as almost all employees are painfully aware, most workers are starving for recognition. Recognition that is tied to specific behaviors is a powerful motivator for increasing productivity. The rationale behind point 3 is to show that you are concerned with the employees' concerns. Through this step you may subsequently be among the first rather than the last to know of sources of irritation among your work force.

4. If necessary, plan a specific follow-up meeting to determine whether the employee's concerns have been resolved. If it is not possible for you to resolve a concern, you need to explain to the employee what you have done and why it was ineffective. In this way, the employee knows that you tried.

A pitfall in the above three steps is the tendency to mix criticism with praise: "Chris, if you would only do this well in accounting, you'd be outstanding." Leave criticism for a separate discussion. Criticism has a tendency to generate criticism. Employees suddenly find it very easy to find fault with the supervisor. If praise is usually mixed with criticism, the praise that is being given is not heard because the employee is waiting for the punch line. However, just as criticism has a tendency to generate criticism, the same effect occurs with praise. Employees suddenly find reasons to compliment a supervisor. The result is a positive and contagious work climate. However, if providing recognition does not maintain productivity in all cases, you may be faced with the problem of motivating a poor performer.

Motivating the Poor Performer

The learning points here assume this is the first-time rather than the twenty-first time discussion of the issue of performance with the employee has taken place. The employee was previously doing an adequate job, but now performance is less than adequate. The steps to follow are:

1. Focus on the problem. Stay away from personalities. For example, rather than saying, "Sam, why are you slowing up production?" you might say, "Sam, there is a problem and I'd appreciate your ideas on how to solve it. Production has decreased by ___ percent and I would appreciate your input on ways to increase it."

Focusing on personalities is tantamount to criticism, which usually puts an employee on the defensive. The employee then feels the necessity for justifying the behavior and consequently resists changing it. And yet, many supervisors feel that their role is that of a disciplinary agent similar to that of a grade school teacher or police officer. The role of the supervisor is to solve problems efficiently. Focusing on the issues rather than on a personality is the only way to solve problems.

2. Ask for the employee's help and discuss the ideas given on how to solve the problem. Employee participation in problem solving helps reduce resistance to change. Equally important is the likelihood that the ideas offered by the employee are good ones. In fact, it may be the case that in the final analysis the poor performance was not due to the employee after all, but rather to improper work procedures.

3. Come to agreement on steps to be taken by each of you. This step is critical. It not only insures the setting of specific goals, but also insures clarity and understanding on the part of the speakers. A key substep is to paraphrase or repeat to the other person what you believe has been said. In this way the pitfall, "you heard what I said but not what I meant," is avoided. An example of paraphrasing is as follows: "Sam, if I hear you correctly, you will check with the computer people by Monday, and you will have the program debugged no later than Friday."

4. Plan a *specific* follow-up meeting. The word *specific* is emphasized to stress the necessity of making clear to the employee when the problem is to be corrected.

In the event that the employee gives answers in step 2 that are clearly excuses that will not solve the problem, company labor relations personnel, union business agents, and research data (Latham & Saari, 1979c) stress that the same learning points should be followed. This procedure allows the employee to save face and to protect his or her self-esteem. The employee knows that you are aware of the problem and the time limit for correcting it. Most employees in these circumstances will correct the situation and will remember that you gave them the opportunity to do so without criticizing them or engaging in disciplinary action.

Discussing Poor Work Habits

Sometimes criticism cannot be avoided. In cases where the poor performance does not improve, or where it is impossible to avoid personalizing the issue (e.g., the employee has been leaving work early), the following points should be covered:

1. Explain to the employee, without hostility, what you have seen and why it concerns you. The phrase *without hostility* was inserted because the discussion should not be an emotional one on your part. You as a manager are paid to solve problems. As previously stated, your role is not to act as a police officer. Your tone should be no different from that of a newscaster.

2. Explain the rationale as to why the behavior cannot continue in words the employee can understand. For example, what happens when a report is late? Does the department really come to a standstill if the employee is absent? If you have a difficult time thinking of a rationale, it may be that the behavior does not constitute a problem, and possibly, the rules should be changed.

3. Ask for and listen openly to the employee's reasons for the behavior. This step is critical for insuring that your decisions are made on the basis of all available facts. In every training class we have encountered, at least one supervisor was on the verge of taking disciplinary action against an employee for coming to work late when it turned out that the employee had cancer. The employee was reluctant to make this fact known to the supervisor. The performance problem that occurred as a result of the medical treatment needed to be corrected, but disciplinary action was clearly not the answer.

4. Focus on *one* specific problem. Do not allow the employee to lead you into a discussion of unrelated issues. For example, you may discuss the fact the employee leaves work early. The employee counters with the perception that his or her work is outstanding in terms of quantity and quality, and thus there is no loss in productivity. You may respond with the observation that the quality of the person's work leaves much to be desired. In the heat of the ensuing argument, the original issue of leaving work early is forgotten.

5. Ask the employee for ideas on ways to solve the problem. Again, participation in problem solving increases commitment to change. In this case, the employee is the problem; the employee's ideas on the subject are a necessity.

6. Offer your help in solving the problem. If you have ideas or suggestions, there is no need for keeping them a secret. By offering your suggestions you are communicating to the employee that you are truly interested in solving the problem rather than finding a way to take disciplinary action.

7. Come to agreement on steps to be taken by each of you. As mentioned earlier, this insures goal setting, clarity, and understanding between you and the employee about what is going to be done to solve the problem.

8. Set a specific follow-up date. This last step is the timetable for insuring that the problem has been resolved.

The opinion of company labor relations personnel and the research data suggest that for minimizing or winning legal and/or union difficulties this first discussion should be labeled a problem-solving meeting. The meeting should be documented as to the date of the meeting, the content of the discussion, the steps that were agreed upon, and the timetable for implementing the steps. The employee should receive a copy of a memo summarizing this information. If a second, third, and fourth meeting are required because the issue has not been resolved, the employee should be given a formal verbal warning, a written letter, and a suspension/termination, respectively.

Salaried employees should be treated no differently from union employees. In too many cases the salaried employee is simply terminated. A union guarantees that a person's security needs will be protected by clearly delineating the steps an organization must follow before the employee can be discharged. An organization can reduce feelings among salaried personnel for the necessity of a union by treating them as fairly as they do their unionized work force.

Disciplinary Action

If the performance problem is not resolved and a subsequent discussion is necessary, the following points should be followed:

1. Define the problem in terms of lack of correction since the previous discussion. In other words, specify the exact issue or issues that have yet to be resolved.

2. Again, explain the rationale in words the employee can understand as to why the behavior cannot continue. Do not simply cite company regulations or a union contract. What is the rationale underlying these regulations?

3. Ask for and listen openly to the employee's reasons for the continued behavior. This step should be followed even if there was a previous discussion on this subject moments earlier. It is imperative that you attempt to collect all the facts before you take disciplinary action.

4. If disciplinary action is necessary, indicate specifically what the action will be, your reasons for taking this action, and when the action will take place.

5. If the action does not require terminating the employee, stress that the employee is responsible for solving the problem, but that you are willing to help anyway you can. The point here is to show that you are not picking on the employee. You should be truly sorry that disciplinary action is needed, but your job is to correct problems as well as praise good performance. It is not your fault that the employee is repeatedly late for work, but it is your responsibility to work with the employee to find answers to the problem.

6. Plan a specific follow-up meeting to praise the employee for correcting the problem.

Overcoming Resistance to Change

Sometimes disciplinary action stems from an unwillingness on the part of an employee to change well-ingrained work habits. Employees do not necessarily resist change because they are stupid or lazy. Employees may resist change because they are afraid that they will not be able to do the job as well as they did prior to when the change was made. Thus their self-esteem as well as their job security may be threatened. In still other cases, employees may realize from past experience that the change generally benefits the organization at their expense (e.g., more work for the same pay). To minimize resistance to change, employees should be encouraged to participate in the decision-making process when the decision will directly affect them. However, the individual supervisor who embraces this philosophy is often in a position where it is impossible to implement it. The decision was made without consulting the supervisor. Where this is the case, the following learning points are appropriate:

1. Clearly describe the details of the change. Replace rumors with fact.

2. Explain why the change is necessary. This step is crucial. People do not like to be manipulated. Things may have been going smoothly from their viewpoint. "Why is someone now causing so much bad feeling and discontent?" "Why do we all of a sudden have to do things differently?" "We just had a change three years ago." "When will the people in corporate headquarters be satisfied?" These are typical questions that a supervisor must be able to answer in words that employees can understand. It is not mandatory that people agree that the change is necessary; it is mandatory that they understand the reasoning behind the change.

3. Discuss how the change will affect the employee. Do not labor on negative aspects, but, if negatives exist, do not attempt to hide them. What employees fear most are changes that they are not prepared to deal with. Unnecessary fear is reduced when employees believe they are being told the truth.

4. Listen openly to the employee's concerns about the change. In some cases this may be analogous to the tell-and-listen approach discussed earlier. Employees feel better after they have had a chance to discuss openly issues that concern them. Moreover, in many cases the employees who are to implement the change may recognize problems that upper management did not consider when they decided on the change. These problems need to be communicated immediately to management. This is one reason why employee participation in decision making is critical for implementing a change successfully.

5. Ask the employee for help in making the change work. This move is more than a simple courtesy. It is a supplemental step to the previous one in encouraging an employee to express concerns and solutions regarding potential problems that management may have overlooked when they decided to introduce the change.

6. If necessary, plan a specific follow-up meeting to assure the employee that you appreciate the ideas and concerns that were mentioned, and to determine the extent to which these issues have been resolved, and whether new issues have appeared.

Handling a Complaining Employee

Many employees like to complain about existing job conditions, not to mention a change in job procedures. It is sometimes tempting to ignore the employee's complaints, to overreact by yelling at the employee, or to engage in a debate with the employee. The result is often a mole hill that turns into a volcano. Key learning points to follow include:

1. Avoid responding with hostility or defensiveness. Hostility and defensive behavior on the part of a supervisor only increase hostility on the part of an employee. The outcome is that the severity of the complaint increases as does the time required on the part of the supervisor to deal with it.

2. Request a full description of the employee's complaint and listen openly. If the employee is speaking rapidly or unintelligibly, slow the speech down to the speed with which you choose to write. For example, you might say, "Kim, this sounds important. Let me get a pencil and paper. I am sorry; I missed several points. Have a seat. Now what was the first point? Sorry, Kim; slow down for just a moment. Your ideas are important and I don't want to miss anything." In short, you are calming the employee by getting the person to dictate to you with a speed that gives you time to both listen and understand what is being said.

3. Restate the complaint to insure understanding. Often the employee does not mean precisely what was said, and the listener did not hear exactly what was meant. Paraphrasing the complaint increases the probability that the two people are focusing on the correct problem.

4. Recognize and acknowledge the employee's viewpoint. This does not necessarily mean that you agree with the viewpoint or that you are going to deal with the complaint in a manner that is satisfactory to the employee. It does mean that you are going to attempt to understand the issue from the perspective of the employee.

5. If necessary, state your position nondefensively. This step ties back to overcoming resistance to change. Explain the rationale why you are not going to change the basis for the employee's complaint.

6. Plan a specific follow-up meeting. This step is necessary to assure the employee that you can see the problem from the employee's perspective, and hopefully to enable the employee to see the issue from either the organization's or your own perspective. If you are in agreement with the employee's complaint and have attempted to resolve it, a followup date is necessary to determine if the complaint has been resolved to the satisfaction of the employee.

CLOSING REMARKS

At Richardson-Merrill Company, Sorcher (personal communication, 1980) has shown that it is not just the supervisor who needs to be trained before a performance appraisal can have a maximum effect on a subordinate's productivity. The subordinate needs to be trained too. Specifically, subordinates need to be trained on how to deal with criticism, how to ask questions and seek facts without appearing defensive, and how to set goals that are difficult but attainable. The learning points described for supervisors regarding recognition, motivating the poor performer, discussing poor work habits, disciplinary action in terms of going to the supervisor's superior, overcoming resistance to change, and responding to complaints would appear to be equally applicable for subordinates in dealing with superiors.

These learning points should not be interpreted as laws. They are guidelines. They work in most situations for both white-collar and blue-collar employers in union and nonunion settings. The underlying theme of the present chapter is that regardless of with whom the supervisor is interacting, the supervisor who receives training in appraising and feeding back the results of the appraisal to employees is more successful than the supervisor who is not trained.

Much has been written on the subject of criticism. Some authors argue for eliminating criticism completely from the appraisal. Others argue that this approach is naive; employees who aren't criticized will not improve their performance. Still others argue that the criticism should be sandwiched in between praise. The results are the same: when criticism is included, performance frequently fails to improve and often drops to a level below where it was prior to the appraisal.

In our opinion, the debate on criticism has been misdirected. Employees need to know where their performance is inadequate. The appropriate question is how this information should be conveyed to the employee. The present training program that emphasizes issues rather than personalities is, in our opinion, an appropriate solution. It maximizes the principles of problem solving discussed by Maier. Moreover, the training program emphasizes the importance of appraisal feedback and goal setting as an ongoing process rather than as a once-a-year activity that a supervisor conducts with each employee.

SUMMARY

Characteristics of effective performance appraisals include allowing subordinates adequate time to prepare to participate in the formal appraisal, demonstrating supportive behavior during the appraisal to the employees, asking the subordinates to discuss problems that may be hampering their performance, minimizing supervisory criticism, encouraging the employees to voice opinions during the appraisal, and setting specific goals to be achieved by the subordinates. Three formal ways of conducting appraisals that incorporate one or more of these characteristics are the tell-and-sell, tell-and-listen, and problem-solving methods.

Tell and sell incorporates the principles of assigned goals and letting employees know how well they are doing in the eyes of the supervisor. The method works best with new employees, trainees, and people who have been socialized to accept an authoritarian leadership style.

The tell-and-listen method increases job satisfaction, but not performance, primarily because no specific goals are set. However, the principles of employee participation and supportive behavior on the part of the supervisors are maximized.

The problem-solving method incorporates the principles of participation, supervisory supportiveness behavior, and goal setting. Criticism is minimized by focusing attention on ways to improve performance rather than chastising past performance. The outcome is increased productivity and job satisfaction for most employees.

Performance appraisals that are given to employees once a year have little or no positive impact on their behavior. Employees should receive feedback on a daily basis. However, if superiors completed performance appraisal forms every day on every employee, the recording of performance appraisal would become an all-consuming activity. Therefore, suggestions were made that can be followed on a daily basis regarding meeting an employee new to an area, giving recognition, motivating a poor performer,

discussing poor work habits, taking disciplinary action, overcoming resistance to change, and dealing with a complaining employee. The underlying theme of these suggestions is that a long-lasting behavior change can
be most easily brought about by (1) maintaining an employee's self-
esteem, (2) expressing a desire to help the employee on the job, (3) looking
for areas to praise rather than criticize, (4) focusing on problems rather
than personalities, (5) explaining the rationale behind rules, and (6) asking
for and listening openly to employee concerns.

Motivating Engineers/ Scientists through Performance Appraisals: A Case Study*

8

INTRODUCTION

The purpose of this chapter is to provide a summary of major points in this book through examination of an actual situation where an organization applied key concepts discussed in chapters 2 through 7. The senior vice president of research and development (R & D) in a large international corporation had requested that ways be found to motivate the organization's engineers and scientists to attain excellence. The company was feeling the impact of an economic recession.

An internal task force, consisting primarily of line managers, had recommended to the president that an efficient way for reducing costs would be to lay off a significant number of employees in R & D. Fortunately for the R & D department, its senior vice president was able to persuade the president that a more effective approach for the company in the long run would be to motivate its engineers and scientists in such a

*This chapter is based on the following research reports:
Latham, G. P. Does participation in setting goals boost engineers' performance? *Chemical Engineering,* 1979, January, 141-144. Copright 1979, McGraw-Hill Co., Inc. Used with permission. Latham, G. P., & Mitchell, T. R. Behaviorial criteria and potential reinforcers for the engineer/scientist in an industrial setting. JSAS *Catalog of Selected Documents in Psychology,* 1976, *6*, 38, 1, 316; Latham, G. P., Mitchell, T. R. & Dossett, D. L. The importance of participative goal setting and anticipated rewards on goal difficulty and job performance. *Journal of Applied Psychology,* 1978, *63*, 163-171.

manner that they would be too valuable to let go. A second task force was immediately formed with the charge of finding the best method(s) to motivate people. The business and professional literature was reviewed. The merits of different theories and approaches for motivating employees were carefully examined. There were proponents and antagonists among the task force for each of the various approaches. After several days of discussions, little progress had been made by the task force—primarily because before managers can decide *how* to motivate employees, it must be determined *what* they want the employees to do. In short, the task force had yet to resolve the most fundamental issue presented to them by the senior vice president, namely, how to define employee excellence?

DEFINING EXCELLENCE

Employee excellence, as noted in Chapter 3, can be defined in terms of cost-related measures, attitudinal or personality traits, or critical job behaviors. A major limitation of defining excellence in terms of dollars generated or lost, number of patents accepted, and the like is that they are frequently excessive or deficient. Cost-related variables can be excessive in that they may be affected by numerous factors over which the engineer or scientist has little or no control, or they can be deficient in that they include only a few, rather than all, of the key elements that constitute the individual's job. In the job of selling, for example, sales volume is usually an *excessive* measure of an individual's effectiveness because it is affected, often to an unknown extent, by such factors as the economic resources of different sales territories, differential effectiveness of the company's advertising campaign in the area where a salesperson is working, and different competitive advantages of the organization from one sales territory to another. In the job of managing, a scientist might be judged to be highly effective in keeping expenditures within the budget, but this measure would clearly be deficient as a comprehensive measure of how well the scientist made use of all available resources. Moreover, cost-related measures should be avoided because they can implicitly encourage a results-at-all-cost mentality that can run counter to corporate ethics policies. This statement does not imply that cost-related variables should never be examined or that they are not crucial to the survival of an organization. It simply means that from a counseling (motivation) and development (training) standpoint, cost-related variables do not inform the employees how or why they are effective or ineffective on the job. Therefore, the employees receive minimum rather than maximum knowledge as to what needs to be continued or done differently.

Performance appraisals based on traits or attitudes can foster misunderstanding and disagreement between managers and their subordinates. For example, a manager could tell engineers that they need to show more initiative, to be better listeners, and to follow through on projects. This could be good advice. But, in its present form, this information is not helpful because it does not indicate exactly what the engineers must do differently. Unfortunately, most of us are not accustomed to speaking in a clear and precise manner. The engineers may interpret the advice in ways in which the manager never intended or become hostile toward the manager because they believe that they are already engaging in these behaviors. And yet, the behaviors that the employees are demonstrating are obviously not the behaviors that the manager wants to see.

With these points in mind, the task force soon realized that excellence should be defined and measured in terms of observable behaviors that are critical to job success or failure. Behaviorally based measures can account for far more job complexity, can be related more directly to what the engineer or scientist actually does, and are more likely to minimize irrelevant biases not under the control of the employee than can cost-related variables or managerial inferences as to a person's attitudes or traits.

The immediate advantages of a behavioral approach to defining excellence are that it not only lends itself to improved measures of job performance, but also (1) lends itself to establishing remedial training programs by pinpointing key skills where an engineer or scientist is deficient, (2) facilitates the writing of comprehensive job descriptions, (3) can be integrated with compensation programs, and (4) can serve as a basis for developing programs for manpower planning, staffing, affirmative action, and career development.

DEVELOPING BEHAVIORALLY BASED
PERFORMANCE MEASURES: BOS

In building behaviorally based measures, engineers and scientists as well as their managers were interviewed regarding specific incidents that they themselves had actually seen make the difference between success and failure in accomplishing a specific objective. Each interview focused on three questions:

1. What were the circumstances surrounding this incident? In other words, what was the situation?

2. What exactly did this engineer or scientist do that was so effective or ineffective? If an engineer was described as being adaptable, analytical, and/or creative, the question was asked as to what the individual did that led the observer to that conclusion. In short, what was the observable behavior? Descriptions of traits or attitudes had to be documented in terms of overt action.

3. How is this incident an example of effective or ineffective behavior? This question is analogous to saying in a diplomatic way, "So what? Tell me what this has to do with job effectiveness."

All incidents that described the same behavior were categorized together to form one behavioral item. Each behavioral item consisted of a statement that described the incidents that formed it. Behavioral items that were similar were grouped to form an overall performance criterion for evaluating engineers and scientists. For example, two incidents describing a scientist's development of a detailed procedure for conducting an experiment formed the behavioral item: "Develops a detailed project plan prior to initiating a project": Almost Never 0 1 2 3 4 Almost Always. This item, along with similar items (e.g., prepares talk prior to the meeting) formed the performance criterion labeled "Planning and Scheduling."

The critical incidents revealed that the effective engineer or scientist in this particular organization is an individual who is good at planning, problem solving, interacting with others, communicating, and maintaining objectivity. Examples of behavioral items within each of these criteria are: develops a plan for structuring a project, seeks out pertinent literature relevant to current work, simplifies projects and reduces costs where feasible, coordinates own work schedule with others, communicates in terms the listener can understand, and recognizes own limitations in areas outside own expertise.

Ineffective engineers or scientists are individuals who frequently get involved in tangential issues or personal interests at the expense of the major objectives of an assignment, do not keep others informed of their activities, insist on doing everything themselves, verbally offend others by consistently pointing out shortcomings rather than solutions, are not concerned with the economic feasibility of a project, do not acknowledge the efforts of others, and accept more assignments and responsibilities than one person can handle. The validity and reliability of BOS developed for engineers and scientists were determined in accordance with the procedures described in Chapter 3.

LIMITATIONS AND ADVANTAGES

A limitation of this approach to defining excellence is that the data collection and analysis are time consuming. Three weeks elapsed before the behavioral criteria were developed. The following advantages, however, more than offset this limitation.

1. Behavioral observation scales (BOS) can be tailor made for the people who will use the appraisal instrument. The appraisal instrument is not based on the opinions, no matter how expert, of outsiders. This alone facilitates commitment to, and understanding of, these performance measures by the people who use them.

2. This approach to measuring excellence provides a comprehensive picture of the key aspects of the engineer's and scientist's job. The result is that the R & D manager is required to focus on all aspects of the job that are critical to job success, rather than only on one or two areas in which the manager may have a personal interest.

3. The emphasis in the performance appraisal is on observable behavior for which an engineer or scientist can be held accountable. Traits and personality variables such as imagination, insightfulness, and loyalty are replaced by overt actions that have been documented by the engineers and scientists themselves as making the difference between success and failure in accomplishing the key aspects of their jobs.

Nevertheless, several members on the task force argued initially that behavioral measures lack the specificity of performance outcomes such as number of trees cut, words typed, or widgets produced. However, in analyzing the jobs performed by engineers/scientists, it became clear to all members of the task force that engineers/scientists produce many different types of outcomes (e.g., designing equipment or developing a new type of tree species). To make comparisons across such outcomes would have been analogous to comparing apples and oranges. When the behavior of engineers/scientists was analyzed, there was great similarity in the behavioral requirements of their different jobs. This similarity was inferred from two sources. First, our content validation procedures (see Chapter 3) showed that these behaviors were comprehensive (Latham & Mitchell, 1976). Second, the appraisal instrument contained behaviors similar to those on behavioral checklists developed for engineers/scientists in other settings (Flanagan, Lange, O'Hagan, & Weislogal, 1949; Landy & Guion, 1970). Thus, the construct validity (see Chapter 3) of the criteria appeared satisfactory.

So, although the outcomes produced by these engineers/scientists were different, the behaviors they emitted were similar. Therefore, from a theoretical and a methodological standpoint, behavioral criteria seemed appropriate. A serious limitation of these behaviorally based performance appraisals is that their effectiveness was dependent upon the objectivity of the manager who did the appraising. To the degree that this person's observations were biased, distorted, or inaccurate, the effectiveness of the performance appraisal for stimulating the productivity of an employee was weakened. For this reason, the managers of the engineers and scientists received training (see Chapter 5) on ways to minimize rating errors when observing and evaluating others.

EMPLOYEE MOTIVATION

The task force was finally in a position to consider the problem of motivation. They now knew what they wanted the engineers and scientists to do. However, they did not know *how* to go about getting the engineers and scientists to do it. One member of the task force pointed out the company's success in applying *goal setting* in several facilities involving line personnel. The task force agreed that goal setting would be appropriate, but agreement could not be reached on how the goals should be set. In reaching agreement, classical and modern organizational theories of management were reviewed.

WHO SHOULD SET GOALS?

Classical organization theory, as espoused by Frederick W. Taylor (1947), states that workers desire security, and dislike job freedom, responsibility, and decision making. Moreover, individuals dislike work and therefore must be closely supervised. A major function of supervision is to set objectives or goals for workers, and to closely supervise them to insure that these goals are attained. Since, according to this theory, employees are motivated primarily by economic needs, monetary incentives should be given to encourage goal acceptance.

The assumptions of modern organization theories, as summarized by Likert (1967), are the antithesis of the above. These theories argue that (1) workers should have responsibility in decisions that affect their performance, (2) employees should participate in setting their own goals, and (3) subordinates are motivated primarily by challenging goals. The key role of a supervisor is to provide supportive leadership and employee counseling to encourage the attainment of those goals. Money is not necessary to bring about goal acceptance.

The task force was divided as to whether assigned or participative goal setting should be implemented. Some people argued that participative decision making was necessary for employee commitment and understanding of the goals. Others argued that assigned goal setting was the norm in the company, and that such goals would insure that the employees work in the correct areas. Still other task force members believed that no goal setting was necessary. These people felt that the primary value of BOS was that they served as an excellent communication vehicle between the manager and the employee. They argued that the BOS served as rules or guidelines of acceptable conduct, and that the engineer and scientist should strive to attain a perfect score. Therefore, the setting of specific goals was not necessary.

There was no way to resolve these arguments on the basis of intuition. Therefore, an experiment was proposed whereby the effects of assigned, participative, and do-your-best goal setting could be systematically compared.

The task force discussed what would be a suitable reward system for recognizing excellence. Several members of the task force argued convincingly that managerial praise by itself should be sufficient to maintain high performance levels.

There is considerable psychological evidence to support this point of view. However, blanket praise which in essence informs an employee that he or she is doing a great job may increase job satisfaction, but it has little impact on job performance because it does not reinforce *specific* job behavior. In fact, blanket praise may have an undesirable effect in that it reinforces *all* behavior. That is, it reinforces those things that the employee is excelling in as well as those things done in a mediocre way. Praise that is made contingent upon a *specific* behavior, however, can be a powerful reinforcer in increasing the frequency with which the employee engages in that behavior. Thus, it was decided that managers should be taught to look for those things that the engineer or scientist is doing well, and comment favorably to the individual about them.

Other members of the task force recalled the desire and competition that engineers and scientists exhibited in trying to be among those who participated in the company's television commercials. They believed that public recognition motivates engineers and scientists. They felt that citing an engineer's or scientist's name in the R & D newsletter for attaining excellence would be perceived by them as highly rewarding.

The remaining members of the task force felt strongly that only a monetary bonus would motivate employees. Other individuals argued that engineers and scientists were professionals who, given an adequate salary, were sufficiently motivated by the work itself. Their argument was that a bonus was simply not necessary.

A decision was reached to test everyone's theories and biases empirically. The task force was beginning to realize that there is no substitute for systematic measurement, particularly regarding human resource problems.

WHAT REWARDS ARE VALUED?

Consequently, the engineers and scientists were interviewed to identify outcomes they would value as rewards for doing a good job. From information obtained in the interviews, a 31-item questionnaire was developed. The 242 engineers and scientists then completed the questionnaire by rating each item on a 5-point scale from "not at all important" to "very important." The results indicated that the five most valued rewards were (1) seeing one's work applied, (2) receiving a salary increase, (3) having one's work put to commercial use, (4) praise from a supervisor, and (5) a monetary bonus. The correlation between the rating of the engineers and scientists was .97. The correlation between the ratings of younger (age 21 to 40) and older engineers and scientists was also .97. These correlations indicate that there were little or no differences in the rewards that are valued between younger versus older engineers and scientists.

The task force was in a quandary about how to treat these data. For one thing, several people in higher management were indeed surprised with the importance these high-level employees attached to money. However, everyone on the task force agreed that the three rewards that would be the easiest to use from an administrative standpoint were managerial praise, public recognition, and a monetary bonus. Thus, the following experimental design shown in Table 8.1 was implemented to test the effectiveness of the different rewards and approaches to goal setting.

The motivation experiment was conducted as follows. Thirty-eight managers were asked to rate each engineer and scientist who reported to them on the BOS. As previously noted, each behavioral item on the BOS had a 0–4 scale underneath it whereby the rater indicated the frequency with which an engineer/scientist had been observed demonstrating each behavior. Excellence was defined by the task force as a score of 165 out of 185 possible points.

EVALUATING GOAL-SETTING TECHNIQUES

The managers were randomly assigned to one of the nine conditions, as shown in Table 8.1. It was noted, however, that the do-your-best groups (7, 8, and 9 in Table 8.1) might implicitly set their own goals because they knew that their peers in the other 6 groups were setting goals. Moreover, because the task force had decided that a score of 165 out of 185 points on the BOS constituted excellence, the possibility existed that

TABLE 8.1

	Assigned Goals	Participative Goals	Do your Best
Praise 、	1	4	7
Public Recognition	2	5	8
Monetary Bonus	3	6	9

engineers and scientists who fell in groups 7, 8, and 9 might feel that they should try to attain 165 points. The fact that these engineers and scientists would know that they were in an experiment, and that their behavior would be compared to others could have induced them to set a specific goal, and the goal could explain why their behavior changed during the course of the experiment. Consequently, it was decided that a tenth condition should be added to the project. Individuals in this group constituted a true control group in that they did not know they were in the experiment, they did not know they were being evaluated on the BOS, they did not receive any goals, and they did not receive any feedback or rewards for doing well on the BOS.*

Members of the task force met with each of four R & D Directors and the people who reported to them to explain all facets of the experiment. In brief, it was explained that the project would be run as follows: Managers in cells 1, 2, and 3 were to evaluate their subordinates using the behavioral observation scales, and then *assign* them goals that they, the managers, felt were difficult but attainable. A typical performance appraisal was as follows:

I have evaluated you on these behavioral items on the BOS, Pat. As you know, this instrument was developed from the input that we received from you and your peers. You are doing very well in the following areas . . . . Over the next six months, I would like you to work on these specific behaviors. . . . You presently have a total score of _____ . I would like to see you work toward a goal of _____ points by the time we have the next appraisal six months from now.

Note that the supervisor was instructed to make the praise specific to the key behaviors that the engineer or scientist was demonstrating effectively. Note also that the manager's emphasis was on the individual's strengths; weaknesses were discussed in terms of goals to work on. Criticism,

---

*The value of a control group is that it is treated exactly the same way as the groups in the experiment with one exception—it does not receive the experimental treatment. In this study, the experimental treatment consisted of goal setting and rewards. If there was any change in employee behavior in the experimental groups different from that of the control group, the task force could conclude that it was due to the goal setting and/or the rewards. The control group "controlled" for other possible explanations because anything else of consequence in the experimental groups was also present in the control group.

such as, "Pat, you have to do better on these specific areas. . . . I am really becoming exasperated with you" was minimized. This is because giving criticism during a performance appraisal can actually *reduce* performance to a level lower than it was prior to the appraisal. Moreover, the employee's performance may remain at the lower level for several months subsequent to the criticism (Kay et al., 1965). This negative effects seems to occur regardless of the order in which the criticism is presented (Hillery & Wexley, 1974). That is, whether the criticism is presented before or after the praise, or sandwiched in between, it still lowers performance.

In instances where criticism could not be avoided, the managers were instructed to shoulder as much of the blame as possible for an employee's low rating, to minimize employee defensiveness. The following quote illustrates the approach taken by the managers:

> *Pat, I am not saying that you don't engage in these behaviors; I am simply saying that I haven't seen you demonstrate them. Over the next six months I would like you to do . . . to make certain that I will see you engage in them.* *

In this way, employees were not put on the defensive as to why they didn't demonstrate specific behaviors in the past. The discussion centered on the future. Thus, employees were aware of the items on which they would be evaluated, and could make a conscious choice as to whether they wanted to do the things necessary to satisfy those requirements during the next six months.

Each of the three groups of engineers and scientists who were assigned goals (groups 1, 2, and 3) differed with respect to the rewards that they were told they could anticipate receiving if they scored at least 165 points on the BOS. Individuals in group 1 were told that they would receive verbal praise and appreciation from their boss for doing well. Individuals in group 2 were told that their name would be publically cited in the R & D newsletter for attaining the standard of excellence. Group 3 individuals were told that they would receive a bonus ranging from 3.5 percent to 9 percent of their annual salary, with the actual amount depending on

---

*Where an employee's low rating was not due to the failure to engage in specific behaviors, but rather for engaging in inappropriate behaviors, the manager followed the learning points discussed in Chapter 7 for correcting poor work habits.

the person's current salary level and the number of points earned above 165. To minimize possible feelings of inequity between employees who were and were not eligible for a monetary bonus, it was stressed that they had been randomly assigned to the three reward conditions, that this was an experiment only, and that as soon as a valid conclusion could be drawn regarding the effectiveness of the three reward systems, all employees would be eligible for the same reward. The concern that employees in the praise and public recognition groups would deliberately perform worse than those in the monetary group to insure that this reward would ultimately be chosen was discounted for three reasons. First, there was no evidence that money was "the" reward that was valued to the exclusion of the other two rewards. Second, the daily task requirements were such that it was believed that no one would jeopardize their job security by lowering their performance so that a monetary reward system would ultimately be implemented. Third, the engineers and scientists were already well paid.

Engineers and scientists who participated in the setting of their goals (groups 4, 5, and 6) were given the following instructions:

"I would like you to evaluate yourself on this BOS that was developed from the input that we got from you and your peers. I am going to fill it out on you, too. Let's get together in about a week and discuss areas of agreement and disagreement, and settle on a score that you would like to aim for as a goal over the next six months."

At this subsequent meeting, the manager and the subordinate *together* decided on the goals that the employee should work toward attaining. The individuals in each of these three groups (4, 5, and 6) were then informed of the rewards that could be anticipated if a score of 165 or higher was achieved.

The supervisors of the engineers and scientists in the do-best condition (7, 8, and 9) provided feedback as to the scores received on all aspects of the BOS. At the end of the appraisal, subordinates were urged to "keep up the good work" if they had done well, and to "really try to do better next time" if this were not true. No goals were assigned or set participatively. However, the employees in these three groups were told exactly where they had done well, where improvement was believed possible, and what reward they could expect if they received a score of 165 or higher on the BOS.

As previously mentioned, the employees in the control group (group 10) did not know they were being evaluated on the BOS nor did they receive feedback from their manager as to how they scored on the BOS. In fact, they did not even know that they were participating in a research project. This was possible because the people who participated in the experiment had been randomly selected from the organization. The individuals in the control group knew that the experiment was taking place, but they did not know about the existence of a control group or about their participation in the group. They assumed that they had not been selected for involvement in the study.

CHECKING THE TWO GOAL-SETTING CONDITIONS

Within a month after the initial appraisal, and five months before the second appraisal in which the rewards were to be dispensed, the employees were asked to respond to two questions using a 5-point scale: (1) "How much influence did you have over the overall goal that was set?" (2) "Compared to your supervisor, how much influence did you have over the overall goal that was set?" These questions were asked in order to learn whether the managers were truly setting goals according to the instructions. (That is, were the managers in the participative condition truly allowing the subordinates to have a say in the goal-setting process?

The data analysis indicated that the managers did an outstanding job in making this study a success. The employees in the participative condition reported significantly more influence over the goals that were set than the employees in the assigned condition. Similarly, the engineers and scientists in the participative condition reported that they had significantly more influence than their supervisors in setting the goals than did the employees in the assigned condition. Moreover, the answers to these questions were not affected by the different rewards that the engineers and scientists were told they could receive.

Goal difficulty was assessed in two ways. First, engineers and scientists were asked to report the specific score (goal) that they were trying to attain on the BOS. Second, each individual was asked to indicate on a 5-point scale how difficult it would be to attain the goal. The former measure assessed the *actual* difficulty of the goals, while the latter measured the employee's perception of the goal's difficulty.

The results showed that engineers and scientists in the participative goal-setting condition set significantly higher goals than the individuals in the assigned goal condition. Nevertheless, despite the fact that the individuals in the participative condition actually set higher goals than those in the assigned condition, they did not perceive it as being more difficult. In short, they set more difficult goals yet felt that they could attain them.

These results suggest that the primary importance of participation in goal setting with engineers and scientists appears to be that it leads to the setting of very difficult goals. When one group of individuals was assigned the goal that was set participatively by individuals in another group, there was no difference in goal attainment, goal acceptance, or performance between the two groups. That participation affects goal difficulty, of course, is of theoretical as well as practical importance since goal setting theory suggests that the higher the goals, the higher the performance. It is interesting to note once again, however, that even though the goals were actually higher in the participative condition, the perceptions of goal difficulty were not significantly different between this group and the groups whose goals were assigned to them.

Goal acceptance was designed in terms of an employee's own determination to attain the goal. The engineers and scientists were asked to respond on a 5-point scale to the question, "How committed are you to attaining your goal?" No significant differences were found among the different conditions. All six groups were between "moderately committed" and "very committed" to attaining their goals.

The two *satisfaction* questions were as follows: (1) "Intrinsic satisfaction means pleasure from successfully accomplishing a task or achieving a challenging goal. Regardless of whether you may receive private recognition, public recognition, or a monetary bonus, how much intrinsic satisfaction do you think you will derive if you attain your goal?", and, (2) "How awkward, embarrassed, or aggravated did you feel during the performance appraisal?" No significant differences were found among the nine groups in terms of satisfaction. Moreover, all six groups indicated that they felt little or no "awkwardness, embarrassment, or aggravation."

Instrumentality refers to the likelihood that a person believes that a particular behavior will lead to a desirable outcome. To assess instrumentality the following question was asked: "Consider the likelihood of favorable or unfavorable consequences of goal attainment in terms of your own job security, future pay incrreases or promotions, coworker respect, etc. In general, how advantageous do you think it will be for you to attain the goal?"

Relevance was assessed by asking: "How useful was the performance appraisal for counseling and development purposes—that is, for discussing your strengths and clarifying areas for improvement?"

Also asked was: "How important do you feel that doing well on the behavioral criteria is to accomplishing the projects that are assigned to you?" The responses to these questions revealed that participation in goal setting had no effect on satisfaction, relevance, or instrumentality. In all cases the employees felt that this approach to performance appraisal was a good one regardless of whether they had been assigned goals or had participated in the goal-setting process.

The practical significance of the results of this study was its demonstration that employee participation may well lead to an upgrading of performance goals. The initial fear expressed by some managers that engineers and scientists might abuse a system that permits participation in setting goals proved groundless. Employee participation led to the setting of higher goals than those that occurred when this responsibility was left solely in the hands of the manager.

FACTORS THAT INCREASED PERFORMANCE

With regard to performance, there was a significant relationship between actual goal difficulty and performance. That is, the more difficult the goal, the higher the performance. Also, the setting of a specific goal, whether assigned or participative, led to the higher performance than either urging people to "do their best" or setting no goal at all. Written comments from the employees who received goals said, in effect, that: "Specific goals encouraged us to develop action plans for translating effort into successful performance." Several individuals in the assigned goal condition wrote that, "receiving a specific goal enabled me to determine for the first time in 15 years what was really expected from me." Moreover, they indicated little anticipated difficulty in meeting the goal that their supervisor was communicating to them in specifics.

An interesting finding of this program was that feedback appears to affect performance only if it is used to set specific goals. Knowledge of results in and of itself did not affect performance, which is exactly what goal-setting theory states. The performance of the engineers and scientists in the do-your-best condition was not significantly higher than that of the group of individuals who did not even know they were in an experiment. This is surprising because the do-your-best groups knew they were in an experiment, that their performance would be compared with employees in the goal-setting groups, that they had to achieve a score of at least 165 to attain the standard of excellence, and that they would receive a specific reward if they attained excellence. Nevertheless, their performance was not significantly better than those individuals who received no feedback at all.

With regard to rewards, the rank ordering in terms of impact on performance was: (1) money, (2) praise, and (3) public recognition. However, the increase in performance due to the money over praise was so small as to be practically insignificant. Thus, from a cost/benefit viewpoint, it is most effective to give praise.* It should be noted, however, that while the rewards did increase performance, the largest performance increases were due to the goals set rather than the rewards that were administered.

CLOSING REMARKS

Participation led to higher goals being set than was the case when the manager unilaterally assigned goals to the worker. Moreover, there was a positive relationship between goal difficulty and performance. Only participative goal setting led to performance increases that were significantly different from those in the do-your-best and control groups. Thus it appears that participation is important to the extent that it influences goal difficulty and hence performance, but goal acceptance can be obtained as easily through assigned as through participatively set goals.

---

*That money was not appreciably more effective than praise in increasing performance may have been due to the fact that money was not given immediately after the employee demonstrated desirable behavior (see Chapter 6 for the importance of tying money directly to performance). It would have been exceedingly difficult to do so from an adminstrative standpoint. However, it should be noted that subsequent interviews with the employees revealed that neither was praise given immediately after desirable behavior occurred. Making praise an immediate outcome of performance is not difficult. If praise had been an immediate outcome of performance it is likely that it would have had a far greater impact on performance than the way money was administered in this study.

So where does all this leave us? In general, the results support participative goal setting. However, if manager know their workers really well, they probably want to take into account individual differences. For example, if a manager has employees who become upset at having goals set for them, participative goal setting should obviously be used. If, on the other hand, certain employees can't make a decision without checking with you first, assign them goals. It's not as important how goals are set, as it is that goals are in fact *set*. After the goals are set, the employee should be praised for the specific things that are being performed well. For far too long managers have clung to the outmoded philosophy, "If you don't hear from me, you can assume you are doing well; if you foul up, you'll hear from me." *Tying goal setting and praise to specific job behaviors is a straightforward method for increasing the motivation level and performance of employees. It is an approach to performance appraisal that works.*

SUMMARY

The senior vice-president of R & D persuaded the president that a more effective approach than laying off employees during an economic recession is to define excellence and motivate employees to attain it. Excellence was defined explicitly in terms of behavioral criteria or standards. Raters received training on ways to minimize rating errors. In addition, they were taught how to assign specific goals, to participate with the employee in specifying goals, or to encourage the employee to "do one's best."

The emphasis in the performance appraisal feedback sessions was on the individual's strengths. Weaknesses were discussed in terms of goals to work on. In this way, employees were not put on the defensive about why they hadn't demonstrated specific behaviors in the past. The discussion was on the future.

High performance was rewarded by praise, public recognition, or a monetary bonus. From a cost/benefit standpoint praise proved to be most effective in increasing performance; public recognition was the least effective. However, the greatest impact on performance was employee participation in setting specific goals. Giving people explicit feedback without setting goals was no more effective than giving them no feedback at all.

Implementing and Maintaining the New Appraisal System

9

How do managers go about implementing the appraisal system discussed in Chapters 2 through 5? Once the system has been developed, what should they look for in determining whether the appraisal process discussed in Chapters 6 through 8 is functioning correctly? Why is it that beneficial programs are sometimes discontinued by people who operate in most areas in a rational manner? What is it about certain programs that cause them to fade away? Conversely, what are the characteristics of those programs that remain healthy and vital? In this chapter, we discuss essential components for bringing about and maintaining a successful performance appraisal system and process. These components are based upon our experiences in implementing the performance appraisal system/process described in the preceding chapters.

IMPLEMENTATION

Unless an organization is knowledgeable of the laws pertaining to performance appraisal we have seldom attempted to implement the appraisal system/process discussed in this book in one grand step. This is because most managers do not see the resolution of human resource problems in terms of effective appraisal procedures. They view the appraisal system in terms of one side of a sheet of paper containing organizationally blessed "buzz words" such as ability, self-starter, gets along well with others, empathy, supervisory skills, and organizes well. They believe the appraisal process consists of a 30 to 45 minute conversation once a year where the manager talks to the employee in general terms about how the employee is performing in relation to these buzz words. The buzz words have generally been defined in one or two sentences by the Personnel Department.

Rather then convincing the manager about the faults of this approach, we have taken a problem-oriented approach and implemented the concepts discussed in this book on a one-step-at-a-time basis without mentioning the word "appraisal." What we have done is capitalize on the word "do" and its variations (doing, did, done, does).

For example, in one situation management wanted to know what it is that one group of loggers *does* that enables them to "walk on water" while a second group is in danger of sinking at any moment. To answer that question, a job analysis (CIT) was conducted to identify the critical job behaviors of loggers. BOS were then developed from the job analysis. We then suggested that management officials be trained, according to the procedures discussed in Chapter 5, to identify these critical behaviors when they are observing loggers on the job. In this way, decisions regarding the signing of contracts and the financing of equipment would be based on performance rather than personalities. Shortly after this training was completed, management asked what could be *done* to improve the job performance of loggers, or how to get them to *do* the key things identified in the job analysis as critical for effective job performance. We then recommended goal setting and the supervisory training discussed in Chapters 6 and 7.

In a second case, the purchasing director observed that her departmental managers were not *doing* their jobs correctly. She wanted to know what could be *done* to get them to work together as a team. Interviews with the individual managers and a representative sampling of their subordinates revealed that the purchasing director had observed a valid problem. A job analysis (CIT) was conducted. All the managers and a representative sampling of subordinates developed BOS. The managers (peers) rated one another anonymously on the extent to which they perceived one another engaging in the behaviors that they as a group reported in the job analysis were critical to one another's success. Team building sessions (see Chapter 6) were then held. The group brainstormed things that each could do in the future to demonstrate the behaviors listed on the BOS in a timely, appropriate manner. Specific behavioral goals were then set.

In a third situation, management was upset with the quality of people who were being hired. We responded with the training program described in Chapter 5 to increase observer skills in recording objectively what was seen. The program emphasizes the need for defining explicitly the key behaviors critical to performing the job effectively prior to conducting an interview. As a result of the training, BOS were developed in the organization. Managers were taught to set goals with the employees on the BOS.

In a fourth situation, management wanted a human relations course for their first-line supervisors because of union-management difficulties. We administered the training program described in Chapter 7. They then wanted a way of determining whether the supervisors were applying *(doing)* what had been taught during training to the job. BOS were developed as a means of assessing supervisory behavior on the job. Because management felt that the superintendents who would be using the BOS had preconceived opinions about individual foremen, the superintendents received the training described in Chapter 5 to minimize rating errors before completing the BOS.

In a fifth situation, management wanted to keep a plant nonunion. The employees were complaining of favoritism in promotion practices. We showed management the value of peer ratings. Management wanted to be certain that the peer ratings were based on what is really important or critical for employees to *do* in the plant consequently, job analysis was performed and BOS were developed. Goals were set in terms of BOS scores. To further reduce the possibility that the supervisors were doing inappropriate things on the job, the modeling training discussed in Chapter 7 was conducted for them.

In a sixth situation, one that we are confronted with frequently, management wanted to find ways of motivating their employees. We described in detail our response to this type of situation in Chapter 8. In brief, before managers can motivate employees, they must specify what it is the employees are supposed to *do* on the job. This specification involves a job analysis and the development of BOS. It is the process of feedback and goal setting that makes this system sustain or bring about high levels of productivity in terms of each individual doing what is critical for fulfilling job requirements.

GUIDELINES FOR ASSESSING THE EFFECTIVENESS
OF THE APPRAISAL PROCESS

Once the performance appraisal system is in place, the key to insuring its use is the performance appraisal process. If the process brings about and maintains high levels of performance, the probability that the system will be used again and again increases.

The critical aspects of the appraisal process, as distinct from the appraisal system, include goal setting, feedback, and allowing employees to participate in decisions that have direct bearing on them. Guidelines for assessing the effectiveness of the appraisal process, therefore, include the following:

1. The employee should be informed prior to the appraisal period what it is that will be appraised.

2. The employee should be informed of the date of the appraisal. The amount of thought and preparation subordinates spend, prior to the appraisal, analyzing their job responsibilities, problems encountered on the job, and the quality of their work correlates positively with improved performance. Thus, both parties should be equally prepared to conduct the appraisal.

3. The appraiser should create an open, supportive atmosphere at the beginning of the appraisal interview. It should be clear to the employee that the emphasis of the discussion is on counseling and development. Thus, the purpose of the appraisal is to help the employee. Threats/ hostility are generally not necessary. As we said in Chapter 1, it is a naive employee who believes that there will be no repercussions for failure to perform the job satisfactorily. To the extent that the supervisor is supportive, employee acceptance of the information that is provided in the appraisal increases.

4. Discussion should focus on identifying problems or obstacles that prevent the employee from performing the job in an optimum manner.

5. The employee and the supervisor should brainstorm ways in which problems or obstacles can be overcome. The solutions should be specific. Agreement should be reached as to who is going to do what by when.

6. The supervisor should continually paraphrase and summarize what was said to avoid the pitfall "you heard what I said, but not what I meant."

"You know where I think I went wrong? I never set target dates!"

Source: Reprinted by permission of Chicago Tribune-New York News Syndicate, Inc.

Figure 9.1

7. Specific goals should be set. The setting of specific goals to be achieved by the subordinate results in up to twice as much improvement in performance than does a discussion of broad general issues (see Fig. 9.1).

8. Criticisms of past performance should be kept to a minimum. The discussion should focus on what the employee is going to do in the future. The employee should have a clear idea of what actions to take to improve performance.

9. Where criticism cannot be avoided, discussion should focus on the problem(s) rather than personalities. Feedback should be clear and specific. The employee should be asked to generate ways of solving the problem.

10. At the end of the interview, a specific follow-up date should be set to determine the extent to which the employee's and/or supervisor's concerns have been eliminated, and progress has been made on the goals that have been set.

11. The evaluative aspect of the appraisal should never come as a surprise to the employee. The supervisor should make known on a daily basis what it is the employee is doing correctly. The demonstration of new behaviors should be praised and reinforced on a continuous basis; established behaviors should be reinforced on an intermittent (variable ratio) basis.

12. An employee whose reduction in grade or suspension/termination is proposed should receive in writing the specification of the critical elements of the employee's job involved in each instance of unacceptable performance. This step should be taken after counseling, a verbal warning, and a written warning have failed to bring about acceptable work behavior.

13. If the employee perceives that the action is unjustified, the employee should be allowed to respond to the action orally and/or in writing. A panel of three "disinterested" members of management should review the proposed action. This recommendation may be perceived as cumbersome by some readers, but this process has kept employees of many companies from feeling the need to join a union.

14. A questionnaire should be developed for subordinates to complete anonymously on the extent to which supervisors are satisfying these guidelines. In addition, questions should be asked concerning the relevancy and comprehensiveness of the BOS. To the extent that changes occur in technology, work flow, or knowledge the BOS may need to be revised.

MAINTAINING THE PERFORMANCE APPRAISAL

In most organizations where we have worked where the appraisal *process* has been executed effectively, the appraisal *system* has survived. However, this has not always been the case.

Based on a review of what has occurred across twelve organizations using different human resource systems to enhance productivity, Hinrichs (1978b) identified several factors associated with the staying power as well as those factors that seemed to be associated with the discontinuation of programs that were in fact of value for the organization in increasing or maintaining high levels of productivity. Because his conclusions are similar to those we have reached based on our own experiences, we have integrated them below.

1. Where the performance appraisal system/process has been successful over the long term, there is an understanding among managers that different measures of productivity are used in different situations. In the area of human resources, productivity is measured appropriately in terms of the frequency with which people exhibit the behavior critical to performing their job successfully.* Critical job behaviors are those that affect the bottom line. Output/input measures and safe work environments do not come about through osmosis. Someone must do something to bring about maximum output with minimum input. It is that measure of "do something" that is critical to accurately measuring the productivity or efficiency of the individual employee. This measure should be based on a detailed job analysis resulting in the development of content valid behavioral observation scales (BOS) for performance appraisal purposes.

2. There must be a significant level of senior management support for the appraisal system/process as opposed to passive toleration. Such support is essential as an umbrella under which new norms and expectations can flourish without the constant pressures to revert to the more comfortable and known ways of operating. Active senior management support is necessary for insuring a high level of commitment by middle managers for the system.

A key reason for the failure of a performance appraisal system/process

---

*Technically, the word productive should be substituted here for the word productivity. Productivity is defined traditionally as output/input. Thus one way of defining productivity for an individual is behavior/effort. In some cases, we may be interested in measuring effort in terms of cost of training/motivational programs designed to impact effort. In most cases, we are interested simply in behavior frequency just as we are interested in machine rate or speed in evaluating the impact on production of a given machine.

is lack of middle management support once the system has been implemented. Middle managers can easily sabotage a human resource program. Thus, middle managers must be rewarded for participating in and supporting the various components of the appraisal process. This participation can most easily be insured by including behaviors on the BOS that are indicative of both objectively observing and rewarding the performance of employees, and stimulating them to increase or maintain a high level of performance. People generally do those things for which they receive recognition for their efforts. Middle managers are no exception. They must see conducting appraisals as critical to their role as managers, or they are not likely to expend much effort on feeding back the results of an appraisal.

3. A "critical mass" must be reached in order for a program to be sustained, or it faces extinction. The appraisal system must be diffused throughout a significant portion of the organization so as to become a way of life for employees. This is why the training on day-to-day appraisals was emphasized in Chapter 7.

The performance appraisal system/process must be installed on key fronts within an organization simultaneously, rather than implementing it in only one area. To maximize chances of success, a shotgun approach rather than a rifle shot should be attempted within the organization. Change has to spread throughout a significant segment of the organization, and be backed by the managers and employees if it is to remain implemented in the organization.

4. The initial strategy should be to go with the winners. That is, managers must be careful to insure that the system/process is implemented in several parts of the organization (i.e., shotgun) where there is a good chance of achieving positive results so that success can be demonstrated early. Once the concepts become widely accepted, it will be easier to tackle the more complex and resistant segments of the organization, because most managers derive reinforcement from the reinforcement of their employees. Nothing increases the credibility of a program more for managers than hearing traditionally skeptical first-line supervisors deriving job satisfaction and economic returns for themselves and the company. Satisfied supervisors and their superintendents have been the major factor in gaining additional management commitment and support for the appraisal system/process described in this book.

5. The implementation of the appraisal system/process should be reviewed quarterly with the vice presidents of both operations and human resources. A major topic of each meeting should be the cooperation and active efforts exerted by the managers reporting to them in making the system a way of life with the people they supervise. These managers should know that if they receive poor evaluations in fulfilling this objective, they run the risk of a transfer, demotion, or, in some cases, termination. This evaluation should be based solely on their job performance in implementing the system rather than their questioning or expressing concern about a particular phase of this approach. In other words, discussion and dissent should be encouraged; passive resistance and sabotage should not be tolerated.

6. There must be one group of people at corporate headquarters who has the charter to put the system in place, and to coordinate and schedule the different components of the system with the immediate needs of various segments of the company.

7. Each segment of the organization must be "seeded" with knowledgeable people to make this system work in their unit. These people serve not only as advocates for the program, but also as resources to whom middle managers can come for assistance when a problem in implementation is anticipated or experienced. In addition, these people, as well as those at corporate headquarters who are responsible for the implementation of the system, should provide every opportunity for the line managers to claim and achieve recognition for the success for the implementation phase. The major responsibility for presenting midproject and final project status reports to a senior manager should be given to them. For example, the consultant to the project may give a broad introduction, outlining the program activities to date, but the responsibility for reporting the data on the project results should be given to the line managers. This is a highly reinforcing activity for most people because it allows them an opportrinity to gain recognition and a feeling of accomplishment. Equally important, this reporting process enables them to identify the appraisal system as their own, and thus increases their commitment to the ongoing success of the process. An added benefit is the respect gained by the corporate and regional consultant who, rather than being resented for the assumption of expertise and credit, is appreciated for establishing the means for them obtaining a sense of recognition, achievement, and responsibility.

Finally, it is important that the corporate and regional experts be aware of current management philosophies regarding human resource management. We have continually been confronted by managers who have been exposed to transactional analysis, sensitivity training, and other psychology fads. From personal and somewhat painful experience, we can state that consultants will have a higher probability of success if they do not challenge the commitment made by managers to these philosophies. Argument against one approach in favor of another produces resentment. It is far wiser to explain the points of unity and agreement among the various approaches.

8. The most lasting performance appraisal systems are those that are based on job analyses, conform to legal requirements, involve the training of multiple raters, and require goal setting, feedback, and reinforcement for effective employee behavior on a frequent basis.

9. Because most managers show a strong preference for live, current information (as opposed to looking backward), and dislike a routine that is highly structured (Mintzberg, 1973), managers should be trained and reinforced for engaging in informal daily appraisals. Furthermore, virtually all appraisal systems result in a need for managerial action regarding highly effective/ineffective subordinates. Since promotions, demotions, salary increases, and bonus systems are seldom at the discretion of the manager (e.g., there may not be any positions open, the manager may not be informed about available slots, decisions on demotions, salaries, and bonuses may be made by a higher level manager) it is imperative that the manager be trained in the application of reinforcement and goal-setting procedures described in Chapters 6 and 7. Both goal setting and feedback can bring about dramatic improvements in performance, which in turn reinforce the appraiser to continue providing feedback and setting goals with employees.

CLOSING REMARKS

In a thoughtful essay, McCall and DeVries (1976) paint a pessimistic future for performance appraisal. They believe that the movement toward objective measurement in performance appraisal, the use of multiple raters, in-depth training of raters, feedback, and setting goals represent an improvement over traditional approaches to appraisal. Still, they argue that these improvements may not be sufficient to overcome those contextual factors in organizations that reduce the effectiveness of performance appraisals. They believe that the nature of managerial work as described by Mintzberg (1973), as well as organizational characteristics, and environmental demands frequently clash with the internal structure of appraisal procedures.

Managerial work is characterized by variety, brevity, and fragmentation according to Mintzberg. The majority of a manager's contacts are ad hoc rather than preplanned. Managers frequently show a strong preference for live, current information. Moreover, Mintzberg found that many managers dislike looking backward or forward.

To the extent that this is true, performance appraisals can clash with managerial preferences because performance appraisal focuses on past performance. It can represent a routine activity that is highly structured, which is especially true where BOS are used every three months or every twelve months. To minimize this clash we emphasize the need for supervisory training described in Chapter 7. This training focuses on dealing with live, current information on a daily basis (e.g., handling complaints, overcoming resistance to change, giving recognition). It emphasizes informal appraisal skills that managers need and appreciate in order to function effectively on the job. It is an essential supplement to the formal appraisal.

Organizational characteristics that can clash with appraisal procedures include managerial philosophies and the extent to which rewards correlate with performance. McCall and DeVries state that participation in setting goals is effective only when it is part of a general managerial philosophy of democracy, or delegation that encourages day-to-day subordinate inputs. If such an atmosphere exists, they argue that the appraisal review for goal setting is redundant. If such an atmosphere does not exist, its utility is said to be marginal. We have shown in Chapter 6 that goal setting can lead to significant increases in performance regardless of whether the goals are assigned or participatively set. The critical factor is that the supervisors behave in a supportive manner.

Second, McCall and DeVries correctly point out that few organizations, when administering merit pay systems, directly reinforce the appropriate conducting of appraisals. Further, because performing appraisals is seldom defined in organizations as critical to fulfilling the managerial role, managers are unlikely to expend much effort on appraisal. Overcoming this problem is straightforward. Higher management must emphasize the importance of performance appraisals to subordinates through examples and rewards.

Environmental demands affecting performance appraisals include the legal requirements reviewed in Chapter 2. The court decisions are largely in agreement with industrial psychology. Appraisal decision should be reliable and valid. The approach we have outlined in this book satisfy these requirements. Thus, these demands should be viewed as aids rather than constraints for performance appraisal.

We believe that the clash between performance appraisals and organizational realities can be minimized if the following suggestions are considered:

1. The appraisal should be designed by a representative sample of the people who will conduct, and feed back as well as receive the results of appraisals. This recommendation is in agreement with the 1978 Civil Service Reform Act.

2. Just as a good photographer does not use one camera for all shots, a good manager knows that one appraisal instrument is not necessarily applicable for all jobs (e.g., line versus staff managers). Several BOS most likely will be necessary for feeding back information to people in widely different jobs. However, we are against using one appraisal procedure for administrative purposes (e.g., promotion, pay) and another procedure for feedback and development. Advising managers that no documentation of the latter is necessary, that information concerning the latter can be kept confidential between the supervisor and the employee only invites litigation problems if appraisal decisions are challenged by a dissatisfied employee (see Chapter 2).

3. The appraisal information must be rich in feedback so that employees obtain a true picture of how well they are performing job responsibilities. BOS that are content valid in the sense that they include a representative sampling of behaviors that are critical to performing the job satisfactorily are essential here. BOS that are completed anonymously by peers and are fed back to the employee by a supervisor are highly desirable for providing rich feedback. The combination of feedback and the setting of specific goals brings about and maintains high productivity at the level of the individual employee.

SUMMARY

Unless an organization is knowledgeable of the laws pertaining to performance appraisal, a problem oriented approach is likely to be most effective in getting the concepts and procedures discussed in this book accepted by management. That is, the procedures should be implemented to solve a specific problem of concern to management rather than sold to them on the need for a new approach to performance appraisal.

Once the appraisal system has been developed, a questionnaire should be designed for employees to complete anonymously as to their perceptions of the effectiveness with which their superiors are implementing the process. The questionnaire should focus on such things as the extent to which the supervisor is supportive of the employee, feedback is explicit, and specific goals are set.

In order to maintain an appraisal system, there must be a significant level of senior management support, middle management must be rewarded for participating in and supporting the process, the system/process must be installed on key fronts within an organization, and there must be people at corporate headquarters and in the regions with the responsibility of "making the system work."

Despite these efforts, the nature of managerial work, organizational characteristics, and environmental demands frequently clash with performance appraisal systems to reduce the effectiveness of the process. This clash can be minimized to the extent that (1) the appraisal system is designed by a representative sample of people who will use the appraisal, (2) BOS are developed for individual jobs or job families, and (3) the appraisal process is rich in feedback for the appraiser–appraisee. If a representative sample of people design the appraisal system, the system is likely to be understood and accepted by the organization. In addition, if BOS are developed for individual jobs or job families, the system will be relevant to the jobs in question. Finally, if the appraisal process emphasizes two-way communication between the appraiser–appraisee, appraisee satisfaction with the appraisal and, more importantly, the desire to demonstrate consistently those behaviors critical to fulfilling job requirements is increased.

Appendix A:
Behavioral Observation Scales Used by a Bowling Lane Corporation

HEAD OFFICE:
4 PINE STREET EXTENSION
DARTMOUTH, N. S., B2Y 2W8
PHONE (902) 469-3365
Owned and Operated by
A. W. Peters Enterprises Limited

BEAZLEY BOWLING LANES
EMPLOYEE DEVELOPMENT CHECKLIST

This checklist has been developed from input received from employees for employee counselling and development. In this way applicants are given a job preview to enable them to see what would be expected of them should they accept a position with Beazley Bowling Lanes. Applicants who believe they could and would meet these job requirements are advised to accept a job with Beazley's.

A second and equally important function of this checklist is that it allows management and employees alike to know what is expected of them and to provide feedback to one another as to areas where they are doing well and areas where improvement is needed. This information is provided a minimum of three times a year. This is done because performance feedback is critical for maintaining employee growth, motivation (goal setting), and job satisfaction.

It is our belief that Beazley employees are adults rather than children. We talk *with* our people rather than *to* them. Communication is a two-way process. For this reason feedback will be provided to employees by management *and* their coworkers; and management will receive feedback from employees by management. In some cases customers will be asked to complete this form. To insure frank, honest feedback, you are asked to complete this form anonymously on the following people:

Do not sign your name. Simply put this form in an envelope, seal it, and leave it in the box in front at my office by (date).

In completing this form circle a 1 if the employee has engaged in a behaviour 0-64 percent of the time, a 2 if the employee has engaged in a behaviour 65-74 percent of the time, a 3 if the employee has engaged in a behaviour 75-84 percent of the time, a 4 for 85-94 percent of the time, a 5 for 95-100 percent of the time.

Your observations are to be based only on the person's behaviour during the past four months. I appreciate your willingness to help one another.

Allan Peters
President

Sir Fish
Restaurants

I. WAITER/WAITRESS

1. Comes to work on time

   Almost never   1   2   3   4   5   Almost always

2. Uses the words "please" and "thank you" when talking to customers

   Almost never   1   2   3   4   5   Almost always

3. Uses the words "please" and "thank you" when talking to fellow employees

   Almost never   1   2   3   4   5   Almost always

4. Tries to remember the names of customers who come to Beazley's three or more times a week

   Almost never   1   2   3   4   5   Almost always

5. Keeps ashtrays clean

   Almost never   1   2   3   4   5   Almost always

6. Keeps counters clean, including creamer bottles and steel shelves

   Almost never   1   2   3   4   5   Almost always

7. Stops talking to a fellow employee as soon as a customer approaches the counter

   Almost never   1   2   3   4   5   Almost always

8. Answers the telephone within three rings regardless of how busy with customers

   Almost never   1   2   3   4   5   Almost always

9. Refuses to gossip about the personal lives of Beazley employees

   Almost never   1   2   3   4   5   Almost always

10. Passes rather than shoves food to customers

    Almost never   1   2   3   4   5   Almost always

11. Cleans the floor when it is dirty

    Almost never   1   2   3   4   5   Almost always

12. Asks customers if everything is satisfactory

    Almost never   1   2   3   4   5   Almost always

13. Swears in front of customers

    Almost always   1   2   3   4   5   Almost never

14. Serves customers within 5 minutes of receiving the order

    Almost never   1   2   3   4   5   Almost always

15. Knows the prices of all food products

    Almost never   1   2   3   4   5   Almost always

16. Knows how to make change

    Almost never   1   2   3   4   5   Almost always

17. Keeps counter stools and legs clean

    Almost never   1   2   3   4   5   Almost always

18. Gives customers their drinks immediately after the food order is taken

    Almost never   1   2   3   4   5   Almost always

19. Asks fellow employees if can help them (for example, changes a cola tank, cuts potatoes for the cook, rents shoes to customers—these are examples only, there are many more)

    Almost never   1   2   3   4   5   Almost always

20. Smokes behind the food counter

    Almost always   1   2   3   4   5   Almost never

21. Smokes a cigarette before checking to see that counter, tables, floor, bar stools, and shelves are clean

    Almost always   1   2   3   4   5   Almost never

22. Talks to customers who have already been waited on while other customers have yet to place their order

    Almost always   1   2   3   4   5   Almost never

23. Complains about other employees within hearing distance of customers

    Almost always   1   2   3   4   5   Almost never

24. Is rude to customers (Says "I'll get to you when I can." "I am busy right now"; continues sitting while a customer waits for service)

    Almost always   1   2   3   4   5   Almost never

25. Smiles when interacting with customers

Almost never   1   2   3   4   5   Almost always

26. Puts hands in hair

Almost always   1   2   3   4   5   Almost never

27. Fingernails are clean

Almost never   1   2   3   4   5   Almost always

28. Asks if can take customers' order rather than walking up to them and just saying "yes"

Almost never   1   2   3   4   5   Almost always

29. Is alert to things that must be restocked, for example: chocolate bars, chips, cigarettes, napkins, sugar

Almost never   1   2   3   4   5   Almost always

30. Asks customers, "How are you today?"

Almost never   1   2   3   4   5   Almost always

31. Anticipates needs of regular customers, for example, "Would you like a cup of coffee this morning?"

Almost never   1   2   3   4   5   Almost always

32. Hair is washed at least twice a week/males come to work clean shaven

Almost never   1   2   3   4   5   Amost always

33. Serves food the way the customer requested it, for example puts mustard on a sandwich if that was the customer's wish

Almost never   1   2   3   4   5   Almost always

34. *Thanks* customer for bringing a complaint to their attention (for example, says, "I appreciate your bringing this to my attention.")

Almost never   1   2   3   4   5   Almost always

35. Gives a big smile when the customer asks for change

Almost never   1   2   3   4   5   Almost always

36. Remembers to include pickles with sandwiches

Almost never   1   2   3   4   5   Almost always

37. Makes suggestions to customers, for example, "Would you like another cup of coffee?"

    Almost never   1   2   3   4   5   Almost always

38. Knows the prices for bowling, for example, league, senior citizen, and holidays

    Almost never   1   2   3   4   5   Almost always

39. Wipes sugar bowls

    Almost never   1   2   3   4   5   Almost always

40. Has body odor

    Almost always   1   2   3   4   5   Almost never

41. Clothes are clean

    Almost never   1   2   3   4   5   Almost always

42. Knows how to work the cash register, for example knows what to do if there is an over or under ring or if the sale is charged to the wrong account

    Almost never   1   2   3   4   5   Almost always

43. Wipes nose with hand

    Almost always   1   2   3   4   5   Almost never

44. Is able to balance total on cash register with cash on hand

    Almost never   1   2   3   4   5   Almost always

45. Says hello to customers when recognizing them outside the bowling alley, for example, downtown

    Almost never   1   2   3   4   Almost always

46. Can change the tape on the cash register

    Almost never   1   2   3   4   5   Almost always

47. Eats food not supplied by Beazley canteen or restaurant in front of customers

    Almost always   1   2   3   4   5   Almost never

48. Asks questions and/or seeks help when doesn't understand something

Almost never   1   2   3   4   5   Almost always

48-154	155-178	179-202	203-226	227-240
very poor	unsatisfactory	satisfactory	excellent	superior

Total = _____

II COOK:

Report your observations of the cook on the behaviour listed under waiter/waitress plus the following:

49. Is careful not to waste food

Almost never   1   2   3   4   5   Almost always

50. Keeps grease off floor and counters

Almost never   1   2   3   4   5   Almost always

51. Uses tongs or spatula to handle food rather than hands

Almost never   1   2   3   4   5   Almost always

52. Cooks meat that looks and/or smells bad

Almost always   1   2   3   4   5   Almost never

53. Comes up with new recipes or ideas for modifying existing recipes

Almost never   1   2   3   4   5   Almost always

54. Prepares for the next shift so that the next cook has minimum rather than maximum work to do

Almost never   1   2   3   4   5   Almost always

55. Consults other cooks for suggestions on ways to help one another

Almost never   1   2   3   4   5   Almost always

56. Customers complain about the quality of the food

Almost always   1   2   3   4   5   Almost never

57. Is open to suggestions from management and employees

Almost never   1   2   3   4   5   Almost always

58. Keeps sink clean

Almost never 1 2 3 4 5 Almost always

59. Runs out of supplies, for example: clams, potatoes, forks, napkins, milk, ketchup and the like

Almost always 1 2 3 4 5 Almost never

60. Anticipates busy and slow days in terms of how much fish to cut and how many potatoes to peel.

Almost never 1 2 3 4 5 Almost always

60-192	193-222	223-205	253-282	283-300
very poor	unsatisfactory	satisfactory	excellent	superior

Total = _____

III MECHANICS

Report your observations of the mechanic on all the behaviour listed under waiter/waitress plus the following:

49. Keeps the ball racks clean

Almost never 1 2 3 4 5 Almost always

50. Washes hands before handling food

Almost never 1 2 3 4 5 Almost always

51. Throws things, and fools around behind the counter

Almost always 1 2 3 4 5 Almost never

52. Is alert for parts that need replacing or tightening, for example, checks for oil leaks, loose bolts, loose chains, parts wearing

Almost never 1 2 3 4 5 Almost always

53. Helps behind the food counter whenever can

Almost never 1 2 3 4 5 Almost always

54. Keeps machines oiled and greased

Almost never 1 2 3 4 5 Almost always

55. Constantly checks cut-out switches

Almost never 1 2 3 4 5 Almost always

56. Gets machine to run without fixing it properly

Almost always   1   2   3   4   5   Almost never

57. Loses tools

Almost always   1   2   3   4   5   Almost never

58. Informs others when a machine is not working properly

Almost never   1   2   3   4   5   Almost always

59. Can make most repairs within 5 minutes because major repairs are minimized through preventive maintenance checks.

Almost never   1   2   3   4   5   Almost always

60. Makes certain that approaches are not sticky

Almost never   1   2   3   4   5   Almost always

61. Makes certain that pins go down correctly

Almost never   1   2   3   4   5   Almost always

62. Knows where tools are

Almost never   1   2   3   4   5   Almost always

63. Knows what tools are needed to make a repair, for example doesn't have to continually run back for more tools

Almost never   1   2   3   4   5   Almost always

64. Asks the mechanic leaving the shift what machines need watching

Almost never   1   2   3   4   5   Almost always

65. Throws tools down rather than taking care of them

Almost always   1   2   3   4   5   Almost never

66. Leaves tools at the location of the last job rather than returning them to where they belong

Almost always   1   2   3   4   5   Almost never

67. Forgets to put washers on

Almost always   1   2   3   4   5   Almost never

68. Can take a sweep apart with only getting hands dirty

Almost never   1   2   3   4   5   Almost always

69. Face and hands are free of grease

Almost never   1   2   3   4   5   Almost always

70. Is constantly looking for things to do, for example, replaces light bulbs, fixes closures on door, unplugs a toilet without being asked

Almost never   1   2   3   4   5   Almost always

71. Keeps the ball runs dusted

Almost never   1   2   3   4   5   Almost always

72. Keeps the approaches free of spots

Almost never   1   2   3   4   5   Almost always

73. Checks washrooms (people loitering, toilets plugged, mirrors dirty)

Almost never   1   2   3   4   5   Almost always

74. Prevents kids from hanging around

Almost never   1   2   3   4   5   Almost always

75. Pulls machines apart during quiet times, for example, Monday or Friday mornings, to see that everything is working

Almost never   1   2   3   4   5   Almost always

76. *Immediately walks rapidly* to the lane where a breakdown occurs (does not stay behind the counter or slowly walk to the machine)

Almost never   1   2   3   4   5   Almost always

77. Keeps customers informed of new developments, for example, tells them about new prices and why they are going into effect, informs them of tournaments, tells them about improvements such as the new rubber fibres

Almost never   1   2   3   4   5   Almost always

78. Cleans air conditioning system once a week, for example, vacuums filters

Almost never   1   2   3   4   5   Almost always

79. Keeps lanes oiled

Almost never   1   2   3   4   5   Almost always

80. Sprays the shoes

Almost never   1   2   3   4   5   Almost always

81. Tools are covered with grease

Almost always   1   2   3   4   5   Almost never

82. Keeps screws and nails in pit area tight

Almost never   1   2   3   4   5   Almost always

83. Checks gear box weekly for oil leaks

Almost never   1   2   3   4   5   Almost always

84. Checks the tension of chains weekly and keeps them oiled

Almost never   1   2   3   4   5   Almost always

85. Wipes machines clean as checking them

Almost never   1   2   3   4   5   Almost always

86. Keeps the pit area clean

Almost never   1   2   3   4   5   Almost always

IV JANITOR

Do not complete section I, II, III on the janitor. Complete only this section on the janitor as well as the *mechanic.* The mechanic is a key person who serves as a backup person to the waiter and the janitor.

87. (1) Keeps the glass doors clean

Almost never   1   2   3   4   5   Almost always

88. (2) Garbage cans are free of odor

Almost never   1   2   3   4   5   Almost always

89. (3) Floor in playroom is kept clean

Almost never   1   2   3   4   5   Almost always

90. (4) Floors are washed with soap and water

Almost never   1   2   3   4   5   Almost always

91. (5) Floors are dry mopped after they are washed

Almost never   1   2   3   4   5   Almost always

92. (6) Score table is clean

Almost never   1   2   3   4   5   Almost always

93. (7) Carpet is vacuumed

Almost never   1   2   3   4   5   Almost always

94. (8) Keeps washroom filled with toilet paper

Almost never   1   2   3   4   5   Almost always

95. (9) Urinals are clean

Almost never   1   2   3   4   5   Almost always

96. (10) Toilets are clean

Almost never   1   2   3   4   5   Almost always

97. (11) Garbage cans are *completely* emptied

Almost never   1   2   3   4   5   Almost always

98. (12) Toilet bowls are kept white

Almost never   1   2   3   4   5   Almost always

99. (13) Bases around toilet bowls are kept clean

Almost never   1   2   3   4   5   Almost always

100. (14) Toilets are plugged

Almost always   1   2   3   4   5   Almost never

101. (15) Hand soap is missing from washroom

Almost always   1   2   3   4   5   Almost never

102. (16) Waters plants

Almost never   1   2   3   4   5   Almost always

103. (17) Washes panel walls

Almost never   1   2   3   4   5   Almost always

104. (18) Washes and wipes door knobs

Almost never   1   2   3   4   5   Almost always

105. (19) Keeps garbage out of walkway and parking lot

Almost never   1   2   3   4   5   Almost always

106. (20) Keeps lawn trimmed

Almost never   1   2   3   4   5   Almost always

107. (21) Empties ash trays thoroughly before vacuuming the rug

Almost never   1   2   3   4   5   Almost always

108. (22) Dusts thoroughly

Almost never   1   2   3   4   5   Almost always

109. (23) Cleans the sinks in the bathroom

Almost never   1   2   3   4   5   Almost always

110. (24) Cleans the mirrors in the bathroom

Almost never   1   2   3   4   5   Almost always

111. (25) Cleans the bathroom walls

Almost never   1   2   3   4   5   Almost always

112. (26) Cleans spots from the carpet rather than only vacuuming over the spots

Almost never   1   2   3   4   5   Almost always

113. (27) Scrubs the ash cans at least once a week

Almost never   1   2   3   4   5   Almost always

114. (28) Washes the wells thoroughly, for example, keeps them free of sticky substances such as spilled pop

Almost never   1   2   3   4   5   Almost always

115. (29) Has to return in the morning to clean things that should have been done the previous night

Almost always   1   2   3   4   5   Almost never

116. (30) Urinals have a deodorant block

Almost never   1   2   3   4   5   Almost always

117. (31) Deodorant stick is kept in wall

Almost never   1   2   3   4   5   Almost always

118. (32) Supplies such as bucket, mop, and detergent are kept in *one* place

Almost never   1   2   3   4   5   Almost always

Mechanic

118-378	379-437	438-496	497-555	556-590
very poor	unsatisfactory	satisfactory	excellent	superior

Janitor

32-102	103-118	119-134	135-150	151-160
very poor	unsatisfactory	satisfactory	excellent	superior

Total = _____

NOTE: To the extent that a mechanic must do the above 32 things because the janitor failed to do them is wrong. The mechanic is expected to report this information to the manager, but the mechanic is a key person who is expected to cover the janitor's duties when the janitor is not present. The mechanic is expected to check on the janitor's work and correct things that the janitor overlooked. Next to the manager the mechanic is the most important person in the bowling alley and thus has the most responsibility.

V ADMINISTRATIVE ASSISTANT

1. Types minimum of 60 words per minute

   Almost never   1   2   3   4   5   Almost always

2. Can take shorthand

   Almost never   1   2   3   4   5   Almost always

3. Can type from a dictaphone machine

   Almost never   1   2   3   4   5   Almost always

4. Answers the phone in a courteous manner

   Almost never   1   2   3   4   5   Almost always

5. Smiles at all employees

   Almost never   1   2   3   4   5   Almost always

6. Smiles at all customers

   Almost never   1   2   3   4   5   Almost always

7. Gossips with employees about other employees

   Almost always   1   2   3   4   5   Almost never

8. Complains in front of customers

Almost always   1   2   3   4   5   Almost never

9. Can use an adding machine

Almost never   1   2   3   4   5   Almost always

10. Can reconcile a bank account

Almost never   1   2   3   4   5   Almost always

11. Pays bills on time

Almost never   1   2   3   4   5   Almost always

12. Maintains and balances cash disbursements journal

Almost never   1   2   3   4   5   Almost always

13. Posts all journals in general ledger

Almost never   1   2   3   4   5   Almost always

14. Able to make adjustments in general ledger

Almost never   1   2   3   4   5   Almost always

15. Handles complete inventory function (includes physically counting purchases such as bowling balls)

Almost never   1   2   3   4   5   Almost always

16. Gathers information (bowling scores, new records, bowling news, bowling tips) for monthly newsletter

Almost never   1   2   3   4   5   Almost always

17. Informs President/General Manager of pressing matters

Almost never   1   2   3   4   5   Almost always

18. Knows how to trace all accounting and cash flows, thereby performing internal control checks

Almost never   1   2   3   4   5   Almost always

19. Tabulates employee performance appraisal reports three times a year

Almost never   1   2   3   4   5   Almost always

20. Keeps issues relevant only to the President/General Manager confidential (refuses to discuss such information with employees)

Almost never   1   2   3   4   5   Almost always

21. Prepares biweekly payroll (multiply hours x rate, make deductions, balance payroll)

Almost never   1   2   3   4   5   Almost always

22. Assists in the collection of amusement machine revenue

Almost never   1   2   3   4   5   Almost always

23. Can operate the copying machine

Almost never   1   2   3   4   5   Almost always

24. Assists in preparation of trophy orders (assembling, engraving)

Almost never   1   2   3   4   5   Almost always

25. Allows people to congregate in front of her desk

Almost always   1   2   3   4   5   Almost never

26. Must be repeatedly asked to do the same thing

Almost always   1   2   3   4   5   Almost never

27. Can compose own letters as directed by President/General Manager

Almost never   1   2   3   4   5   Almost always

28. Organizes a filing system that is easily learned by the President/ Manager and keeps it up to date on a daily basis (items are promptly filed)

Almost never   1   2   3   4   5   Almost always

29. Keeps executive offices clean (vacuum, dust, water plants)

Almost never   1   2   3   4   5   Almost always

30. Can drive all company vehicles for performing company business

Almost never   1   2   3   4   5   Almost always

30-96	97-111	112-127	127-141	142-150
very poor	unsatisfactory	satisfactory	excellent	superior

Total = _____

VI PROGRAM DIRECTOR/LANE INSPECTOR

1. Provides input to the General Manager regarding effectiveness of all personnel on all of the above behaviours, thus serving as a Lane inspector/consultant to the General Manager

Almost never   1   2   3   4   5   Almost always

2. Thinks of ideas for increasing business

   Almost never   1   2   3   4   5   Almost always

3. Is repeatedly asked to do the same thing

   Almost always   1   2   3   4   5   Almost never

4. Works long hours when necessary (for example over 40 hours)

   Almost never   1   2   3   4   5   Almost always

5. Spot checks the lanes during weekends (for example drops in unexpectedly at a lane for 10 minutes)

   Almost never   1   2   3   4   5   Almost always

6. Fair and consistent in dealing with employees (does not show favoritism to any one employee)

   Almost never   1   2   3   4   5   Almost always

7. On special occasions such as customer birthday parties, stays with the party showing the people how to bowl and helps them to have a good time

   Almost never   1   2   3   4   5   Almost always

8. Takes charge of at least one shift per week

   Almost never   1   2   3   4   5   Almost always

9. Keeps storage room in Pine Street spotless

   Almost never   1   2   3   4   5   Almost always

10. Comments positively on the scores of customers

    Almost never   1   2   3   4   5   Almost always

11. Praises people for a good shot

    Almost never   1   2   3   4   5   Almost always

12. Sends out invitations for a bowling tournament in a timely manner

    Almost never   1   2   3   4   5   Almost always

13. Helps individuals to form teams to bowl in a tournament

    Almost never   1   2   3   4   5   Almost always

14. Gets trophies to customers on schedule

    Almost never   1   2   3   4   5   Almost always

15. Actively promotes the selling of shoes

    Almost never   1   2   3   4   5   Almost always

16. Actively promotes the selling of bowling balls

    Almost never   1   2   3   4   5   Almost always

17. Asks for and listens openly to concerns of league captains

    Almost never   1   2   3   4   5   Almost always

18. Offers help in solving league problems

    Almost never   1   2   3   4   5   Almost always

19. Comes to agreement with the league on steps to be taken to resolve a problem

    Almost never   1   2   3   4   5   Almost always

20. Gets involved in too many things at the same time

    Almost always   1   2   3   4   5   Almost never

21. Staff knows where to get hold of program director at all times

    Almost never   1   2   3   4   5   Almost always

22. Forgets little things has been asked to do

    Almost always   1   2   3   4   5   Almost never

23. Is able to set priorities on a daily basis. Sets up a check list of key things is going to accomplish each day

    Almost never   1   2   3   4   5   Almost always

24. Is upset by what employees think of him/her; for example, is overly worried what people will think if he/she reports to the General Manager an employee who did not do something properly

    Almost always   1   2   3   4   5   Almost never

25. Asks people to do things rather than ordering

    Almost never   1   2   3   4   5   Almost always

26. Asks fellow employees for their ideas for promoting business

    Almost never   1   2   3   4   5   Almost always

27. Asks customers for their ideas for promoting business

    Almost never   1   2   3   4   5   Almost always

28. Makes customers comfortable through casual conversation about their background and interests

Almost never   1   2   3   4   5   Almost always

29. Expresses a desire to help customers improve their bowling scores

Almost never   1   2   3   4   5   Almost always

30. Makes it clear that has confidence that the customers can improve their bowling

Almost never   1   2   3   4   5   Almost always

31. Asks customers if there is anything can do to help them

Almost never   1   2   3   4   5   Almost always

32. Avoids responding with hostility or defensiveness when receiving a complaint

Almost never   1   2   3   4   5   Almost always

33. Recognizes and acknowledges the other person's viewpoint

Almost never   1   2   3   4   5   Almost always

34. States the company's position nondefensively

Almost never   1   2   3   4   5   Almost always

35. Delegates work that should do by self

Almost always   1   2   3   4   5   Almost never

36. Completes assigned jobs

Almost never   1   2   3   4   5   Almost always

37. Meets deadlines

Almost never   1   2   3   4   5   Almost always

38. Keeps customers informed of changes, for example, tells them about new prices and why they are going into effect, informs them of tournaments, tells them about improvements in the lanes

Almost never   1   2   3   4   5   Almost always

38–122	123–141	142–160	161–179	180–190
very poor	unsatisfactory	satisfactory	excellent	superior

Total: _____

VII MANAGER/GENERAL MANAGER/PRESIDENT

1. Employees feel free to go to manager with problems

   Almost never   1   2   3   4   5   Almost always

2. Takes one to two full days off per week

   Almost never   1   2   3   4   5   Almost always

3. Shows concern for own health (refuses to work excessive hours, for example, 60 to 70 hours per week)

   Almost never   1   2   3   4   5   Almost always

4. Trains managers to have the same skill levels as self

   Almost never   1   2   3   4   5   Almost always

5. Trains mechanics to have the same level of expertise as self

   Almost never   1   2   3   4   5   Almost always

6. Tells employees the names of fellow employees who complained about them

   Almost always   1   2   3   4   5   Almost never

7. Is proactive in that is constantly looking for potential problems and finds solutions before the problem materializes

   Almost never   1   2   3   4   5   Almost always

8. Does work that should delegate to others

   Almost always   1   2   3   4   5   Almost never

9. Delegates work that should do

   Almost always   1   2   3   4   5   Almost never

10. Meets deadlines

    Almost never   1   2   3   4   5   Almost always

11. Insures that cooks/waiters/waitresses, mechanics and janitors are trained in all aspects of their jobs

    Almost never   1   2   3   4   5   Almost always

12. Treats all employees in a fair, consistent, uniform manner (does not show favoritism)

    Almost never   1   2   3   4   5   Almost always

13. Is constantly smiling when interacting with customers

Almost never   1   2   3   4   5   Almost always

14. Lets employees know their weekly work schedule no later than Thursday of the previous week

Almost never   1   2   3   4   5   Almost always

15. Meets employees' needs in a timely manner (for example, tools, etc.)

Almost never   1   2   3   4   5   Almost always

16. Explains to employees exactly what is expected of them—employees know their job responsibilities

Almost never   1   2   3   4   5   Almost always

17. Rules and regulations are clearly explained

Almost never   1   2   3   4   5   Almost always

18. Sees that the machines are in good working order

Almost never   1   2   3   4   5   Almost always

19. Sees that the inside and outside of the building is in good condition, including parking lot, washrooms, walls, and entranceway

Almost never   1   2   3   4   5   Almost always

20. Knows the layout of the lanes, for example, where the switches and breakers are

Almost never   1   2   3   4   5   Almost always

21. Makes certain that the staff is not sitting around when there is work to be done

Almost never   1   2   3   4   5   Almost always

22. Helps employees when they fall behind, for example, works behind the lunch counter

Almost never   1   2   3   4   5   Almost always

23. Says hello to all employees

Almost never   1   2   3   4   5   Almost always

24. Insures there is enough staff working to handle the customers

Almost never   1   2   3   4   5   Almost always

25. Insures that there are not too many staff working in relation to the small number of customers

Almost never   1   2   3   4   5   Almost always

26. Insures that the shoes behind the counter are stored in a logical order

Almost never   1   2   3   4   5   Almost always

27. Makes certain that the lanes are properly stocked, including the restaurant

Almost never   1   2   3   4   5   Almost always

28. Is thought highly of by the league presidents

Almost never   1   2   3   4   5   Almost always

29. Checks to see that bowling balls are in clean playing shape

Almost never   1   2   3   4   5   Almost always

30. Makes certain that the waiters/waitresses know that they are to take instructions from the cook

Almost never   1   2   3   4   5   Almost always

31. Insures that people are paid a salary that is in line with their performance and job responsibility

Almost never   1   2   3   4   5   Almost always

32. Checks statements to insure that bills were not overpaid

Almost never   1   2   3   4   5   Almost always

33. Insures that the lanes are clean

Almost never   1   2   3   4   5   Almost always

34. Meets deadline in making bank deposits

Almost never   1   2   3   4   5   Almost always

35. Comes into the lanes at *unexpected* times to see that the place is working smoothly

Almost never   1   2   3   4   5   Almost always

36. Consults employees for their ideas on ways of making their job better

Almost never   1   2   3   4   5   Almost always

37. Employees know where to get hold of manager at all times

Almost never   1   2   3   4   5   Almost always

38. Must repeatedly be asked to do the same thing

Almost always   1   2   3   4   5   Almost never

39. Forgets things has been asked to do

Almost always   1   2   3   4   5   Almost never

40. Is able to set priorities on a daily basis; sets up a checklist of key things is going to accomplish each day

Almost never   1   2   3   4   5   Almost always

41. Asks people to do things rather than ordering them

Almost never   1   2   3   4   5   Almost always

42. Asks fellow employees for their ideas for promoting business

Almost never   1   2   3   4   5   Almost always

43. Asks customers for their ideas for promoting business

Almost never   1   2   3   4   5   Almost always

44. Makes customers comfortable through casual conversation about their background and interests

Almost never   1   2   3   4   5   Almost always

45. Gets involved in the personal lives of employees

Almost always   1   2   3   4   5   Almost never

46. Avoids responding with hostility or defensiveness when receiving a complaint

Almost never   1   2   3   4   5   Almost always

47. Recognizes and acknowledges the person's viewpoint

Almost never   1   2   3   4   5   Almost always

48. States the company's position nondefensively

Almost never   1   2   3   4   5   Almost always

49. Completes assigned job

Almost never   1   2   3   4   5   Almost always

50. Praises employees for things they do well

   Almost never   1   2   3   4   5   Almost always

51. Asks employees if there is anything can do to make their job easier

   Almost never   1   2   3   4   5   Almost always

52. Expresses a desire to help employees do their job

   Almost never   1   2   3   4   5   Almost always

53. Stresses the importance of safety to employees

   Almost never   1   2   3   4   5   Almost always

54. Asks employees for their help in solving a problem

   Almost never   1   2   3   4   5   Almost always

55. Explains the rationale for rules and regulations

   Almost never   1   2   3   4   5   Almost always

56. Clearly describes the details of a change in policy or procedure to employees

   Almost never   1   2   3   4   5   Almost always

57. Explains why the change is necessary

   Almost never   1   2   3   4   5   Almost always

58. Listens to an employee's concern about the change

   Almost never   1   2   3   4   5   Almost always

59. Asks employees for their help in making a change work

   Almost never   1   2   3   4   5   Almost always

60. Criticizes an employee in front of another employee

   Almost always   1   2   3   4   5   Almost never

60–122	123–222	223–252	253–282	283–300
very poor	unsatisfactory	satisfactory	excellent	superior

Total: _____.

Employees who do not perform their job duties (that is, if their total number of points falls in the very poor or unsatisfactory range) will receive a verbal warning. The words "verbal warning" will be used by the Manager in the discussion with the employee. If further discussion is required within a three-month period the employee will receive a written warning. If performance is not satisfactory within the following three-month period the employee will be asked to leave Beazley Bowling Lanes.

Please record critical incidents that support your observations. Since this list is not intended to be exhaustive for any one job, please make additional comments in the space below:

DATE: _____

EMPLOYEE'S SIGNATURE:

_____

SUPERVISOR'S SIGNATURE:

_____

Appendix B: Behavioral Observation Scales for Managers in _____ Company's Strategic Planning Group (SPG)

Manager _____

Date _____

This checklist contains key job behaviors that managers have reported as critical for improving their contribution as SPG managers to the effectiveness/efficiency of Northwest (N.W.) operations.

Please consider the above named individual's behavior on the job for the past six months. Read each statement carefully. Circle the number that indicates the extent to which you believe this person has demonstrated this behavior. For each behavior a 4 represents almost always or 95 to 100 percent of the time. A 3 represents frequently or 85 to 94 percent of the time. A 2 represents sometimes or 75 to 84 percent of the time. A 1 represents seldom or 65 to 74 percent of the time. A 0 represents almost never or 0 to 64 percent of the time.

An example of an item is shown below. If a manager comes to meetings on time 95 to 100 percent of the time you should circle a 4. If the manager hardly ever comes to meetings on time, you should circle 0.

Example: Comes to meetings on time.

Almost Never   0   1   2   3   4   Almost Always

I TEAM PLAYING

1. Invites the input of SPG managers on issues that will directly affect them before making a decision

   Almost Never   0   1   2   3   4   Almost Always

2. Explains to SPG the rationale behind directives, decisions, and policies that may or will affect other divisions

   Almost Never   0   1   2   3   4   Almost Always

3. Keeps SPG informed of *major* changes in the department regarding people, policies, projects, construction, etc.

   Almost Never   0   1   2   3   4   Almost Always

4. Continually seeks input of SPG as a group on capital policy and plans rather than engaging primarily in interactions with individual managers

   Almost Never   0   1   2   3   4   Almost Always

5. Is open to criticism and questioning of decisions from SPG members at SPG meetings

   Almost Never   0   1   2   3   4   Almost Always

6. Supports SPG decisions

   Almost Never   0   1   2   3   4   Almost Always

7. Spends time learning about other SPG members' ongoing operations (e.g., their targets, time tables, interrelationships of targets within and between departments)

   Almost Never   0   1   2   3   4   Almost Always

8. Develops ways of combining departmental objectives with the overall objectives of N.W. operations

   Almost Never   0   1   2   3   4   Almost Always

9. Admits when doesn't know the answer

   Almost Never   0   1   2   3   4   Almost Always

10. Participates in SPG discussions (e.g., asks questions; brainstorms with group)

    Almost Never   0   1   2   3   4   Almost Always

11. Encourages candid comments (e.g., not offended by loss of temper by others)

    Almost Never   0   1   2   3   4   Almost Always

12. Acknowledges the expertise of fellow SPG members

    Almost Never   0   1   2   3   4   Almost Always

13. Looks for ways to support fellow SPG members (e.g., ideas, man hours)

    Almost Never   0   1   2   3   4   Almost Always

14. Keeps discussion in SPG meetings on key SPG issues

    Almost Never   0   1   2   3   4   Almost Always

15. Generates new ways of tackling new or ongoing problems

    Almost Never   0   1   2   3   4   Almost Always

16. Solicits comments from SPG members on the effectiveness of the structure of the organization

    Almost Never   0   1   2   3   4   Almost Always

    Total Score = _____

II PLANNING/FORECASTING

1. Operates on a crisis basis

    Almost Always   0   1   2   3   4   Almost Never

2. Sets goals that are difficult, but attainable

    Almost Never   0   1   2   3   4   Almost Always

3. Establishes a realistic timetable to get the job done

    Almost Never   0   1   2   3   4   Almost Always

4. Planning/forecasting is based on investigation of facts

    Almost Never   0   1   2   3   4   Almost Always

5. Surfaces important issues for which there may be no immediate answers

    Almost Never   0   1   2   3   4   Almost Always

6. Identifies problems not previously considered by SPG that may affect N. W. operations

   Almost Never   0   1   2   3   4   Almost Always

7. Identifies opportunities to improve the value of N.W. assets

   Almost Never   0   1   2   3   4   Almost Always

8. Has broad overall strategy statements for the department that define where the department is to be 5 years from now

   Almost Never   0   1   2   3   4   Almost Always

9. Measures the success of the department and functional areas against the standards of SPG and/or N.W. operations and PPD

   Almost Never   0   1   2   3   4   Almost Always

10. Talks about day-to-day issues at SPG meetings only to the extent that they surface a new condition or situation that affects long-term strategies of SPG and/or N.W. operations

    Almost Never   0   1   2   3   4   Almost Always

11. Finds ways of incorporating/integrating the programs and objectives of the corporate office with those of the department/functional areas

    Almost Never   0   1   2   3   4   Almost Always

12. Identifies jobs, job requirements, as well as manpower needs and skills that are anticipated within the next 3 to 5 years in areas of own responsibility

    Almost Never   0   1   2   3   4   Almost Always

13. Establishes measures for evaluating the efficiency of the department/ functional area to determine whether operating within an acceptable margin

    Almost Never   0   1   2   3   4   Almost Always

14. Establishes mechanisms for spotting trends/patterns on key departmental/functional areas

    Almost Never   0   1   2   3   4   Almost Always

                                        Total Score = _____

III INTERACTIONS WITH SUBORDINATES

1. Communicates objectives of SPG to the people he/she works with

   Almost Never   0   1   2   3   4   Almost Always

2. Requires managers to engage in planning and forecasting

   Almost Never   0   1   2   3   4   Almost Always

3. Encourages key managers to consider the value of team building activity for their respective departments

   Almost Never   0   1   2   3   4   Almost Always

4. Clearly defines the role responsibilities of the key managers

   Almost Never   0   1   2   3   4   Almost Always

5. Communicates measurable standards against which people will be evaluated

   Almost Never   0   1   2   3   4   Almost Always

6. Solicits divergence of thinking on issues

   Almost Never   0   1   2   3   4   Almost Always

7. Sends key people to seminars for developmental purposes

   Almost Never   0   1   2   3   4   Almost Always

8. Attracts and trains people necessary to perform functions that will be critical within the next 3 to 5 years

   Almost Never   0   1   2   3   4   Almost Always

9. Changes the organization to fit the people who are reluctant to transfer, retire, be promoted, etc. (rather than insisting upon an organization that is designed to accomplish the work that is expected of it)

   Almost Always   0   1   2   3   4   Almost Never

10. Procrastinates in dealing with poor performers

    Almost Always   0   1   2   3   4   Almost Never

11. Encourages subordinates to express their ideas in written form on 1 to 2 pages

    Almost Never   0   1   2   3   4   Almost Always

12. Holds people accountable for technical levels of performance as well as dollars (e.g., speed, efficiency, rates, rejection)

Almost Never   0   1   2   3   4   Almost Always

13. Is frequently seen in the work areas of the people who report to the manager as well as their people (e.g., "shows the flag")

Almost Never   0   1   2   3   4   Almost Always

14. Shows sensitivity in implementing change with people

Almost Never   0   1   2   3   4   Almost Always

15. Increases a feeling of belongingness in the departments for which he/she is responsible

Almost Never   0   1   2   3   4   Almost Always

16. Encourages the elimination of a we-they attitude among salaried and hourly employees

Almost Never   0   1   2   3   4   Almost Always

17. Conveys a high concern for safety

Almost Never   0   1   2   3   4   Almost Always

18. Makes self accessible to people who report to him or her

Almost Never   0   1   2   3   4   Almost Always

19. Delegates responsibility commensurate with the authority of people

Almost Never   0   1   2   3   4   Almost Always

20. Holds the key people accountable for motivating and training their people

Almost Never   0   1   2   3   4   Almost Always

Total Score = _____

SUMMARY COMMENTS

1. What is _____ doing that you believe is effective and you would like to see him/her continue doing?

2. What would you like to see _____ start doing, stop doing, or do differently?

Please record observations of critical incidents to support your ratings.

Bibliography

Albermarle Paper Company v. *Moody,* U.S. Supreme Court Nos. 74–389 and 74–428, 10 FEP Cases 1181, 1975.

Amir, Y., Kovarsky, Y., & Sharan, S. Peer nominations as a predictor of multistage promotions in a ramified organization. *Journal of Applied Psychology,* 1970, *54,* 462–469.

Anastasi, A. *Psychological testing.* New York: Macmillan, 1976.

Andrews, I.R., and Henry, M.M. Management attitudes toward pay. *Industrial Relations,* 1963, *3,* 29–39.

Arvery, R.D. *Fairness in selecting employees.* Reading, Mass.: Addison-Wesley, 1979.

Atkin, R.S., & Conlon, E.J. Behaviorally anchored rating scales: Some theoretical issues. *Academy of Management Review,* 1978, *3,* 119–128.

Bakke v. *Regents of the University of California,* 17 FEB, 1978.

Bandura, A. *Social learning theory.* Englewood Cliffs, N.J.: Prentice-Hall, 1977.

Barrett, R.S. The influence of the supervisor's requirements on ratings. *Personnel Psychology,* 1966, *19,* 375–387.

Bassett, G.A. & Meyer, H.H. Performance appraisal based on self-review. *Personnel Psychology,* 1968, *21,* 421–430.

Bayroff, A.G., Haggerty, H.R., & Rundquist, E.A. Validity of ratings as related to rating techniques and conditions. *Personnel Psychology,* 1954, *7,* 92-113.

Beatty, R.W., Schneier, S.E., & Beatty, J.R. An empirical investigation of perceptions of ratee behavior, frequency, and ratee behavior change using behavioral expectation scales. *Personnel Psychology,* 1977, *33,* 647-658.

Beer, M. *Note on performance appraisal.* Boston, Mass.: Intercollegiate Case Clearing House, 1977.

Bem, D.J. Self-perception theory. In L. Berkowitz (Ed.), *Advances in experimental social psychology.* New York: Academic Press, 1972.

Berkshire, J.R., & Highland, R.W. Forced-choice performance rating: A methodological study. *Personnel Psychology,* 1953, *6,* 355-378.

Bernardin, H.J. Behavioral expectation scales versus summated rating scales: A fairer comparison. *Journal of Applied Psychology,* 1977, *62,* 422-427.

Bernardin, H.J. Effects of rater training on leniency and halo errors in student ratings of instructors. *Journal of Applied Psychology,* 1978, *63,* 301-308.

_____, & Buckley, M.R. A consideration of strategies in rater training. Unpublished manuscript, 1979.

_____, & Pence, E.G. The effects of rater training: Creating new response sets and decreasing accuracy. *Journal of Applied Psychology,* 1980, *65,* 60-66.

_____, & Walter, C.S. Effects of rater training and diary-keeping on psychometric error in ratings. *Journal of Applied Psychology,* 1977, *62,* 64-69.

_____, Alvares, K.M., & Cranny, C.J. A recomparison of behavioral expectation scales to summated scales. *Journal of Applied Psychology,* 1976, *61,* 564-570.

Blanz, F., & Ghiselli, E.E. The mixed standard scale: A new rating system. *Personnel Psychology,* 1972, *25,* 185-200.

Blum, M.L., & Naylor, J.C. *Industrial psychology: Its theoretical and social foundations.* New York: Harper & Row, 1968.

Borman, W. C. Effects of instructions to avoid halo error on reliability and validity of performance evaluation ratings. *Journal of Applied Psychology,* 1975, *60,* 556–560.

———, Format and training effects on rating accuracy and rater errors. *Journal of Applied Psychology,* 1979, *64,* 410–421.

Brito v. Zia Company, 478 F.2d. 1200 (1973).

Brogden, H.E., & Taylor, E.K. The dollar criterion: Applying the cost accounting concept to criterion construction. *Personnel Psychology,* 1950, *3,* 135–154.

Burke, L.K., & Rayloe, W.K. Rater training and experience. *Journal of Applied Psychology,* 1950, *34,* 381–383.

Burke, R.J., Weitzel, W., & Weir, T. Characteristics of effective employee performance review and development interviews: Replication and extension. *Personnel Psychology,* 1978, *31,* 903–919.

Burnaska, R.J. The effects of behavior modeling training upon managers' behaviors and employees' perceptions. *Personnel Psychology,* 1976, *29,* 329–335.

Campbell, J.P. The cutting edge of leadership: An overview. In J.G. Hunt & L.L. Larson (Eds.), *Leadership: The cutting edge.* Carbondale, Ill.: Southern Illinois University Press, 1977.

———, Dunnette, M.D., Lawler, E.E., & Weick, K.E. *Managerial behavior, performance, and effectiveness.* New York: McGraw-Hill, 1970.

Carroll, S.J., Jr., & Tosi, H.L., Jr. *Management by objectives: Applications and research.* New York: Macmillan, 1973.

Cox, J.A., & Krumholtz, J.D. Racial bias in peer ratings of basic airmen. *Sociometry,* 1958, *21,* 292–299.

Cronbach, L.J. Test validation. In R.L. Thorndike (Ed.), *Educational measurement* (2nd ed.). Washington, D.C.: American Council on Education, 1971.

Cummings, L.L., & Schwab, D. *Performance in organizations: Determinants and appraisals.* Glenview, Ill.: Scott, Foresman & Company, 1973.

Curtis, B., Smith, R. E., & Smoll, F. L. Scrutinizing the skipper: A study of leadership behaviors in the dugout. *Journal of Applied Psychology,* 1979, *64,* 391–400.

Deci, E. L. The effects of contingent and noncontingent rewards and controls on intrinsic motivation. *Organizational Behavior and Human Performance,* 1972, *8,* 217–229.

DeCotiis, T., & Petit, A. The performance appraisal process: A model and some testable propositions. *Academy of Management Review,* 1978, *3,* 635–646.

DeJung, J. E., & Kaplan, H. Some differential effects of race of rater and ratee on early peer ratings of combat attitude. *Journal of Applied Psychology,* 1962, *46,* 370–374.

DeNisi, A. S., & Mitchell, J. L. An analysis of peer ratings as predictors and criterion measures and a proposed new application. *Academy of Management Review,* 1978, *3,* 369–374.

Dickerson v. *United States Steel Corp.,* 582 F.2d. 827, 17 FEP 1589 (3d Cir. 1978).

Domingo v. *New England Fish Company,* 445 F. Supp. 421 (W.D. Wash., 1977).

Dossett, D. L., Latham, G. P., & Mitchell, T. R. The effects of assigned versus participatively set goals, KR, and individual differences when goal difficulty is held constant. *Journal of Applied Psychology,* 1979, *64,* 291–298.

Downs, S., Farr, R.M., & Colbeck, L. Self-appraisal: A convergence of selection and guidance. *Journal of Occupational Psychology,* 1978, *51,* 271–278.

Drucker, P. *Management: Tasks, responsibilities, and practices.* New York: Harper & Row, 1973.

Dunnette, M. D. *Personnel selection and placement.* Belmont, Calif.: Brooks Cole, 1966.

_____ . Mish-mash, mush, and milestones in organizational psychology. In H. Meltzer & F. R. Wickert (Eds.), *Humanizing organizational behavior.* Springfield, Ill.: Charles C Thomas, 1976.

_____ , & Borman, W. C. Personnel classification systems. *Annual Review of Psychology,* 1979, *30,* 477–525.

Edwards, K. A. Fair employment and performance appraisal: Legal requirements and practical guidelines. In D. L. DeVries (Chm.), Performance appraisal and feedback: Flies in the ointment. Symposium presented at the annual meeting of the American Psychological Association, Washington, D. C., September 1976.

Equal Employment Opportunity Commission. Guidelines on employee selection procedures. *Federal Register,* 1970, *35,* 12333–12336.

_____ . Uniform Guidelines on Employee Selection. *Federal Register,* 1978, *43,* 38290–38309.

_____ . Adoption of questions and answers to clarify and provide a common interpretation of the Uniform Guidelines on Employee Selection Procedures. *Federal Register,* 1979, *44,* 11996–12009.

Fay, C. H., & Latham, G. P. Effects of training and rater scale of minimizing rating errors. Unpublished manuscript, 1980.

Feldman, J. M. Beyond attribution theory: Cognitive processes in employee performance evaluations. Paper presented at the annual meeting of AIDS, New Orleans, 1979.

Fiske, D. W. Variability among peer ratings in different situations. *Educational and Psychological Measurement,* 1960, *20,* 283–292.

_____ , & Cox, J. A. The consistency of ratings by peers. *Journal of Applied Psychology,* 1960, *44,* 11–17.

Fivars, G. The critical incident technique: A bibliography. *JSAS Catalog of Selected Documents in Psychology,* 1975, *5,* 210.

Flanagan, J. C. The critical incident technique. *Psychological Bulletin,* 1954, *51,* 327–358.

_____ , Lange, C., O'Hagan, A., & Weislogel, M. *Critical requirements for research personnel.* Pittsburgh, Pa.: American Institute for Research, 1949.

French, W. L., & Bell, C. H., Jr. *Organization development: Behavioral science interventions for organization improvement.* Englewood Cliffs, N.J.: Prentice-Hall, 1978.

Friedman, B. A., & Cornelius, E. T. III. Effect of rater participation in scale construction on the psychometric characteristics of two rating scale formats. *Journal of Applied Psychology,* 1976, *61,* 210–216.

Ghiselli, E. E. Dimensional problems of criteria. *Journal of Applied Psychology*, 1956, *40*, 1-4.

Goldstein, A. P., & Sorcher, M. *Changing supervisory behavior.* New York: Pergamon, 1974.

Gordon, L. V., & Medland, F. F. The cross-group stability of peer ratings of leadership potential. *Personnel Psychology,* 1965, *18,* 173-177.

Greller, M. M. Subordinate participation and reaction to the appraisal interview. *Journal of Applied Psychology,* 1975, *60*, 544-549.

Griggs v. *Duke Power Company,* 401 U.S. (1971), 3 EPD 8137.

Grunwald, H., & Duncan, R. An interview with Fidel Castro. *Time Magazine,* February 4, 1980, 48-49.

Guion, R. J. Criterion measurement and personnel judgments. *Personnel Psychology,* 1961, *14,* 141-149.

Guion, R. M. *Personnel testing.* New York: McGraw-Hill, 1965.

Hakel, M. D., Hollman, T. D., & Dunnette, M. D. Accuracy of interviewers, C.P.A.'s, and students in identifying the interests of accountants. *Journal of Applied Psychology,* 1970, *54,* 115-119.

Hall, W. B. Employee self-appraisal for improved performance. *Tools for improved personnel relations.* New York: American Mangement Association, 1951.

Heneman, H. G. III. Comparisons of self and superior ratings of managerial performance. *Journal of Applied Psychology,* 1974, *58,* 638-642.

Herzberg, F. One more time: How do you motivate employees? *Harvard Business Review,* 1968, 53-62.

Hillery, J. M., & Wexley, K. N. Participation in appraisal interviews conducted in a training situation. *Journal of Applied Psychology,* 1974, *59,* 168-171.

Hinrichs, J. R. An eight-year follow-up of a management assessment center. *Journal of Applied Psychology,* 1978a, *63,* 596-501.

———. *Practical management of productivity.* New York: Van Nostrand Reinhold, 1978b.

Hollander, E. P. Buddy ratings: Military research and industrial implications. *Personnel Psychology,* 1954a, *7,* 385-393.

_____. Peer nominations on leadership as a predictor of the pass-fail criterion in naval air training. *Journal of Applied Psychology,* 1954b, *38,* 150-153.

_____. The friendship factor in peer nominations. *Personnel Psychology,* 1956, *9,* 435-447.

_____. The reliability of peer nominations under various conditions of administration. *Journal of Applied Psychology,* 1957, *41,* 85-90.

_____. Validity of peer nominations in predicting a distant performance criterion. *Journal of Applied Psychology,* 1965, *49,* 434-438.

Industrial-Organizational Psychology of the American Psychological Association. *Principles for the validation and use of personnel procedures.* Discussion Draft, Author, 1980.

Ivancevich, J. M., Donnelly, J. H., & Lyon, H. L. A study of the impact of management by objectives on perceived need satisfaction. *Personnel Psychology,* 1970, *23,* 139-151.

James v. *Stockham Valves and Fittings Co.,* 559 F.2d. 310, cert. denied 434 U.S. 1034 (1978).

Jenkins, G. D., & Taber, T. A. A Monte Carlo study of factors affecting three indices of composite scale reliability. *Journal of Applied Psychology,* 1977, *62,* 392-398.

Kane, J. S., & Lawler, E. E., III. Methods of peer assessment. *Psychological Bulletin,* 1978, *85,* 555-586.

Kavanagh, M. J. The content issue in performance appraisal: A review. *Personnel Psychology,* 1971, *24,* 653-669.

_____, MacKinney, A. C., & Wolins, L. Issues in managerial performance: Multitrait-multimethod analysis of ratings. *Psychological Bulletin,* 1971, *75,* 34-49.

Kay, E., Meyer, H. H., & French, J. R. P., Jr. Effects of threat in a performance appraisal interview. *Journal of Applied Psychology,* 1965, *49,* 311-317.

Kearney, W. J. Behaviorally anchored rating scales — MBO's missing ingredient. *Personnel Journal,* 1979, *58,* 20-25.

Kirkland v. *New York Department of Correctional Service,* 7 FEB 700, 1974.

Klimoski, R. J., & London, M. Role of the rater in performance appraisal. *Journal of Applied Psychology,* 1974, *59,* 445-451.

Korman, A. K. The prediction of managerial performance: A review. *Personnel Psychology,* 1968, *21,* 295-322.

Krackhardt, D., McKenna, J., Porter, L. W., & Steers, R. M. Goal setting, supervisory behavior, and employee turnover: A field experiment. Technical Report No. 17, Graduate School of Management, University of Oregon, 1978.

Kraut, A. I. Prediction of managerial success by peer and training-staff ratings. *Journal of Applied Psychology,* 1975, *60,* 14-19.

Kubany, A. J. Use of sociometric peer nominations in medical education research. *Journal of Applied Psychology,* 1957, *41,* 389-394.

Lancaster, H. Failing system: Job tests are dropped by many companies due to antibias drive. *Wall Street Journal,* September 3, 1975, 1; 19.

Landy, F. J., & Farr, J. L. Performance rating. *Psychological Bulletin,* 1980, *87,* 72-107.

———, & Guion, R. M. Development of scales for the measurement of work motivation. *Organizational Behavior and Human Performance,* 1970, *5,* 93-103.

———, Barnes, J. L., & Murphy, K. R. Correlates of perceived fairness and accuracy of performance evaluation. *Journal of Applied Psychology,* 1978, *63,* 751-754.

———, Farr, J. L., Saal, F. E., & Freytag, W. R. Behaviorally anchored scales for rating the performance of police officers. *Journal of Applied Psychology,* 1976, *61,* 750-758.

Latham, G. P. The development of job performance criteria for pulpwood producers in the southeastern United States. Unpublished master's thesis, Georgia Institute of Technology, 1969.

———. Does participation in setting goals boost engineers' performance? *Chemical Engineering,* January 1979, pp. 141-144.

———, & Baldes, J. J. The "practical significance" of Locke's theory of goal setting. *Journal of Applied Psychology,* 1975, *60,* 122-124.

———, & Beach, H. D. Training interviewers in the critical incident technique. Workshop conducted at the annual meeting of the Canadian Psychological Association, Windsor, Ontario, June, 1974.

_____ , & Dossett, D. L. Designing incentive plans for unionized employees: A comparison of continuous and variable ratio reinforcement schedules. *Personnel Psychology*, 1978, *31*, 47-61.

_____ , & Kinne, S. B. Improving job performance through training in goal setting. *Journal of Applied Psychology*, 1974, *59*, 187-191.

_____ , & Locke, E. A. Increasing productivity with decreasing time limits: A field replication of Parkinson's law. *Journal of Applied Psychology*, 1975, *60*, 524-526.

_____ , & Locke, E. A. Goal setting: A motivational technique that works. *Organizational Dynamics*, Autumn 1979, 68-80.

_____ , & Mitchell, T. R. Behavioral criteria and potential reinforcers for the engineer/scientist in an industrial setting. *JSAS Catalog of Selected Documents in Psychology*, 1976, *6*, 38, 1, 316.

_____ , & Saari, L. M. The effects of holding goal difficulty constant on assigned and participatively set goals. *Academy of Management Journal*, 1979a, *22*, 163-168.

_____ , & Saari, L. M. The importance of supportive relationships in goal setting. *Journal of Applied Psychology*, 1979b, *64*, 163-168.

_____ , & Saari, L. M. The application of social learning theory to training supervisors through behavioral modeling. *Journal of Applied Psychology*, 1979c, *64*, 239-246.

_____ , & Wexley, K. N. Behavioral observation scales for performance appraisal purposes. *Personnel Psychology*, 1977, *30*, 255-268.

_____ , & Yukl, G. A. A review of research on the application of goal setting in organization. *Academy of Management Journal*, 1975a, *18*, 824-845.

_____ , & Yukl, G. A. Assigned versus participative goal setting with educated and uneducated woods workers. *Journal of Applied Psychology*, 1975b, *60*, 299-302.

_____ , & Yukl, G. A. The effects of assigned and participative goal setting on performance and job satisfaction. *Journal of Applied Psychology*, 1976, *61*, 166-171.

_____ , Fay, C. H., & Saari, L. M. The development of behavioral observation scales for appraising the performance of foremen. *Personnel Psychology,* 1979, *32,* 299-311.

_____ , Mitchell, T. R., & Dossett, D. L. The importance of participative goal setting and anticipated rewards on goal difficulty and job performance. *Journal of Applied Psychology,* 1978, *63,* 173-171.

_____ , Pursell, E. D., & Wexley, K. N. *Predicting logging performance through behavioral accounting.* Tacoma, Wash.: Human Resource Planning and Development, Weyerhaeuser Company, 1974.

_____ , Saari, L. M., Pursell, E. D., & Campion, M. A. The situational interview. *Journal of Applied Psychology,* 1980, in press.

_____ , Wexley, K. N., & Pursell, E. D. Training managers to minimize rating errors in the observation of behavior. *Journal of Applied Psychology,* 1975, *60,* 550-555.

_____ , Wexley, K. N., & Rand, T. M. The relevance of behavioral criteria developed from the critical incident technique. *Canadian Journal of Behavioural Science,* 1975, *7,* 349-358.

Lawler, E. E. III, The multitrait-multirater approach to measuring managerial job performance. *Journal of Applied Psychology,* 1967, *51,* 369-381.

_____ . *Pay and organizational effectiveness: A psychological view.* New York: McGraw-Hill, 1971.

Lawshe, C. H. Statistical theory and practice in applied psychology. *Personnel Psychology,* 1959, *22,* 117-124.

Lazer, R. I., & Wikstrom, W. S. *Appraising managerial performance: Current practices and future directions.* New York: Conference Board, 1977.

Levine, J., & Butler, J. Lecture versus group discussion in changing behavior. *Journal of Applied Psychology,* 1952, *36,* 29-33.

Lewin, A. Y., & Zwany, A. Peer nominations: A model, literature critique and a paradigm for research. *Personnel Psychology,* 1976, *29,* 423-447.

Likert, R. A technique for the measurement of attitudes. *Archives of Psychology,* 1932, No. 140, 44-53.

_____ . *New pattern of management.* New York: McGraw-Hill, 1961.

_____ . *The human organization.* New York: McGraw-Hill, 1967.

Lissitz, R. W., & Green, S. B. Effect of the number of scale points on reliability: A Monte Carlo approach. *Journal of Applied Psychology,* 1975, *60,* 10-13.

Locke, E. A. Toward a theory of task motivation and incentives. *Organizational Behavior and Human Performance,* 1968, *3,* 157-189.

_____ . The nature and causes of job satisfaction. In M. Dunnette (Ed.), *Handbook of Industrial and Organizational Psychology.* Chicago: Rand McNally, 1976.

_____ . The ubiquity of the technique of goal setting in theories and approaches to employee motivation. *Academy of Management Review,* 1978, *3,* 594-601.

_____ . Latham versus Komaki: A tale of two paradigms. *Journal of Applied Psychology,* 1980, *65,* 16-23.

Maier, N. R. F. *The appraisal interview.* New York: Wiley, 1958.

Maloney, P. W., & Hinrichs, J. R. A new tool for supervisory self-development. *Personnel,* 1959, *36,* 46-53.

Mayfield, E. C. Management selection: Buddy nominations revisited. *Personnel Psychology,* 1970, *23,* 377-391.

_____ . Value of peer nominations in predicting life insurance sales performance. *Journal of Applied Psychology,* 1972, *56,* 319-323.

McCall, M. W., & DeVries, D. L. Appraisal in context: Clashing with organizational realities. In D. DeVries (Chm.), Performance appraisal and feedback: Flies in the ointment. Symposium presented at the annual meeting of the American Psychological Association, Washington, D.C., September 1976.

McCormick, E. J. Job and task analysis. In M. Dunnette (Ed.), *Handbook of Industrial and Organizational Psychology.* Chicago: Rand McNally, 1976.

_____ . *Job analysis: Methods and applications.* New York: AMACOM, 1979.

Meyer, H. H. The pay-for-performance dilemma. *Organizational Dynamics,* Winter 1975, *3,* 39-50.

_____ . The annual performance review discussion: Making it constructive. *Personnel Journal,* 1977, *56,* 508–511.

_____ , & Kay, E. A. Comparison of a work planning program with the annual performance appraisal interview approach. Behavioral Research Report No. ESR17, General Electric Company, 1964.

_____ , Kay, E., & French, J. R. P., Jr. Split roles in performance appraisal. *Harvard Business Review,* 1965, *43,* 123–129.

Miller, L. M. *Behavior management: The new science of managing people at work.* New York: Wiley, 1978.

Miner, J. B. Management appraisal: A capsule review and current references. *Business Horizons,* 1968, *11,* 83–96.

_____ . Psychological testing and fair employment practices: A testing program that does not discriminate. *Personnel Psychology,* 1974, *27,* 49–62.

Mintzberg, H. *The nature of managerial work.* New York: Harper & Row, 1973.

Mitchell, T. R., & Wood, R. E. Supervisor's responses to subordinate poor performance: A test of an attributional model. *Organizational Behavior and Human Performance,* 1980, *25,* 123–138.

Mitnick, M. M. Equal employment opportunity and affirmative action: A managerial training guide. *Personnel Journal,* 1977, *56,* 492–497; 529.

Mobley, W. H. The link between MBO and merit compensation. *Personnel Journal,* 1974, *53,* 423–427.

Moody v. *Albermarle Paper Co.,* 474 F.2d. 134 (Ca-4, 1973), 5 EPD 8470.

Moses, J. L., & Byham, W. C. *Applying the assessment center method.* New York: Pergamon Press, 1977.

Nagle, B. F. Criterion development. *Personnel Psychology,* 1953, *6,* 271–289.

Nemeroff, W. F., & Wexley, K. N. Relationships between performance appraisal interview outcomes by supervisors and subordinates. Paper presented at the annual meeting of the Academy of Management, Orlando, Florida, 1977.

O'Reilly, A. P. Skill requirements: Supervisor-subordinate conflict. *Personnel Psychology,* 1973, *26,* 75-80.

Osburn, H. G., & Manese, W. R. *How to install and validate employee selection techniques.* Washington, D.C.: American Petroleum Institute, 1972.

Parker, J. W., Taylor, E. K., Barrett, R. S., & Martens, L. Rating scale content: III. Relationships between supervisory- and self-ratings. *Personnel Psychology,* 1959, *12,* 49-63.

Pati, G. C., & Reilly, C. W. Reversing discrimination: A perspective. *Human Resource Management,* Winter 1977, 25-35.

Pettway v. *American Cast Iron Pipe Co.,* 7 FEB 1115, 1974.

Peters, L. H., & O'Connor, E. J. Situational constraints and work outcomes: The influence of a frequently overlooked construct. *Academy of Management Review,* 1980, *5,* 391-397.

_____ , & Rudolf, C. J. The behavioral and affective consequences of performance-relevant situational variables. *Organizational Behavior and Human Performance,* 1980, *25,* 79-86.

Porter, L. W. Turning work into nonwork: The rewarding environment. In M. D. Dunnette (Ed.), *Work and nonwork in the year 2001.* Monterey, Calif.: Brooks Cole, 1973.

_____ , & Steers, R. M. Organization, work, and personal factors in employee turnover and absenteeism. *Psychological Bulletin,* 1973, *80,* 151-176.

Prien, E. P., & Ronan, W. W. Job analysis: A review of research findings. *Personnel Psychology,* 1971, *24,* 371-396.

Pursell, E. D., Dossett, D. L., & Latham, G. P. Obtaining validated predictors by minimizing rating errors in the criterion. *Personnel Psychology,* 80, *33,* 91-96.

Rand, T. M., & Wexley, K. N. A demonstration of the Byrne similarity hypothesis in simulated employment interviews. *Psychological Reports,* 1975, *36,* 535-544.

Reeves v. *Eaves,* 15 FEB 441, 1977.

Roadman, H. E. An industrial use of peer ratings. *Journal of Applied Psychology,* 1964, *48,* 211-214.

Robertson, D. E. New directions in EEO Guidelines. *Personnel Journal,* 1978, *57*, 360-363; 394.

Ronan, W. W., & Latham, G. P. The reliability and validity of the critical incident technique: A closer look. *Studies in Personnel Psychology,* 1974, *6*, 53-64.

_____, Latham, G. P., & Kinne, S. B. The effects of goal setting and supervision on worker behavior in an industrial situation. *Journal of Applied Psychology,* 1973, *58*, 302-307.

_____, & Prien, E. P. *Toward a criterion theory: A review and analysis of research and opinion.* Greensboro, N.C.: The Richardson Foundation, 1966.

_____. *Perspectives on the measurement of human performance.* New York: Appleton-Century-Crofts, 1971.

Rowe v. *General Motors,* 4 FEP 445, 1972.

Ryan, T. A., & Smith, P. C. *Principles of industrial psychology.* New York: Ronald, 1954.

Saari, L. M., & Latham, G. P. The validity of trainer ratings in an organizational setting. Unpublished manuscript, 1980.

Schmidt, F. L., & Johnson, R. H. Effect of race on peer ratings in an industrial situation. *Journal of Applied Psychology,* 1973, *57,* 237-241.

_____, & Kaplan, L. Composite vs. multiple criteria: A review and resolution of the controversy. *Personnel Psychology,* 1971, *24,* 419-434.

Schwab, D. P., Heneman, H. G., & DeCotiis, T. A. Behaviorally anchored rating scales: A review of the literature. *Personnel Psychology,* 1975, *28*, 549-562.

Seiler, L. H., & Hough, R. L. Empirical comparisons of the Thurstone and Likert techniques. In G. F. Summers (Ed.), *Attitude measurement.* Chicago: Rand McNally, 1970.

Sharf, J. C. Executive committee recommendation to APA "testing committee." *The Industrial-Organizational Psychologist,* 1979, *16,* 39-41.

Skinner, B. F. *The behavior of organisms.* New York: Appleton-Century-Crofts, 1938.

Slater, P. E. Contrasting correlates of gorup size. *Sociometry,* 1958, *21*, 129-139.

Smith, P. C. Behaviors, results, and organizational effectiveness: The problem of criteria. In M. D. Dunnette (Ed.), *Handbook of Industrial and Organizational Psychology*. Chicago: Rand McNally, 1976.

Smith, P., & Kendall, L. M. Retranslation of expectations: An approach to the construction of unambiguous anchors for rating scales. *Journal of Applied Psychology*, 1963, *47*, 149–155.

Smith, R. E., Smoll, F. L., & Hunt, E. B. Training manual for the coaching behavior assessment system. *JSAS Catalog of Selected Documents in Psychology*, 1977, *7*, 2. (Ms. No. 1406)

Spool, M. Training programs for observers of behavior: A review. *Personnel Psychology*, 1978, *31*,, 853–888.

Springer, D. Ratings of candidates for promotion by co-workers and supervisors. *Journal of Applied Psychology*, 1953, *37*, 347–351.

Stanton, E. S. The discharged employee and the EEO laws. *Personnel Journal*, 1976, *55*,, 128.

Stockford, L., & Bissell, H. W. Factors involved in establishing a mangement-rating scale. *Personnel*, 1949, *26*, 94–116.

Tavernier, G. Public servants rate their own performance. *International Management*, 1977, *32*, 19–21.

Taylor, F. W. *Principles of scientific management*. New York: Norton, 1947.

Teel, K. S. Self-appraisal revisited. *Personnel Journal*, 1978, *57*, 364–367.

The Industrial-Organizational Psychologist. *In-Basket correspondence*. The Industrial-organization Psychologist, 1980, *17*, 10–17, 42–43.

Thorndike, R. L. *Personnel selection: Test and measurement techniques*. New York: Wiley, 1949.

Thorton, G. C., III. The relationship between supervisory- and self-appraisals of executive performance. *Personnel Psychology*, 1968, *21*, 441–455.

Thorton, G. L., III. Psychometric properties of self-appraisals of job performance. *Personnel Psychology*, 1980, *33*, 236–271.

Thurstone, L. L. Attitudes can be measured. *American Journal of Sociology,* 1928, *33,* 529-554.

Toops, H. A. The criterion. *Educational and Psychological Measurement,* 1944, *4,* 271-297.

Trattner, M. H. Comparison of three methods for assembling aptitude test batteries. *Personnel Psychology,* 1963, *16,* 221-232.

United States v. *City of Chicago,* 8 EPD (1976).

United States v. *South Carolina,* 434 U.S. 1026, 16 FEP 501 (1978).

United Steelworkers v. *Weber,* U.S. F 1979.

Van Der Veen, F., & Fiske, D. W. Variability among self-ratings in different situations. *Educational and Psychological Measurement,* 1960, *20,* 83-93.

Vroom, V. H., & Maier, N. R. F. Industrial social psychology. *Annual Review of Psychology,* 1961, *12,* 413-446.

Wade v. *Mississippi Cooperative Extension Service,* 372 F. Supp. 126 (1974), 7 EPD 9186.

Wallace, S. R. Criteria for What? *American Psychologist,* 1965, *30,* 411-417.

Wanous, J. P. Effects of realistic job previews on job acceptance, job attitudes and job survival. *Journal of Applied Psychology,* 1973, *58,* 327-332.

———. *Organizational entry: Recruitment, selection, and socialization of newcomers.* Reading, Mass.: Addison-Wesley, 1980.

Warmke, D. L., & Billings, R. S. Comparison of training methods for improving the psychometric quality of experimental and administrative performance ratings. *Journal of Applied Psychology,* 1979, *64,* 124-131.

Waters, L. K., & Waters, C. W. Peer nominations as predictors of short term sales performance. *Journal of Applied Psychology,* 1970, *54,* 42-44.

Watkins v. *Scott Paper Co.,* 11 EPD 1089, 1976.

Webster, E. C. (Ed.). *Decision making in the employment interview.* Montreal: Eagle, 1964.

Weitz, J. Selecting supervisors with peer ratings. *Personnel Psychology,* 1958, *11*, 25-35.

Wetzel v. *Liberty Mutual Insurance Co.,* 16 EPD 8348 (WD Pa. 1978).

Wexley, K. N. Roles of performance appraisal in organizations. In S. Kerr, *Organizational Behavior,* Columbus, Ohio: Grid Publishing Co., 1979.

_____ , & Latham, G. P. *Developing and training human resources in an organization.* Goodyear Publishing, Inc., 1980.

_____ , & Nemeroff, W. F. Effects of racial prejudice, race of applicant, and biographical similarity on interviewer evaluations of job applicants. *Journal of Social and Behavioral Sciences,* 1974, *20*, 66-78.

_____ , & Nemeroff, W. F. Effectiveness of positive reinforcement and goal setting as methods of management development. *Journal of Applied Psychology,* 1975, *60*, 446-450.

_____ , & Yukl, G. A. *Organizational behavior and personnel psychology.* Homewood, Ill.: Irwin, 1977.

_____ , Sanders, R. E., & Yukl, G. A. Training interviewers to eliminate contrast effects in employment interviews. *Journal of Applied Psychology,* 1973, *57*, 233-236.

_____ , Singh, J. P., & Yukl, G. A. Subordinate personality as a moderator of the effects of participation in three types of appraisal interviews. *Journal of Applied Psychology,* 1973, *58*, 54-59.

_____ , Yukl, G. A., Kovacs, S. Z., & Sanders, R. E. Importance of contrast effects in employment interviews. *Journal of Applied Psychology,* 1972, *56*, 45-48.

Wherry, R. J., & Fryer, H. Buddy ratings: Popularity contest or leadership criteria? *Personnel Psychology,* 1949, *2*, 147-159.

Whisler, T. L., & Harper, S. F. (Eds.). *Performance appraisal: Research and practice.* New York: Holt, Rinehart, & Winston, 1962.

Whitla, D. K., & Tirrel, J. E. The validity of ratings of several levels of supervisors. *Personnel Psychology,* 1954, *6*, 461-466.

Williams, S. E., & Leavitt, H. J. Group opinion as a predictor of military leadership. *Journal of Consulting Psychology,* 1947, *11*, 283-291.

Yukl, G. A., & Latham, G. P. Consequences of reinforcement schedules and incentive magnitudes for employee performance: Problems encountered in an industrial setting. *Journal of Applied Psychology,* 1975, *60*, 294–298.

_____ , Latham, G. P., & Pursell, E. D. The effectiveness of performance incentives under continuous and variable ratio schedules of reinforcement. *Personnel Psychology,* 1976, *29*, 221–231.

_____ , Wexley, K. N., & Seymore, J. D. Effectiveness of pay incentives under variable ratio and continuous reinforcement schedules. *Journal of Applied Psychology,* 1972, *56*, 19–23.

Name Index

Subject Index